PARADISE REDEFINED

Paradise Redefined

*Transnational Chinese Students and
the Quest for Flexible Citizenship
in the Developed World*

VANESSA L. FONG

STANFORD UNIVERSITY PRESS
STANFORD, CALIFORNIA

Stanford University Press
Stanford, California

Printed in the United States of America on acid-free,
archival-quality paper

Library of Congress Cataloging-in-Publication Data
Fong, Vanessa L., 1974–   author.
  Paradise redefined : transnational Chinese students and
the quest for flexible citizenship in the developed world /
Vanessa L. Fong.
     pages cm
  Includes bibliographical references and index.
  ISBN 978-0-8047-7266-2 (cloth : alk. paper)—
ISBN 978-0-8047-7267-9 (pbk. : alk. paper)
   1. Chinese students—Foreign countries. 2. Foreign
study—China. 3. Transnationalism. . China—
Emigration and immigration. I. Title.
  LB2376.6.C6F66 2011
  370.116—dc22

                                    2011005567

Typeset by Classic Typography in 10/12.5 Palatino.

Contents

Acknowledgments   vii

1. Introduction   1
2. Is the Moon Rounder Abroad? How Chinese
   Citizens See the World   40
3. Choosing the Road Less Traveled: How and
   Why Chinese Citizens Decide to Study Abroad   67
4. The Floating Life: Dilemmas of Education,
   Work, and Marriage Abroad   95
5. When Migrants from the Same Hometown Meet,
   Tears Fill Their Eyes: Freedoms Won and Lost
   Through Transnational Migration   142
6. The Road Home: Decisions About Returning
   to China or Staying Abroad   191

   Notes   223
   Works Cited   241
   Index   265

Acknowledgments

I thank Nicole Newendorp, Nancy Abelmann, Sung won Kim, Qin Wenjuan, Lin Shu, Fang Lue, Jee Young Noh, Zhou Shuyi, Fang Shixin, Yang Yan, Zhang Cong, Chen Chen, Li Wei, Hu Minglie, and two anonymous reviewers at Stanford University Press for carefully reading my entire manuscript and providing detailed and very helpful suggestions. I am grateful to Stacy Wagner, Carolyn Brown, and Mimi Braverman at Stanford University Press for their support and advice throughout the publication process. For advice about various portions of this book and the research that went into it, I thank Katherine Masyn, Natasha Warikoo, Rachel Murphy, Erica James, Manduhai Buyandelgeriyn, Sonja Plesset, James L. Watson, Hirokazu Yoshikawa, Bilal Malik, Natsuko Kuwahara, Chih-Ting Chang, Hilary Chart, Stephanie Hsieh, Beaudry Kock, Paul Kuttner, Minkyung Lee, Arzu Mistry, Andres Sevtsuk, Wu Ning, Laura Batt, Fatou Camara, Charlene Desir, Andres Guerra, Meera Pathmarajah, Minnie Quach, Steve Song, Phitsamay Sychitkokhong, Jay Wang, Maggie Yuan, Tiffany Chao, Janet Kwok, Andrew Conning, Vanessa Beary, Tiffanie Ting, Adrienne Keene, Brendan Randall, Russell Carlock, Rebecca Rolland, Ai Goto-Araki, Injeong Kim, Kathleen Lynch, Erin McCloskey, Karen Wiener, Ji Eun Yang, Anusuya Banerjee, Miriam Boatright, Chen Mulian, Cheng Wen-Ju, Feng Yi, Julianne Fylstra, Clayton Harmon, Hsu Yu-Li, Hu Xinyue, Huang Linghui, Kim Kyojin, Li Lushi, Lu Ruyi, Magari Noriko, Janhvi Maheshwari, Christin Park, Qin Weijia, Natalie Roote, James Simpson, Song Ge, Tan Ying, Magdalena Wierzbicka, Zhang Dan, Kijoo Cha, Hsun-Yu Chan, Manlai Cheng, Yookyung Choi, He Ji,

Huyan Qianqian, Jun Eun Jeong, Stephanie Kimura, Kwan Hoi Yum, Liu Jing, Liu Xiyun, Min Sook-Weon, Yukiko Koga, and Amanda Wallace.

I am grateful for the questions and comments I received from audience members when I presented portions of this book at Harvard University, Oxford University, Cambridge University, the University of Michigan at Ann Arbor, Amherst College, Brown University, Georgetown University, New York University, the University of California at Los Angeles, Davidson College, Yale University, the London School of Economics, and the University of Nevada at Las Vegas, and at meetings of the American Anthropological Association, the American Educational Research Association, the Association for Asian Studies, the Society for Medical Anthropology, and the Society for Psychological Anthropology.

I am most deeply indebted to the people in my study, some of whom have shared their lives with me for over a decade. I thank the staff and administrators at the Harvard Graduate School of Education, especially my assistant, Anne Blevins, for helping me with technical, administrative, and research issues, my research assistants in China and the United States for helping me with data entry and collection, my colleagues and students at the Harvard Graduate School of Education for giving me advice and suggestions that have helped improve this book, my mentors and friends in the Harvard Anthropology Department and at Amherst College for helping to shape the way I think about the issues in this book, and my friends and family for their support through the process of research and writing.

The research for the longitudinal project that resulted in this book was funded by a Beinecke Brothers Memorial Fellowship, an Andrew W. Mellon Grant, a National Science Foundation Fellowship, a grant from the Weatherhead Center at Harvard University, a postdoctoral fellowship at the Population Studies Center of the University of Michigan at Ann Arbor, an Andrew W. Mellon Foundation Demography Fund Research Grant, a grant from the Wenner-Gren Foundation for Anthropological Research, a National Academy of Education/Spencer Foundation Postdoctoral Fellowship, a Visiting Fellowship at the Centre for Research in Arts, Social Sciences, and Humanities at Cambridge University, a grant from the Harvard University China Fund, grants from the Harvard University Asia Center, a grant from the Harvard University William F. Milton Fund, and a National Science Foundation CAREER Award.

PARADISE REDEFINED

CHAPTER 1

Introduction

GAO NENG seemed an unlikely candidate for study abroad in 1999, when I first met her in the northeastern Chinese coastal city of Dalian when she was 13.[1] She was the only child of factory workers, each of whom earned just under 1,000 yuan (US$121) per month.[2] Her family lived in a one-bedroom apartment and could not afford the luxuries that some other Dalian families had, such as a cell phone, microwave oven, computer, car, or air conditioner. I visited Gao Neng in Dalian again in 2002, when she was 16 and attending a college prep high school. I talked with her and her parents over the phone at least once a year before and after that. In all this time I never heard them mention any plans for her to study abroad.

I arrived in Dalian again in 2004, when Gao Neng was 18. I hoped to visit her and some of her former classmates. But when I called her home phone, her parents told me they had spent 60,000 yuan (US$7,255) of their life savings and had borrowed money from relatives to send their daughter to Ireland, where she was attending English-language classes while working as a salesclerk. They hoped she would learn enough English to qualify for admission to a college in Ireland and save enough money from work to pay tuition there and to repay their relatives' loans. When I visited Gao Neng in Ireland a month later, she told me that she was almost as surprised as I was that she was able to study abroad. She learned only after she had taken her college entrance exam that her parents had begun the process of applying for a visa for her to study in Ireland without even telling her. They wanted her to give the Chinese college entrance exam her best shot and hoped she could get into a good college in China and save them the expense of sending her abroad. But when Gao Neng failed to get into any four-year college in China, she was delighted to learn that her parents were already preparing to send her to Ireland. "I thought my family was too poor, so I didn't dare mention my dream of study abroad to them, but my Ma understood my heart too well," she told me.

I was similarly surprised by the study-abroad trajectories of other Chinese youth I first met in Chinese schools and homes in Dalian in the late 1990s, when I was trying to learn what life was like for the first generation born after China's one-child policy began in 1979. I found that adolescent singletons (only children) were facing unprecedented levels of parental pressure and competition in the educational system and the job market. Every child was expected to become a winner in a pyramidal socioeconomic system that allowed only a small minority to win. Singletons were the sole focus of parents' financial and emotional investment, and they were expected to eventually get work that paid enough to enable them to become the main providers of funds for their elderly parents' retirement, nursing care, and medical expenses. Chinese singletons of both genders and all kinds of aptitudes and socioeconomic statuses were therefore raised with the kind of heavy parental investment, high expectations, consumption demands, and educational aspirations common among children of highly educated professionals in developed countries, even though opportunities for higher education and white-collar work were more limited in China than in developed countries. After publishing these findings in *Only Hope: Coming of Age Under China's One-Child Policy* in 2004, I returned to Dalian, eager to continue following the lives of the singletons I had gotten to know. I wanted to see what would happen next as they started college or careers. I learned, however, that many of them had left for Australia, Europe, Japan, New Zealand, North America, or Singapore.

I had not expected so many of them to study abroad. To get a student visa to enter a developed country, a Chinese citizen has to show embassy officers proof of sufficient funds to pay for tuition and living expenses without working. The junior high school, college prep high school, and vocational high school where I first met most of the Chinese citizens in my study were academically and socioeconomically average by urban Dalian standards.[3] Few of them seemed wealthy enough to pay for study abroad or were high-achieving enough to qualify for scholarships abroad. Most Dalian residents I knew had no close relatives abroad and had never been outside China. When I first met them in the late 1990s, few of them knew how to use the Internet, much less how to use it to research study-abroad options. Among respondents to my 1999 survey, 87 percent (N = 2,193) indicated that they had no computer at home, and 18 percent (N = 2,195) indicated that their families had no phone of any kind.[4] (N is the number of respondents who answered a specific question on the survey I administered to 2,273 teenagers in 1999 or the resurvey I administered to 1,365 of the 1999 survey respondents in 2008–2010; N is different for each question because some respondents answered some survey questions but not others.)

Yet, when I taught English conversation to the 2,273 students who completed my 1999 survey and asked them to raise their hands if they would like to study abroad someday, the vast majority raised their hands. Many asked me about how they might get opportunities to study abroad and what life abroad was like for Chinese citizens. I tried to answer their questions as best as I could, based on what I knew about the experiences of Chinese citizens in the United States and on research I did on the Internet about international student experiences in other developed countries. Those students especially interested in study abroad were disproportionately represented among those I got to know well, because my English-language proficiency and knowledge about life abroad were part of the reason they befriended me in the first place. Still, I could tell that interest in study abroad was not limited to them. Even when waiting at bus stops, riding the bus, or shopping or waiting in lines at stores, I often overheard conversations about study abroad among strangers who were not paying attention to me and probably did not know that I was not a Chinese citizen.

By 2010, 20 percent of the 1,365 1999 survey respondents I resurveyed had studied abroad, and an additional 11 percent had gone abroad solely for tourism, work, business, or other purposes.[5] They joined a growing wave of transnational students from China. Xiang Biao and Wei Shen analyzed statistics published by the Chinese Ministry of Education and found that 179,800 Chinese citizens went abroad to study in 2008 alone, making China the source of the largest proportion of transnational students in the world.[6] Even among the 619 respondents to the longer version of my 2008–2010 surveys who had never been abroad, 64 percent indicated on the most recent survey they completed between 2008 and 2010 that they would like to someday go abroad for study, work, and/or immigration.[7]

In retrospect, I realize that I had underestimated the extent to which obstacles to study abroad could be overcome by a confluence of four factors: (1) the heavily concentrated financial resources that would be invested in Chinese singletons by their parents and some of their aunts, uncles, and grandparents; (2) the rapid increase in urban Chinese families' incomes and the value of their assets (especially housing) that would occur as a result of China's rapid economic growth and rural to urban migration; (3) the expansion of international education infrastructure (such as foreign-language schools in China and abroad, homestay programs abroad, partnerships between study-abroad brokers [*zhongjie*] in China and schools in developed countries, and international student recruitment programs and websites run by these brokers and schools) that would result from developed countries' increased interest in developing countries like China as growing markets for educational services; and (4) the eagerness to study abroad that was already widespread among Dalian teenagers at the time I started my research in the late 1990s. I had assumed that study abroad was unlikely even for those who seemed to desire it most. I was not entirely wrong. The desires of some of those who had seemed the most knowledgeable about and interested in study abroad as teenagers waned as they learned more about the risks and sacrifices that study abroad entailed and as they found reasonably satisfactory opportunities in China. However, I was surprised to learn that some others who had seemed less knowledgeable about, less financially capable of, and less interested in study abroad actually did end up leaving China to study in other countries.

I kept in touch with 92 of the survey respondents with whom I was closest after they graduated from the schools where I conducted my initial survey and participant observation. When some of them and their friends and cousins left China to study in Australia, Britain, Ireland, Japan, and the United States, I followed them to those countries, at first thinking that what I observed of their experiences would just be a minor part of the larger story of the transition from adolescence to young adulthood that I would tell about their cohort, all of whom I was determined to track for the rest of their lives. But as more and more of them started studying abroad and as I started hearing even from many of those who stayed in China that they were planning to study abroad and that many of their friends and cousins were studying abroad, I realized that study abroad was becoming more common for their generation than I ever imagined it could be. I therefore spent the first decade of the twenty-first century following these students on their journeys abroad, trying to figure out why they chose to study abroad despite the obstacles, what they experienced abroad, how their experiences changed them, and how they decided whether to stay abroad or return to China.

This book reveals what I learned about the motivations, experiences, and perspectives of transnational Chinese students who studied at colleges, universities, and language schools in developed countries and who hoped that such education would increase their access to social and cultural citizenship in the developed world—and sometimes to legal citizenship in developed countries—while also trying to maintain their social, cultural, and legal citizenship in China. I look at how they won and lost various kinds of freedom through the process of study abroad and at how and why they decided to stay abroad or return to China. I follow them on their journeys from China to developed countries, and in some cases back again, and explore how the process of study abroad transformed them, leading them to redefine what they considered paradise and where they could find it.

The Developed World as One Imagined Community

Benedict Anderson argued that nationalism emerged once people were able to see themselves as part of an "imagined community" resulting from the emergence of a shared language, print capitalism, and, most important, the educational pilgrimages that ambitious youth made to national centers.[8] In describing how Chinese leaders encouraged Chinese citizens to imagine themselves as part of a transnational Confucian community of East and Southeast Asians, Aihwa Ong suggested that Anderson's idea of imagined communities could also apply to "imaginaries . . . brought together by the reconfigurations of global capitalism."[9] Arjun Appadurai argued that the speed and ubiquity of global cultural flows have broken down national boundaries in unprecedented ways, causing people worldwide to "no longer see their lives as mere outcomes of the givenness of things, but often as the ironic compromise between what they could imagine and what social life will permit."[10] Building on these ideas, I argue that the increasingly globalized nature of the media, language, and educational pilgrimages available to young Chinese citizens in cities like Dalian encourages them to aspire to belong to an imagined developed world community composed of mobile, wealthy, well-educated, and well-connected people worldwide.[11]

Transnational students play a key role in the building and maintenance of this imagined developed world community. They are a rapidly growing sector of the student population in developed countries[12] and have also been highly influential as agents of globalization in their home countries[13] and in their host countries.[14] As Anderson noted, "There was, to be sure, always a double aspect to the choreography of the great religious pilgrimages: a vast horde of illiterate vernacular-speakers provided the dense, physical reality of the ceremonial passage; while a small segment of literate bilingual adepts drawn from each vernacular community performed the unifying rites, interpreting to their respective followings the meaning of their collective motion."[15] So it was in Dalian, as in other cities in China and the rest of the developing world from where a minority was drawn to study in developed countries, where they would learn to interpret the imagined community of the developed world for their home communities. Many Chinese citizens wanted to become part of that minority. They believed that pilgrimages to developed countries would not only help them become citizens of the developed world but also facilitate efforts to make China part of the developed world. Ideally, developed world citizenship would add to rather than replace their Chinese citizenship. Many transnational Chinese students told me that, after they secured social, cultural, and/or legal citizenship in a developed country, they would channel developed countries' cultural and economic capital into China by working in transnational businesses and organizations that would help to transform China into a developed country. Chinese citizens dreamed that their pursuit of developed world citizenship would enable them to eventually help remake China in the image of the developed world paradise they imagined they would find abroad.

Chinese citizens in my study often experienced and discussed the developed world as if it were one imagined community, sharing one culture, system, and citizenship status. They contrasted how things were done in China (*zhongguo*) by Chinese people (*zhongguoren*) with how things were done in "foreign [mostly developed] countries" (*waiguo*) by "foreigners" (*waiguoren*), as though all the foreign countries were part of one single country and all the foreigners shared the same nationality. They sometimes mistook the products or customs of one developed country for another. They believed that credentials, experience, and social, cultural, or legal citizenship gained in any developed country could open the door to any other developed country, and they assumed that developed countries set the standards by which success everywhere was measured.

Many Chinese citizens who wanted to study abroad were not determined to study in one particular developed country but rather willing to study in whichever developed country seemed most likely to grant them a visa at the time they applied. Some told me that they wanted to study in a developed country but had no idea which one would be best for them. They asked me for advice about which country they should choose. Others were trying to decide between two, three, or more of their favorite developed countries. Many did have some preferences for studying in particular developed countries based on factors such as how much they liked the cultures, environments, and climates of those countries, how many of their friends and relatives were already in those countries or interested in going with them to those countries, how prestigious and easily transferable to other countries those countries' skills, knowledge, educational credentials, and work experiences would be, how easy it would be in those countries for them to get low-skilled work while they were students and professional work once they graduated, and how likely those countries were to grant them permanent residency rights or legal citizenship if they wanted it. But those who could not get visas to enter their top-choice developed country were quite willing to settle for the developed country that was their next choice, fifth choice, or even last choice. Even while they were living in a developed country, they still sometimes referred to that country as "abroad" (*waiguo*) instead of by its name (e.g., Australia, Britain, Ireland, Japan, the United States). Some who were dissatisfied with the first developed country they studied in ended up moving to a different developed country in search of better opportunities. They talked about such moves between developed countries the same way they talked about moving from one city in China to another and not in the way they talked about the much more life-changing and potentially permanent move they made from China to a developed country.

Chinese citizens' tendency to elide differences between different developed countries derived partly from inadequate knowledge about those countries and the differences between them, in the same way that Orientalist discourses derived partly from inadequate knowledge about non-Western countries and the differences between them.[16] But the Chinese concept of *waiguo* was not just a form of reverse Orientalism. It was also based on recognition of real similarities between different developed countries' cultures, laws, political economies, and ways of integrating and not integrating transnational migrants like themselves. These similarities resulted from the strong alliances those countries shared, which enabled people, goods, media, ideas, money, capital, credentials, skills, and jobs to flow quickly and easily between them, and particularly between those countries' elite (whom Chinese citizens in my study hoped to join). As Saskia Sassen argued, large cities with strong transnational linkages tend to produce denationalized elite who sometimes share greater affinities with their counterparts in the globalized cities of other countries than with the nonelite of their own countries.[17] These denationalized elite formed an imagined community of the developed world that had some of the characteristics a country might have.

Individuals and countries that were part of the developed world shared with each other common economic systems, cultural understandings, business practices, academic canons, standards for educational credentials, interests in movies, TV shows, sports, and music, Internet communities, and a lingua franca (English, which most college-educated citizens of non-Anglophone developed countries such as Japan, France, Germany, and Spain could also speak). These were also shared by some Chinese citizens living in China or abroad as social and cultural citizens of the developed world, but not by the majority of Chinese citizens.

Most transnational corporations were based in developed countries, and it was easier for their employees to transfer from a branch in one developed country to a branch in another developed country than it was for Chinese citizens working in Chinese branches of transnational corporations to transfer to branches of those same corporations in developed countries. People doing the same job in different developed countries were likely to have similar salaries and standards of living, but those doing the same job in China were likely to have much lower salaries and standards of living. Employers and universities in developed countries valued education and work experience acquired in other developed countries more highly than education and work experience acquired in China.

Borders between Anglophone countries were even more porous, as were borders between European Union (EU) countries. Political and military alliances between subgroups of developed countries (and sometimes a few of the most developed of the developing countries) have also been formalized through international organizations such as the EU, the North Atlantic Treaty Organization (NATO), the Group of 8 (G8), the Commonwealth of Nations, the North American Aerospace Defense Command (NORAD), and the Organization for Economic Cooperation and Development (OECD). Most developed countries are politically and militarily allied with each other and are understood to be under the protection of the US military. China, on the contrary, has no political or military alliances with any developed countries. It is no wonder, then, that Chinese citizens looking (mostly from the outside) at this exclusive but internally coherent imagined community of developed countries and developed world citizens would talk about it as though it were all one country.[18]

In this book I portray the imagined community of the developed world as it was seen through the eyes of the Chinese citizens in my study. I therefore focus on what the developed countries had in common and how they differed from China rather than on how they differed from each other. Although I recognize that the differences between different developed countries (and between different neighborhoods, cities, towns, regions, subcultures, ethnic groups, and socioeconomic classes within each developed country) are significant, descriptions of such differences are mostly beyond the scope of this book. Chinese citizens did talk with each other and with me about differences they perceived between developed countries. But it was hard for me to figure out which of those perceived differences were due to real, systematic differences between those countries, which were due to differences between different kinds of places (e.g., rural versus urban, affluent versus impoverished) within each country, which were due to differences between the kinds of Chinese citizens who went to each country, and which were due to stereotypes that exaggerated small or nonexistent differences between countries.[19]

Therefore, although I do describe a few unique policies and historical developments in particular developed countries when they are necessary for contextualizing the opportunities and constraints faced by Chinese citizens in those countries, I do not generalize about each developed country and how it differs from other developed countries. Nor do I assess the fairness and accuracy of the generalizations that Chinese citizens made about those countries and their citizens. Many of their comments seemed like overgeneralizations about entire countries based on a few experiences that they had in particular settings with particular individuals in those countries. I cannot tell how or how much their generalizations differ from what I would find if I did a systematic study of each phenomenon among the entire population of each country, because I did not do that kind of study in any of the countries discussed in this book. My goal is not to present fair and accurate generalizations about "what developed countries are really like" (a task beyond the scope of this, and probably any, book) but rather to present a portrait of how transnational Chinese students in my study subjectively experienced their interactions with those countries and how these subjective experiences transformed the way they thought about the developed world, China, and their own hopes, goals, and concerns. I focus on aspects of the experience of study abroad that seemed pervasive across the experiences of many Chinese citizens studying in many different countries. Despite the diversity of personalities, perspectives, and socioeconomic and academic backgrounds among Chinese citizens in my study, most had a lot in common when it came to their motivations for and experiences of study abroad. Despite the diversity of policies, cultures, and socioeconomic conditions among the countries in which they studied (and the subcultures, neighborhoods, towns, cities, and regions within each country), these countries were all part of the developed world and operated by the rules of the global neoliberal system, and as such they shared many commonalities with regard to how they interacted with transnational Chinese students. These commonalities are the focus of this book.

Developed Countries and Developed World Citizenship

Chinese citizens sometimes talk about how "foreign countries are like paradise" (*waiguo jiuxiang tiantang*).[20] I heard them make this comparison when they looked at photos that friends and relatives took abroad of pristine beaches and bright blue skies that seemed far less polluted than what they saw in their own Chinese cities, when those friends and relatives told them about things they had abroad that most Chinese citizens wanted but could not get (such as cars, large houses, and salaries that were many times more than what most Chinese citizens earned), and while they watched movies and TV shows from abroad (such as *Growing Pains, True Lies,* and *Home Alone*) and marveled at the fun, exciting lives that characters in developed countries seemed to enjoy amid luxurious material surroundings. Some used this comparison to explain why Chinese citizens who went abroad decided not to return to China. "Of course someone who has seen paradise wouldn't want to come back to hell," a 56-year-old retired factory worker told me and her friend while the three of us were having lunch at a restaurant in China. She was trying to console her friend, a 51-year-old businesswoman, who had started crying when she talked about how her daughter had left China to attend college in Japan at age 19 and was still reluctant to leave her office job there to return to China at age 27.

Some Chinese citizens who were studying abroad or had returned from abroad compared the developed countries they studied in to paradise sincerely, but others made it ironically, contrasting the disappointing developed country they studied in with the paradise that they imagined all developed countries were. Many believed that paradise could be found in China as well. Like Li Zhang, who heard Chinese citizens describe their expensive private homes as their "private paradise,"[21] I sometimes heard Chinese citizens using the term *paradise* to describe places in China (such as particularly prestigious and luxurious hotels, restaurants, universities, and homes) that could be considered part of the developed world.

As a term that refers to an imagined community of elite individuals worldwide, most of whom live in societies characterized by a combination of high per capita gross domestic product (GDP), power, and prestige, rather than to any specific geographic area, race, ethnicity, or nation-state, *developed world* seems to be the English phrase that best captures popular Chinese ideas about the kind of paradise Chinese citizens associate with affluent lifestyles in China and the Chinese term *waiguo* (which literally means "outside the country," "abroad," or "foreign countries"). The term *foreign countries* (*waiguo*) usually referred to Australia, Britain, Canada, Japan, New Zealand, Singapore, the United States, and the Western European countries. Chinese citizens said that developing countries were also "foreign countries" (*waiguo*) when asked about them, and they understood that *waiguo* referred to all foreign countries, not just developed foreign countries, when they saw it in a textbook, legal document, or my survey. In casual conversations, however, they used *waiguo* to refer primarily to developed countries, preferring to refer to developed countries by their names (e.g., Mexico, Cuba, Vietnam) rather than generalizing about them. Chinese citizens often talk about how China is a "poor" (*qiong*), "backward" (*luohou*) "developing country" (*fazhanzhong guojia*) that needs to "develop" (*fazhan*) and "modernize" (*xiandaihua*) in order to "catch up to" (*ganshang*) "wealthy/developed countries" (*fada guojia*), which are also known as "advanced countries" (*xianjin guojia*) or simply as "foreign countries" (*waiguo*). They assume that citizens of the developed world have "high quality" (*gao suzhi*), whereas citizens of the developing world do not. Chinese educational, economic, and fertility limitation policies were explicitly intended to raise the "quality" (*suzhi*) of the Chinese population so that China could become part of the developed world.[22]

Chinese citizens' classification of a country's level of development did not depend entirely on objective standards such as per capita GDP. They rarely talked about countries they considered less developed than China. When talking about developed countries (*fada guojia*), they never mentioned countries such as Qatar, the United Arab Emirates, Kuwait, or the Bahamas, each of which has a per capita GDP similar to those of developed countries but lack the power, prestige, and geopolitical alliances of those countries.

Although the term *foreigner* (*waiguoren*) was most commonly used to describe racially white citizens of Western developed countries, it was also sometimes used to describe nonwhite citizens of Western and non-Western developed countries. Immigrants from developing countries (including China) were usually described in terms of their national origins regardless of their legal citizenship status or where they were living. Nonwhite citizens of developed countries who did not have clearly identifiable origins in particular developing countries were sometimes described just as foreigners (*waiguoren*) and other times with racial categories, depending on context. I was occasionally described as a foreigner (*waiguoren*) by Chinese citizens who wanted to emphasize my developed country citizenship. More commonly I was described as a "Chinese person" (*zhongguoren*), "ethnically Chinese person" (*huaren*), "Chinese descendant" (*huayi*), or "Chinese American" (*meiji huaren*).

Chinese citizens in my study wanted to become part of the developed world by acquiring social, cultural, and sometimes legal citizenship in the developed world. Most nonimpoverished citizens of developed countries who do not have criminal records are part of the developed world. As with any kind of citizenship, developed world citizenship has social, cultural, and legal aspects that are connected but not inseparable. Building on the work of others who have examined what citizenship categories mean for transnational people,[23] I draw distinctions between legal, social, and cultural citizenship in my discussions of the kinds of rights, freedoms, and opportunities that Chinese citizens tried to acquire abroad. I use the term *legal citizenship* to refer to a set of legal rights based on how one is classified by documents such as passports and residency cards, the terms of which are defined and enforced by local, national, and international legal systems. I use the term *social citizenship* to refer to a status that gives one access to certain standards of living, education, health, income, mobility, prestige, and comfort. I use the term *cultural citizenship* to refer to a status of belonging to a community in ways that are felt by the individual and recognized by others.

Most aspects of citizenship are not things that one either has or does not have but rather fuzzy statuses that an individual can have more or less of at any given moment. The boundaries between those who have a certain kind of social and cultural citizenship and those who do not are subject to more contestation and interpretation than the boundaries between those who have a certain kind of legal citizenship and those who do not. But even legal citizenship can mean different things for different individuals. Legal permanent residency status grants an immigrant most (but not all) of the legal rights that full legal citizens have, whereas children, prisoners, those who face discrimination because of their race, gender, ethnicity, religion, or sexual orientation, and those with records of criminal convictions or severe mental illnesses or disabilities can have some but not all of the legal rights possessed by others with identical citizenship documents. As James Holston pointed out, even those who share the same legal citizenship status can have unequal access to legal rights in a system of "differentiated citizenship."[24]

Although social, cultural, and legal citizenship can be acquired and used independently from each other, they can also affect, supplement, and sometimes even substitute for each other. One can be a full legal citizen of the developed world only if one has legal citizenship in a developed country, but one can be a social and cultural citizen of the developed world even without legal citizenship in any developed country. Legal citizenship and physical residence play a large role in determining whether one is part of the developed world or the developing world, but they are not the only relevant factors. In a world of global cultural flows, interconnected political economies, and increasingly mobile people, it is possible to be part of the developing world even while living in a developed country, or to be part of the developed world even while living in a developing country. Citizens of the developed world can enjoy developed world rights in almost any country, even if they are not legal citizens of any developed country. Wealthy, well-educated, and well-connected Chinese citizens living in China, with the same wealth, prestige, and ability to travel freely between China and developed countries that most middle-class citizens of developed countries have, can be considered part of the developed world. On the other hand, legal citizens of developed countries who are poor, suffer discrimination, or have been convicted of crimes are often excluded from the developed world even though they live in developed countries.

Like the Chinese migrants described by Julie Chu and by Frank Pieke and his collaborators, Chinese citizens in my study saw going abroad not only as a physical journey but also as a journey from one category of personhood to another.[25] What they wanted most was the prestige, comfort, geographic mobility, and high standard of living enjoyed by cultural and social citizens of the developed world. Legal citizenship in a developed country was valued not for its own sake but as a means to this end.

As Andrew Kipnis pointed out, legal citizenship in a developed country can provide an instant set of developed world capabilities and freedoms even to those who do not have the incomes, careers, or education that would entitle them to full social or cultural citizenship in the developed world.[26] Legal citizens of developing countries who are social and cultural citizens of the developed world face some of the same obstacles that nonelite legal citizens of developing countries face when they try to get visas or permanent residency rights abroad. But some can use their developed world prestige, wealth, skills, knowledge, education, credentials, and social networks to get around those obstacles. Even legal citizens of developing countries who lack permanent residency rights in a developed country can use their social and cultural citizenship in the developed world to gain some, if not all, of the same legal, cultural, and social rights that citizens of developed countries have. Legal citizens of developing countries who have large amounts of money to invest or skills and credentials that are in high demand worldwide can quickly and easily get visas to most countries they want to visit while enjoying salaries and living standards comparable to what they would have in developed countries, even while they are living in developing countries.

Social and cultural citizenship in a developed country can also facilitate one's application for permanent residency or legal citizenship there. Permanent residency documents confer most of the same rights that full legal citizenship does while also allowing the holder to retain all the rights associated with legal citizenship in other countries. Those who have full legal citizenship rights in one country and legal permanent residency rights in one or more other countries thus have flexible legal as well as social and cultural citizenship, which allows them to move quickly and freely between countries and systems, seeking advantages and avoiding disadvantages wherever they appear. "Flexible citizenship" of the kind described by Aihwa Ong[27] can offer an especially wide range of the freedoms and capabilities that Amartya Sen considered the most important determinant of human well-being.[28]

Although legal citizenship in a developed country can help an individual to attain the freedoms and capabilities associated with developed world citizenship, it is neither necessary nor sufficient for attainment of those freedoms and capabilities.[29] Writing about twentieth-century societies in which the deterritorialization of individuals was less common than it has become in the global neoliberal system of the twenty-first century, Thomas Humphrey Marshall and others who have built on his work described "civil" and "political" citizenship (both of which are part of my concept of legal citizenship) as necessary (though insufficient) foundations for social and cultural citizenship.[30] As processes of globalization and transnational migration have accelerated, however, scholars of citizenship have increasingly seen legal citizenship as a useful but not always necessary facilitator for social and cultural citizenship, which increasingly transnational processes of neoliberalization often allow to operate independently of legal citizenship.[31] Ong defined cultural citizenship as "a dual process of self-making and being-made . . . in shifting fields of power that include the nation-state and the wider world."[32] Building on Ong's definition, I argue that cultural citizenship processes can transcend national boundaries, as individuals are made and make themselves in the context not only of the societies in which they live and hold legal citizenship but also of the global neoliberal system, which assumes that all who acquire developed world discipline, skills, and affluence can become social and cultural citizens of the developed world, regardless of where they live or what is written on their passports. At the same time, even those with legal citizenship and residency in a developed country can be denied developed world social and cultural citizenship, as is the case for those who have criminal records, are impoverished, or suffer discrimination.[33] Those unable or unwilling to become full legal citizens of a developed country could still obtain a more limited kind of legal citizenship in that country by acquiring documents (such as the US green card) that grant permanent residency rights in that country without requiring that they give up legal citizenship rights in any other country. Even full legal citizens of a developed country are not guaranteed social and cultural citizenship in the developed world. Even someone without any kind of legal citizenship in any developed country can still attain social and cultural citizenship comparable to or even better than the social and cultural citizenship of most legal citizens of developed countries by getting degrees from prestigious colleges and universities of the developed world and by getting work (in any developed or developing country) that provides them with levels of income, prestige, and mobility comparable to those enjoyed by professionals and businesspeople in developed countries. Regardless of whether they live in China or abroad and whether they have passports issued by China or by a developed country, those who have developed world social and cultural citizenship can have capabilities and freedoms similar to those of most citizens and residents of developed countries.

I use the term *developed countries* to refer to nation-states, such as Australia, Canada, Japan, Singapore, the United States, and most countries of Western Europe, that consistently place at the top of per capita GDP rankings and recognize each other as political and military allies. On the other hand, I use the term *developed world* to refer not to any specific ethnicity, geographic region, or nation-state but rather to an imagined global community of affluent, powerful, and prestigious people. The developed world consists of a global neoliberal community defined more by the wealth, mutual recognition, and cultural and social citizenship of its members than by legal citizenship or geographic or national boundaries. The developed world is a loosely organized and flexibly bounded but increasingly powerful, exclusive, and united formation of individuals worldwide; most of these individuals are residents and legal citizens of developed countries, but some of them are residents and legal citizens of developing countries. The global neoliberal system disproportionately draws support from and favors the perspectives of the developed world, which has disproportionate social, cultural, economic, military, and political power.

Ever since I began doing research in China, I have struggled to find English words that adequately describe the goals toward which the Chinese citizens I met were striving, which I now call the developed world, developed world citizenship, and developed countries. At first I used the term *First World*,[34] a phrase coined by the French demographer Alfred Sauvy in 1952, when he drew an analogy between the nonindustrialized countries and the "third estate" (*tiers état*), which in prerevolutionary France referred to commoners who could be contrasted with the clergymen (the "first estate") and the nobility (the "second estate").[35] During the Cold War, the term *Third World* referred to regions that were not aligned with either the capitalist bloc ("First World") or the socialist bloc ("Second World"). I stopped using First World and Third World, however, because these terms seemed increasingly outdated as the Cold War receded further into the past. Similarly, I started out using Immanuel Wallerstein's distinction between "core regions" and "peripheral regions" but found that his emphasis on regions was increasingly inadequate for addressing the deterritorializable citizenship statuses granted by the global neoliberal system that grew out of the capitalist world system he described.[36]

I also tried using the term *wealthier societies* but stopped once I realized that wealth was not the only factor that determined membership in the developed world.[37] If wealth were all that mattered, then Chinese citizens in my study would be talking about and trying to study in countries such as Qatar, the United Arab Emirates, Kuwait, or the Bahamas, all of which have per capita incomes similar to those of developed countries. My surveys, interviews, and participant observation, however, all suggested that those countries were rarely mentioned by Chinese citizens in my study and were never considered places to attend school.

I have used, and continue to use, the term *Western countries* when discussing Australia, New Zealand, Europe, and North America. I am careful, however, to use that term only when emphasizing cultural, geographic, and linguistic similarities and alliances between those countries. I avoid conflating "Western" with "developed" because "Western" does not fit Asian developed countries such as Singapore and Japan.

I considered using the terms used by citizens of developing countries described in other studies, such as *outside* or *the donor countries* that Karen Hansen observed Zambians using when they referred to developed countries.[38] Yet these terms seemed either too broad or too narrow to fit the community that Chinese citizens imagined when they spoke of the paradise they wanted to join.

Another problem with terms such as *core regions, outside, donor countries, Western countries,* and *wealthier societies* lies in how they tie developed world status to geographically bounded regions or legally bounded nation-states. To adequately describe the community imagined by Chinese citizens in my study, I needed terms that could apply to individuals as well as to regions, territories, alliances, and nation-states. I tried using the terms *elite* or *global elite*,[39] which put the emphasis on individuals, but stopped using them because they sounded awkward as descriptors for countries.

I finally settled on the terms *developed countries, developed world,* and *developed world citizens* because "developed" and "developing" are the only terms among the ones I considered that could be translated directly into commonly used Chinese terms with similar meanings (e.g., developing countries [*fazhanzhong guojia*] and developed countries [*fada guojia*]) and because these terms have also been used frequently in Anglophone scholarship to describe the goals toward which Chinese citizens and leaders aspired. Many Anglophone anthropologists and cultural studies scholars have criticized discourses of development and the privileging of developed countries as the models that all other countries should emulate at all costs.[40] But Anglophone economists, demographers, and public health researchers have helped promote such discourses,[41] which have also been dominant in China since the post-Mao economic reforms that began in the 1970s and to a lesser extent since the establishment of the People's Republic of China in 1949. Although the sense of impoverishment and dissatisfaction experienced by Chinese citizens in my study results partly from their acceptance of assumptions underlying development discourses, it is clear that they and their government no longer perceive any alternatives to these discourses when it comes to determining the goals toward which they should strive. The Chinese government tried to present Maoism as an alternative to development discourses for a few decades (1949–1976) after the founding of the People's Republic of China. But it could not get rid of the teleological imperatives of development discourses entirely, because Maoism itself was based partly on the goal of catching up with the industrial and military standards of the developed countries. After Mao Zedong's death in 1976, Chinese leaders and citizens stopped resisting integration into the global neoliberal system and instead sought to raise their position within this system by trying to become as economically, educationally, and demographically similar to developed countries and developed world citizens as possible.

There are no clear rules to determine which countries can be classified as "developed countries" or which individuals can be classified as part of the "developed world." Efforts to come up with such rules in international discourses and among international organizations (e.g., the United Nations [UN], the International Monetary Fund [IMF], the World Bank, the G8, the OECD, and the World Trade Organization [WTO]) are controversial. Some countries, such as Australia, Britain, Canada, Japan, the United States, and most Western European countries, are always classified as developed countries regardless of the criteria used; other countries, such as Qatar, the United Arab Emirates, Kuwait, the Bahamas, and most Eastern European countries, are sometimes categorized as developed countries and sometimes as developing countries. Most Chinese citizens in my study wanted to study in the countries that were always classified as developed. China itself is usually classified as among the most developed of the developing countries, and most of its policies and the efforts of its citizens are geared toward transforming China into a developed country and bringing as many of its citizens as possible into the developed world as quickly as possible. This process, which Chinese citizens call development (*fazhan*) and modernization (*xiandaihua*), is one in which the Chinese citizens in my study are heavily invested, because it could potentially redefine China and most Chinese citizens as part of the paradise that many currently have to go abroad to find.

Global border control systems limit the mobility of legal citizens of the developing world while allowing legal citizens of the developed world to travel quickly and easily almost anywhere in the world. Legal citizenship in any developed country usually gives one the right to enter any other developed country, either without a visa or with a short-term tourist visa automatically granted upon one's arrival at the airport. The process of getting visas, permanent residency rights, and legal citizenship from developed and developing countries alike is also quicker, easier, and less likely to result in denials for legal citizens of developed countries than for legal citizens of developing countries, who have to provide much more evidence that they are not likely to become security threats or undocumented immigrants. Most developing countries, on the other hand, are too dependent on income from travelers from developed countries and at too little risk of having them stay as undocumented immigrants to be selective about admitting them. They therefore quickly, easily, and almost automatically grant visas and immigration documents to citizens of developed countries. Governments of developing countries that have tense relationships with some developed countries require more waiting and documentation from citizens of those countries who apply for visas or permanent residency rights documents but are still likely to approve most of those applications eventually. Many developing countries (including China) are as restrictive as developed countries are about granting visas or permanent residency rights to legal citizens of other developing countries that rank below them in development hierarchies, but they treat legal citizens of other developing countries that rank above them close to how they treat legal citizens of developed countries.

On the other hand, legal citizens of developed countries who lack social and cultural citizenship in the developed world lack the capabilities (such as wealth, skills, knowledge, education, credentials, and social networks) that would enable them to take advantage of the legal rights guaranteed by their legal citizenship. Their legal right to quick, easy, and automatic entry into other countries cannot be used if they lack the money and vacation time to travel to those countries. Although they have the legal right to live, work, and get subsidized education in the developed country in which they live, they can still end up with educational attainment, jobs, and incomes that are worse than those of Chinese citizens (in the same developed country or in China) who have more social and cultural citizenship in the developed world. Legal citizens of developed countries can even be legally excluded from the developed world if their inadequate developed world social and cultural citizenship results in criminal records that cause them to be denied many of the legal rights that other legal citizens of their countries have, in both national and transnational contexts. Getting visas, permanent residency rights, or naturalization documents in developed or developing countries can even be more difficult for legal citizens of developed countries with criminal records than for legal citizens of developing countries without criminal records.

The Global Neoliberal System

Neoliberalism (defined by David Harvey as a "theory of political economic practices that proposes that human well-being can best be advanced by liberating individual entrepreneurial freedoms and skills within an institutional framework characterized by strong private property rights, free markets, and free trade")[42] is accepted and promoted to varying degrees by most countries and individuals that are part of the developed world or seeking to join it.[43] The global neoliberal system is the twenty-first century version of the capitalist world system described by Immanuel Wallerstein.[44] The capitalist world system dominated the global economy from the sixteenth to the twentieth century and was based on an international division of labor in which core regions dominated by exchanging expensive professional services and manufactured goods for cheap labor and raw materials from peripheral regions. As the dominant engine of a twenty-first century world with increasingly rapid and efficient transportation and communication technologies, the global neoliberal system resembles the capitalist world system that gave birth to it but locates itself more in the bodies of disciplined, deterritorializable individuals than in particular regions or nation-states.[45]

Although transnational migration has occurred for as long as nations have existed, it has never been as quick, easy, and inexpensive as it has become in the twenty-first century.[46] As new technologies have made transportation,[47] market exchanges,[48] communication,[49] and media flows[50] easier, faster, and cheaper, transnational migration has become possible and sometimes even necessary for an ever-increasing proportion of the world's population. In the global neoliberal system that dominates the twenty-first century world, economic, cultural, and social capital can be much more fluid and transnational than the physical means of production (such as machines, factories, and transportation infrastructures) that undergirded the political economy of the capitalist world system of previous centuries. As the significance of knowledge, skills, and information in determining global power relationships has increased, so have possibilities for individuals to develop citizenship rights and privileges that transcend the socioeconomic classifications of the countries and regions in which they reside or have legal citizenship. The demands, desires, and needs of transnational migrants have helped to transform the social, political, and economic systems and infrastructure of many countries and have compelled their governments to seek stronger geopolitical alliances and better integration with global systems.

The global neoliberal system has become increasingly powerful and pervasive worldwide as the proportion of countries and individuals who submitted to neoliberal governmentality increased.[51] Although it is based on the same hierarchies, exchanges, and technologies that structured the capitalist world system, the global neoliberal system offers individuals greater opportunities for deterritorialization, flexible citizenship, and transcendence of state sovereignties.[52] Centers and peripheries are no longer tied to geographic regions as they were in the capitalist world system Wallerstein described; rather, they are located in easily portable skills, credentials, bank accounts, and citizenship documents. The developed center could be located in the office of a corporate manager in New York, but it could also be located in Dalian, in the office of a Dalian native with US university degrees and permanent residency rights documents who is managing the Dalian branch of a multinational corporation and getting paid the same as her counterpart in New York. The developing periphery could likewise be located in either Dalian or New York, in the body of a Chinese janitor vacuuming floors in the same office building owned by the same multinational corporation. Chinese citizens in my study wanted to study abroad not because they wanted to move closer to a geographic center but because they wanted to make the leap from a trajectory that they feared would lead them to the life of a janitor onto a trajectory that they hoped would lead them to the life of a manager. The freedoms and capabilities of the manager and the janitor were seen as so different that some Chinese citizens believed that they needed to study on the other side of the earth to have a chance at eventually becoming a manager rather than a janitor in the same building in China.

A visa to go abroad was seen as a hard-won opportunity to begin a process that could eventually enable one to settle down in a developed country or to live as a social, cultural, and possibly legal citizen of the developed world even after returning to China. Although some Chinese citizens in my study saw study abroad as the first step toward permanent immigration, most were more ambivalent. They wanted to stay in a developed country long enough to acquire social, cultural, and sometimes legal citizenship in that country, but they also wanted to eventually return to China with the ability to go abroad again at any time and the ability to enjoy the same freedoms and capabilities they would enjoy in developed countries. A 24-year-old office worker applying for permanent residency rights in Australia told me six years after she left China to attend a university in Australia, "If China develops well, I'll just stay there, and if not, I'll go somewhere else. I can't abandon my parents in China after all they've done for me, but if I go back to China, I may never earn back the money they spent to send me abroad. I'd prefer to live in China, but I don't want to be stuck there. It's not that I don't love my country—I do, but China's too scary—every few years something like SARS happens, and I don't want to be stuck there if things go bad. And if I'm in China and see a good opportunity abroad, I want to be able take it. So I'll only want to return to China as an Australian citizen, so that I can go abroad again anytime I want. I have to get citizenship in Australia before I can go back to China; if I don't, I'll be stuck in China again, with nothing to show for all my family sacrificed. Maybe China will have a bright future, or maybe not, but if conditions in China are bad in the future, I would feel gloomy if I were locked in there and couldn't get out."

Chinese citizens in my study hoped that, by going abroad, they would transform themselves from citizens of the developing world into citizens of the developed world. Many of them hoped that, after living a few years or a few decades in a developed country, they would be able to eventually return to China—but as social, cultural, and perhaps legal citizens of the developed world and thus armed with developed world levels of wealth, developed world skills and credentials that would qualify them to receive developed-world-level salaries, and perhaps legal permanent residency rights in a developed country that would enable them to travel almost anywhere in the world anytime they wanted. What they feared was that they would never attain the developed world citizenship they desired, even after studying abroad, and that they would have to choose between returning to China empty-handed, to resume their old lives as citizens of the developing world, and remaining part of the developing world, as stigmatized, impoverished, undocumented immigrants, even while living in a developed country.

Research Methods

This book draws on data from an ongoing longitudinal mixed-method study of a cohort of Chinese citizens born under China's one-child policy. I have been conducting this study since 1997. All my survey data come from respondents who attended the Dalian schools where I taught English between 1998 and 2000. I surveyed students in all the homerooms (*banji*) in grades 8 and 9 during fall 1999 at the junior high school (*chuzhong*), all the homerooms in grades 10, 11, and 12 during spring or fall 1999 at the regular college prep high school (*putong gaozhong*), and one homeroom in grade 12 and most of the homerooms in grades 10 and 11 during fall 1999 at the vocational high school (*zhiye zhongzhuan*).

Most homerooms had 40–50 students, although the largest homeroom had 56 students and the smallest had 31 students. Students in each homeroom sat in the same seat in the same classroom all day, every day, while teachers of different subjects came into the homeroom at different times to teach different lessons. My survey asked these students about their academic interests, educational histories, family structures, gender socialization, socioeconomic conditions, and interactions with their parents. Each school contributed about a third of the respondents to my 1999 survey.[53] A comparison of my survey respondent lists with school enrollment lists showed that 9 percent of the 2,489 students enrolled in the homerooms I surveyed either declined to complete my survey or were not in class at the time I conducted the survey.[54]

The schools where I conducted my survey in 1999 enrolled students from a wide range of socioeconomic backgrounds, although the most disadvantaged teenagers in Dalian (e.g., those who were severely disabled or lacked urban residential registration) were excluded, and the most elite teenagers (who were more likely to attend private schools, keypoint high schools, or schools in developed countries) were underrepresented. On the high school application form for those who graduated from junior high school in 1999, school types were ranked by selectivity in the following order, from most selective to least selective: (1) keypoint college prep high schools (*zhongdian gaozhong*); (2) ordinary/regular college prep high schools (*putong gaozhong*); (3) private college prep high schools (*minban gaozhong*); and (4) professional high schools, vocational high schools, professional vocational high schools, adult education vocational high schools, and technical high schools (*zhongdeng zhuanye xuexiao, zhiye gaozhong, zhiye zhongzhuan, chengren zhongzhuan,* and *jigong xuexiao,* respectively). The college prep high school I surveyed belonged in the second most selective category, and the vocational high school I surveyed

belonged in the least selective category. The junior high school I surveyed had the widest range of achievement levels and socioeconomic
statuses, because it was located in a socioeconomically average school
district and admitted all primary school graduates in its district without regard to their exam scores or ability to pay. Chinese junior high
schools and primary schools were compulsory and inexpensive; they
were not given official state-sanctioned rankings and were attended
by almost all urban citizens who were not severely disabled. Some
junior high schools and primary schools had especially good reputations that drew children whose parents could afford the extra fees
and bribes required of students from outside the school's district, and
some others had especially bad reputations that caused most of the
wealthiest parents of students in those districts to pay extra fees and
bribes to enroll their children at other schools. But many junior high
schools (including the one where I administered my survey) had average reputations that did not attract or repel a lot of students.

During almost two years of participant observation (1998–2000)
at the schools where I conducted my 1999 survey, I worked as an
unpaid English conversation teacher, giving lessons in each of the 46
homerooms I surveyed and offering extra English-related classes and
activities for interested students from various homerooms during
breaks, study halls, and lunch periods. When I was not teaching, I sat
with students, observing their classes, meetings, study hall periods,
breaks, and lunch periods throughout the school day.

After respondents to my 1999 survey graduated, I kept in touch
with 92 of them and their families, visiting some of them during the
1–3 months I spent in Dalian almost every year between 2002 and
2010.[55] I also communicated with them by phone, e-mail, and instant
messaging when I was not in China.[56] Between 1997 and 2010, I lived
in the homes of nine Chinese families and visited the homes of hundreds of other Chinese citizens, most of whom were survey respondents or their friends or relatives. They and their parents invited me
to their homes initially to provide tutoring or advice about how they
might get opportunities to study or work abroad, and later because
we became friends.

The first few years after my survey respondents graduated from the
schools where I had met them, I focused on staying in touch with as
many of them as possible. I hoped to do longitudinal research about
how they dealt with the challenges of higher education, careers, childbearing, and the rearing and education of their own children, for the

rest of their lives. I was surprised, though, to find that when I called their landline home phone numbers in China to arrange visits, I was told by some of their parents that they were studying abroad. I began talking on the phone with those who had gone abroad, and I visited some of them in Australia, Britain, Ireland, Japan, and the United States, not because I wanted to focus on study abroad as a research topic but merely because I did not want to lose touch with them.

I initially thought that those who studied abroad would constitute only a tiny proportion of those in my study and thus only a small part of the broader story I would tell in this book, which I thought would be about how singletons of their generation pursued higher education and careers during the transition from adolescence to young adulthood, mostly in China and occasionally abroad. As increasing numbers of the singletons I had met in China began studying abroad, though, I realized that study abroad was becoming more common than I had imagined it could be and that even many of those who had not studied abroad were talking about wanting to. I wondered whether it was just a matter of time before most of the other singletons I knew in Dalian studied abroad as well. If I did not start paying attention to transnational migration, I could miss out on an important period of their lives or even lose touch with them altogether. I decided, then, that the study-abroad process itself should be the focus of this book.

When some of the Chinese youth in my study started studying in Australia, Britain, Ireland, Japan, and the United States, I followed them to those countries, living with them in the crowded houses and apartments they shared with other transnational students of similar ages, most of whom shared their linguistic, socioeconomic, and demographic backgrounds. Between 2003 and 2010, I spent more than a year (intermittently, a few days, weeks, or months at a time) conducting participant observation and interviews in those countries, sharing rooms, meals, and social activities with transnational students whom I had first met in China and getting to know hundreds of their Chinese classmates, roommates, friends, and co-workers abroad. Sometimes they had extra rooms, beds, or cots for me to sleep on (usually because a roommate or housemate had just moved out or was temporarily in China or elsewhere for a visit). Other times, I slept on a couch or on the floor in a sleeping bag I brought with me.

I visited transnational students in my study whenever I had time to travel, usually before or after my annual trip to China but sometimes when I happened to pass through or close to the cities or towns where they were studying while I was traveling to give lectures, attend academic conferences, or visit family and friends who were not in my study. Many of my trips were made on "Round the World" plane tickets that offered considerable flexibility for last-minute itinerary changes, so long as I traveled in only one direction around the world, from my local airport in Boston to other cities in the United States, then to various cities in Japan, China, Australia, Ireland, and Britain, and finally back to Boston. Once I bought the ticket (which cost US$3,500–$5,000 and was good for one year), I could use it in accordance with those rules to fly to up to 15 cities worldwide on airlines that were part of the appropriately named Oneworld alliance, which was yet another global system for facilitating the transnational mobility of developed world citizens with the time, money, knowledge, and documents to travel quickly and easily through many countries on one trip.

When I lived with Chinese citizens abroad, many acquaintances of those I first met in Dalian initially thought I was yet another newly arrived student from Dalian. When I went with them to bars, eateries, churches, parties, schools, stores, and parks in the developed countries in which they were studying, I was sometimes asked by natives of those countries if I could speak English and I was praised for the quality of my English when I did speak it. Even after I explained my citizenship status, education, work background, and reason for visiting, most of the Chinese citizens in my study and their Chinese and non-Chinese acquaintances abroad still treated me as yet another member of the transnational Chinese community in the country in which they lived, which in a way I was. I had inherited my US citizenship from my father, who had been a Chinese citizen before he left Beijing (then Beiping), China, in the 1940s to attend college in the United States, where he eventually became a naturalized US citizen before spending the 1970s working in international trade in Taiwan, where he met and married my mother, who was 20 years younger than him. I inherited his legal US citizenship when I was born in Taiwan in 1974, went with them to the United States in 1977, and stayed in the United States continuously until 1997, when I began my research in China. My academic interest in China was initially sparked by my curiosity about my family's background and that of the Chinese immigrants I grew up with in Southern California, and my ability to conduct research in China was facilitated by my native fluency in Mandarin Chinese. I explained to Chinese citizens that my social, cultural, and legal citizenship was similar to what their children might have if they are raised in a developed country as legal citizens of that country. Many of them told me that they hoped that any children they raised abroad would be as fluent in Chinese and interested in China as I was.

Meanwhile, I was also trying to stay in touch with everyone else I had first met in Dalian, as I hoped (and still hope) to continue following the trajectories of their education, careers, childbearing, and child rearing, regardless of where they end up living. I continued to call, e-mail, and visit as many of them as possible, in China and abroad, but this grew increasingly difficult as more of them migrated all over China and the world, frequently changing their phone numbers, home addresses, and e-mail and instant messenger addresses. At first I relied on their parents, who were far less likely to migrate, to keep me in touch with them after they left home. Even this became more difficult, however, because many of their parents (most of whom lacked e-mail or instant messenger addresses and some of whom lacked cell phones) sold their homes and moved to other parts of the same city, sometimes using the difference between the price of their more valuable old homes near the city center and their less valuable new homes in the suburbs to finance their children's transnational migration. I worried that my plans to follow them longitudinally for the rest of their lives would be jeopardized by all this migration. I knew I had to reestablish contact with more of them by doing a systematic resurvey of respondents to my 1999 survey if my longitudinal study was to continue.

I began that resurvey in 2008. Between June 1, 2008, and December 31, 2010, I tried to track down and survey all 2,273 of the respondents who had completed my survey in 1999. By December 31, 2010, I had survey responses from 1,365 of them.[57] My research assistants and I started with those with whom I had stayed in touch after 1999 and with those whose families were still using the landline phone numbers they had given me in 1999. We asked them to help us find the current contact information of their former classmates, whether they were in Dalian, other places in China, or abroad. Most survey respondents had kept in continuous contact with at least a few of their classmates, and some had kept in touch with most of their classmates. Even those who were living abroad or in other cities in China kept in touch with their classmates by e-mail, phone calls, occasional visits to Dalian, instant messaging, and social networking websites. Students in each homeroom had spent most of their waking hours together in the same classroom for two or three years, and some of the junior high school students had spent six years of primary school together in addition to spending three years of junior high school together.[58] As a result, most respondents had become lifelong friends with at least some of their classmates. Some homerooms had organized their own reunions before.

As I collected surveys, I discovered that many alumni that I had lost touch with after they graduated were also studying abroad. I conducted phone interviews with them and also interviewed some of them in person when they and I were in China. I organized homeroom reunions in Dalian during the summers of 2009 and 2010 for all the alumni who had completed my survey in 1999. A total of 362 showed up for the 47 homeroom reunions I organized in 2009, and 404 showed up for the 34 homeroom reunions I organized in 2010.[59] Altogether, 522 alumni came to at least one of these reunions. Of these, 244 attended their reunions both years (2010 and 2009), and an additional 278 attended one reunion but not the other.

These reunions enabled me to get back in touch with many alumni whom I had lost touch with after they graduated, including many of those whom I had never gotten to know well even while I was their English teacher. Some who were living abroad or in other Chinese cities were also able to come because they happened to be in Dalian on vacation during their homeroom's reunion. A few even purposefully scheduled their visits to Dalian to coincide with their homeroom's reunion dates. Most who came were motivated more by a desire to see their former classmates, some of whom they had not seen since they graduated, than by a desire to see me. They helped prevent my study from becoming too affected by selection bias based on interest in me and what I could teach about English and about life in the United States.

Some alumni declined my invitation to the reunions because they were too busy or did not have warm feelings toward me or their former classmates. Others, sometimes in the same homeroom, still had the photos they had taken with me a decade ago or the notes they had taken based on my English lessons. I was moved when alumni I had not seen for a decade recalled specific details of my English lessons. One recalled how I drew a book with a smiling, bespectacled worm sticking out of it to teach them the English word *bookworm* and said that the term could be used to describe me. Another told me that she had been impressed with how I drank boiled tap water instead of buying new bottles of water even though I could afford to buy them, followed my example, and saved lot of money over the years as a result. Some recalled the time I did an awkward imitation of Michael Jackson's dance moves as I taught them the song "Beat It," and many recalled the time I played Rapunzel and beat my hands against the air like a mime as I pretended to be trapped behind the glass window of a tower in an adaptation of the musical *Into the Woods* that I directed and performed with their classmates for a schoolwide talent show.

Alumni reacted with amused surprise when they saw that thin classmates were now fat, fat classmates were now thin, unusually short and unusually tall classmates were now of average height, classmates of average height had grown into giants, and tomboyish girls who used to have boyish haircuts now had waist-length hair, makeup, jewelry, and frilly dresses. Some could no longer recognize many of their classmates or remember the names of those whose faces they recognized; others not only recognized each classmate but also impressed everyone by reciting each classmate's name, class registration number, and seat assignments. They shared memories, laughing and joking about the foibles of their teachers and classmates and shedding new light on my understandings of friendships and conflicts that I had not fully understood when I observed them a decade ago. Several men play-wrestled and rode piggyback on each other just as they had when they were 14, even though they were now 24. Almost every homeroom had several alumni who were dating or had married their classmates. Some of these couples had been secretly dating since adolescence (against school rules, which prohibited dating), and others had not been particularly close as adolescents but married after getting to know each other better later on. These couples' classmates teased them about how their secret romances had been obvious all along, or they reacted with exaggerated shock at how unlikely some couples seemed (the troublemaker who married the teacher's pet, for instance).

Some alumni at these reunions had returned to Dalian from study abroad, either for permanent residence or for a short visit, and regaled their classmates with stories about life abroad. I was struck by how most of them told their classmates only about what they liked about life abroad. Even some who had told me in more private settings that they had been unhappy abroad told their classmates only about the fun, amusing, and admirable things they saw and did abroad. Others did not talk much to their classmates about their experiences abroad, preferring instead to talk about their current life in China and about their shared memories of high school or junior high school. Most of those I interviewed over the phone but did not already know well were similarly reluctant to tell me about bad experiences they had had abroad. Most of the unpleasant experiences I describe in this book were ones that I observed or heard about while living with Chinese citizens abroad or ones I was told about over the phone by those who considered me a close friend. The Chinese citizens in my study seemed reluctant to talk about any unpleasant aspects of life, in China or abroad, around those who had never been abroad and were not their close friends. This may be part of the reason that many Chinese citizens who got information about life abroad from those they did not know well assumed that developed countries were "like paradise."

I asked alumni to fill out paper surveys at each homeroom reunion.[60] My research assistants and I also sent surveys by e-mail or instant messenger services to those who could not attend the homeroom reunions because they were abroad, in other Chinese cities, or in Dalian but too busy to come; we asked them to complete the surveys and send them back to us by e-mail or instant messenger. In addition, we conducted brief phone and instant messenger surveys (asking only a few key questions about study and work abroad, marriage, and childbearing) with those who were too busy to complete surveys by e-mail or instant messenger or who lacked regular Internet access.[61] I also asked alumni who had attended the homeroom reunions to help me find their classmates who had not attended and ask them to e-mail me their completed surveys as well. The homeroom reunions were an incentive for those who were not living in Dalian to send me their surveys, as many were grateful to me for organizing the reunions even if they themselves could not attend, and they also wanted to make sure I had their contact information so that I could keep them posted on the dates and locations of future reunions just in case they were able to return to Dalian on those dates.

The surveys were important for helping me see the big picture of transnational migration among survey respondents, who were likely to be more similar to youth throughout Dalian and other Chinese cities than those who befriended me, among whom fans of the United States and the English language were disproportionately represented. Survey respondents were selected just because they had attended the socioeconomically and academically average schools where I had taught in 1999 and not because they were particularly interested in me.

I had wondered whether those who kept in touch with me were much more likely to study abroad than their classmates who had lost touch with me. What if the ones I kept in touch with were actually an unusual group of Americaphiles who differed greatly from the vast majority of Chinese citizens of their age, most of whom had no interest in study abroad? If that had been the case, I would have focused this book on how and why the few who studied abroad became so different from most of their peers and what that meant for them and their society. I found, however, that even among the 1,273 respondents to my 2008–2010 surveys who had not been in contact with me at any time between 1999 and 2008, 29 percent had been abroad (including 17 percent who had studied abroad), and 64 percent of the 590 of them who completed the long version of my survey and had never been abroad wanted to live abroad eventually.[62]

I had also wondered whether those I got to know well were disproportionately likely to study in developed countries. Did a large proportion of 1999 survey respondents uninterested in staying in touch with me study in Africa, the Caribbean, or Central or South America? If that had been the case, I might have tried to talk more with them so that I could write about the emergence of a new subculture of Chinese youth who chose to study in developing countries, perhaps for reasons similar to those of some citizens of developed countries who chose to study in developing countries rather than developed countries.[63] I found, however, that none of the 1,365 respondents to my 2008–2010 surveys had ever attended classes in Africa, South Asia, the Caribbean, Central America, or South America and that only 6 of those respondents had ever stepped foot in any of those regions. Nor did anyone at the class reunions talk about wanting to study in those regions. This finding helped convince me that the desire to study in developed countries rather than developing countries was common among many kinds of youth in Dalian, not just among those who had kept in touch with me.

Because many people in my study know each other and may read this book, I have tried to make it hard for individuals I quote or describe to be recognized by readers who know them.[64] All names in this book are pseudonyms, except for those of published authors I cite and those of public figures I never met.[65]

Defining the Boundaries of a Global Ethnography

Global ethnography and multisited fieldwork are necessary for studying global processes and transnational people. A major challenge of such research, however, is that of figuring out where and how to draw the boundaries of one's research.[66] Ethnography can only illustrate how a particular group of people interact with social processes that are always more complex than the portrait that a single book can present. Ethnography cannot represent the full reality of a group of people even in the geographically bounded villages that used to be its main subjects, much less the full reality of a global phenomenon. It is therefore important to clarify what group of people and which processes an ethnography is illustrating, particularly in a global, multisited study like mine, where the boundaries of the group and the processes studied are not obvious.

I use the phrase *in my study* to describe the Chinese citizens I first met in China between 1997 and 2010 and those I met through the social networks of Chinese citizens I first met in China during that period. I refer to the 2,273 Chinese citizens I first surveyed in 1999 as "survey respondents." I refer to the survey respondents and all the other Chinese citizens whom I first met in China or in other countries through the social networks of Chinese citizens I first met in China as "Chinese citizens in my study."

Survey respondents from Dalian had much in common with most urban Chinese citizens of their generation. According to my 1999 survey, 94 percent (N = 2,167) of survey respondents had no siblings and 5 percent (N = 2,167) had one sibling[67] and 98 percent (N = 2,171) belonged to the Han ethnic group, which made up 92 percent of the Chinese population in 2000.[68] Their ages ranged from 13 to 20 when I first surveyed them in 1999 and from 24 to 31 when I last surveyed them in 2010. Most of the Chinese citizens in my study grew up in Dalian, although some of them grew up in other (mostly northeastern) Chinese cities but were introduced to me in Australia, Britain, Ireland, Japan, or the United States by Chinese citizens I first met in Dalian.

Because much of this book focuses on how transnational Chinese students in my study pursued developed world citizenship that could enhance or replace the Chinese citizenship they had before studying abroad, I should clarify that Chinese citizenship for them consists of the kind of social, cultural, and legal citizenship held by people who are legal residents of cities in mainland China, hold passports (*huzhao*), household registration (*hukou*), and identity cards (*shenfenzheng*) issued by the government of the People's Republic of China, grew up speaking Mandarin Chinese as their only native dialect, are of Han Chinese ethnicity, and were born and raised in mainland China to parents who were also born and raised in mainland China. These conditions fit the vast majority of people in my study, and they fit everyone in my study that I got to know well. The Chinese citizenship of the vast majority of people in my study may differ from the citizenship of people who were born with rural Chinese citizenship, those born in other countries to at least one Chinese parent, those who have one parent who is a Chinese citizen and one parent who is a citizen of another country, citizens of Hong Kong, Macao, or Taiwan, or those who are registered as belonging to one of the 55 Chinese non-Han minority ethnicities recognized by the Chinese government.[69]

Rural Chinese citizens have a kind of citizenship that is different from and less desirable than that of urban Chinese citizens.[70] The process of changing one's household registration from rural to urban in China is actually similar to the process of becoming a naturalized citizen of another country. The experiences of rural Chinese citizens are beyond the scope of this book, because almost everyone in my study was born and raised in a city and had household registration documents from a mainland Chinese city rather than from a rural county. Respondents to my 1999 survey were recruited from urban schools that usually allowed only citizens of Dalian city to enroll. Only 3 percent of the 972 respondents to the birthplace question on my 2008–2010 survey indicated that they were born in rural areas. Because I did most of my participant observation in Dalian city, the vast majority of other people I met in China were also citizens of Dalian city. Even abroad, most of those who were introduced to me by Chinese citizens I first met in China were citizens of Dalian or other northeastern Chinese cities where Mandarin was the main or only dialect of Chinese spoken, because those I first met in China tended to befriend others with the same citizenship status, native dialect, and backgrounds even while they studied abroad.

Although Hong Kong, Taiwan, and Macao are recognized by most countries (albeit controversially in the case of Taiwan) as part of "China," they are historically, socially, economically, politically, demographically, and geopolitically quite different from mainland China and are as restrictive as foreign countries about allowing entry by residents of mainland China.[71] In many ways, they are already part of the developed world. Some aspects of what I write about "China" and "Chinese citizenship" may also be true of Hong Kong, Taiwan, and Macao and citizenship in those places, but they lie beyond the scope of my study. Even though they have strong relationships with the southern provinces of mainland China, Hong Kong, Taiwan, and Macao have relatively weak relationships with the northeastern areas of mainland China where most of the Chinese citizens in my study grew up. When asked to name places outside mainland China where they had ever lived for at least 6 months, only 2 of the 285 who answered that question mentioned Hong Kong, only 1 mentioned Macao, and none mentioned Taiwan. Most considered these places part of China and thus too similar to their own cities to be worthwhile places to study, given that it was as difficult and as expensive to study in Hong Kong, Taiwan, or Macao as it was to study in foreign countries.

I use the phrases *transnational Chinese students* or *transnational students in my study* to refer to current and former Chinese citizens in my study who have ever taken classes outside China.[72] Many of their experiences and perspectives may be shared by other Chinese citizens who have left China but did not attend classes while abroad (e.g., the 5 percent of the 1,365 respondents to my 2008–2010 surveys who worked without attending classes outside China, and the additional 7 percent who have been outside China, mostly as tourists, but did not work or attend classes while abroad).[73] My focus in this book, however, is on the perspectives and experiences of those who studied abroad, because they constituted the majority of transnational Chinese citizens in my study and because the pursuit of some kind of educational goal abroad—whether it was a college degree, graduate degree, or just greater proficiency in a developed country's language and culture—was important to all the transnational Chinese citizens in my study that I got to know well. The 253 transnational respondents who answered the longer version of my 2008–2010 survey first left China at an average age of 23, and 93 percent of them first left China between ages 18 and 28. Because they first left China during a life stage that dominant contemporary urban Chinese norms deemed the proper time to pursue higher education, the pursuit of some kind of education was on the minds of most of the transnationals in my study, even when their main purpose for going abroad was to work, do business, marry, or immigrate and even when they had visas based on those purposes rather than student visas. My study focuses on how a cohort of urban, mostly singleton Chinese citizens born and raised with extremely high educational expectations experienced the transition from adolescence to young adulthood. Youth in my study are therefore more likely to prioritize educational goals than the kinds of Chinese emigrants described in previous studies,[74] most of whom were past their 20s or had grown up in communities in which education was not the main goal of people in their age group.

All the transnational students in my study were born with Chinese citizenship in mainland China, although some eventually became naturalized citizens of other countries as young adults. I use the term *transnational* in its broadest, most literal sense to refer to anyone who crosses a border between two countries, including "immigrants" (who intend to live in a country other than the one they were born in for the rest of their lives), "sojourners" (who intend to return to their homelands for permanent residence after long stays abroad), and "tourists" (who intend to return to their homelands after short stays abroad). I do not distinguish between these different kinds of transnational individuals in my study because their intentions about when and whether to return to China (or to go abroad again after returning to China) are uncertain and frequently changing, making it impossible for them or me to know at this stage if they are going to be sojourners, immigrants, or tourists. Some who entered developed countries on tourist, student, work, or business visas eventually tried to immigrate, while others who received immigration visas, permanent residency rights, or even legal citizenship from developed countries actually returned to China for permanent residence.

I do not use the phrase *in my study* to refer to Chinese citizens I first met in the United States at schools I attended or taught at or to refer to anyone who was not born in mainland China, regardless of their ethnicity, legal citizenship, or when or how I met them. Some of the Chinese citizens in my study introduced me to transnational students who were born in Japan, the Republic of Korea, Taiwan, Hong Kong, and a variety of European, African, Middle Eastern, South Asian, Southeast Asian, Central Asian, North American, and South American countries. I do not address their experiences in this book, however, because they are too different from the transnational students in my study to be within the scope of this research. I also met many Chinese citizens who were transnational students at Harvard University, where I was a student for six years and have been a faculty member for more than seven years, but I have not written about their experiences in this book. Transnational students I met outside my study differed from transnational students in my study in significant ways. For instance, the transnational students who were my classmates or students at Harvard had more prestigious academic credentials and thus more opportunities for upward mobility and freedom to choose education, work, and migration pathways that fit their intellectual passions than the vast majority of transnational students in my study, most of whom attended far less prestigious foreign-language schools, for-profit, technical, or community colleges, or low-ranked universities. Of the hundreds of transnational students in my study who told me about schools they attended, only six attended universities ranked among the top 100 in the world university rankings published in 2010 by Quacquarelli Symonds, Jiaotong University, or *The Times Higher Education*.[75]

Although transnational students outside my study have helped me think about the broader context of transnational migration, I do not include information about their experiences in this book because I have not surveyed, interviewed, or conducted participant observation among them in any systematic way and because discussing their experiences in this book could give readers the mistaken impression that the opportunities and options they had were also available to the transnational students in my study, the vast majority of whom attended socioeconomically and academically average high schools that differed significantly from the elite keypoint high schools that most of the Chinese citizens I met at Harvard attended. Unlike transnational students in my study, my students and former classmates at Harvard all had scholarships or wealthy families that enabled them to devote most of their time to studying without doing low-skilled, low-wage work to support themselves. Students like them were not well represented in the social networks of transnational students in my study, most of which consisted of financially struggling young Chinese transnational students who got to know each other in low-prestige schools, low-wage work settings, and crowded shared rooms, apartments, and houses in developed countries.

Of the hundreds of transnational Chinese students introduced to me by transnational students I had first met in Dalian, only a few were from areas of China where a dialect different from Mandarin was spoken. Linguistic divisions separated the Chinese citizens in my study, most of whom spoke only Mandarin, from Chinese people who spoke other Chinese dialects (such as Cantonese or Min Nan dialects) that were as unintelligible to those who knew only Mandarin as Spanish would be to those who knew only English. Some who grew up in Hong Kong, Taiwan, or Macao could not even speak or understand Mandarin. Although most mainland Chinese citizens were fluent in Mandarin because it was the official language of the educational system and the media in mainland China, many Chinese citizens from the southern and western parts of China preferred to speak their native dialects among friends. Those who spoke only Mandarin felt left out or suspicious that they were being talked about when Chinese people from other regions spoke with each other in another Chinese dialect. Transnational students in my study were therefore most likely to befriend other students from northeastern China who spoke only Mandarin Chinese, even while they were living abroad and had many opportunities to meet Chinese people who spoke other dialects.

Chinese people were engaged in transnational migration for several centuries before the establishment of the People's Republic of China (PRC) in 1949.[76] During the autarkic Maoist era (1949–1978), however, most of the Chinese people who engaged in transnational migration were from places outside the control of the mainland Chinese government, such as Taiwan, Hong Kong, and Southeast Asia.[77] Even in the 1980s and 1990s, when the policies of "reform and opening up" (*gaige kaifang*) were transforming China, most Chinese citizens still had to have great wealth, scholarships, or strong transnational family and hometown business networks before they could go abroad.[78] In the 2000s, however, processes of globalization, fertility decline, and rapid economic growth combined to make transnational migration increasingly possible, even for Chinese citizens who lacked those advantages.

Unlike the multigenerationally transnational Chinese families common in many previous studies of Chinese emigration,[79] the vast majority of the transnational students in my study were the first in their families to go abroad. Only 6 percent of my 275 transnational student survey respondents indicated that at least one of their parents first left China before or during the year the respondent first left China. Unlike previous generations of transnational migrants from China, most transnational students in my study went abroad alone, without scholarships, significant wealth, jobs, extensive transnational social networks, or much knowledge about their destinations. They were part of a new wave of emigrants from China who saw transnational migration as a form of education, tied to the transition from adolescence to adulthood, that could permanently transform them into citizens of the developed world even if they eventually returned to China for permanent residence. As pioneers without established roadmaps for transnational migration, they struggled to define the meaning and purpose of their quest for developed world citizenship. Many were torn between their desire to follow established paths toward permanent immigration in developed countries that had been more common for previous generations of Chinese emigrants and their desire to carve out new paths toward flexible developed world citizenship that would allow them to return to China after several years of education abroad without losing the capabilities they had won abroad.

CHAPTER 2

Is the Moon Rounder Abroad?

How Chinese Citizens See the World

MANY CHINESE CITIZENS referred to developed countries as paradise (*tiantang*) and assumed that they would be happier in those countries than they were in China. Sometimes when they talked about developed countries too much, their friends and relatives asked them, "Is the moon rounder abroad?" suggesting that they were silly to think that everything was better abroad, even the moon, which presumably was the same everywhere. Yet some were not deterred. They believed that life really was better abroad, and they were determined to see for themselves by going abroad.

Although Chinese citizens of all ages in my study agreed that developed world citizenship was desirable, opportunities for attaining it were most abundant for young people who had not yet finished their education, established careers, or started families and thus had the time and flexibility to devote to the quest for developed world citizenship.[1] Opportunities for study abroad became more widely available just as the generation of Chinese citizens most likely to desire them entered the life stage that developed countries' embassies and Chinese families deemed most appropriate for study abroad.

Most transnational students in my study were singletons born after China's one-child policy began in 1979. They were raised with high ambitions and intense parental investment. China's participation in the global neoliberal system subjected Chinese citizens—especially those born under China's fertility limitation policies—to the discipline of that system, which privileges developed world citizens and encourages everyone else to try to acquire developed world citizenship.[2] They perceived study abroad as the next logical step in their journey toward full developed world citizenship.

Seeing China Through a Global Neoliberal Lens

The complaints most Chinese citizens in my study made about China were part of a global narrative about the teleological, dichotomous, unilineal evolutionist division of the world into developed countries that sit at the top of the global social, economic, and political hierarchy and developing countries that must, can, and should play by the rules of the global neoliberal system in order to become developed. This narrative portrays developed countries as existing in the present and developing countries as existing in the past and denies their contemporaneity and mutual influence.[3] This narrative has saturated everyday and official discourses in developing and developed countries. Its roots lie in the imperialist or colonialist campaigns that originated in Western Europe,[4] but it was later adopted by other countries that rose to the top of the capitalist world system. This system emerged in Western Europe during the fifteenth century and spread until it encompassed almost every part of the world.[5] Teleological discourses were disseminated by the developed world to explain and justify the inequalities that structured the capitalist world system and, later, the global neoliberal system that emerged from it and to legitimize that system by promising an evolutionist path by which everyone could someday become part of the developed world if they submitted to the discipline of those systems.

To promote their goal of making China part of the imagined community of the developed world, Chinese state leaders allowed Chinese newspapers, magazines, and television stations to focus heavily on sports and entertainment from the developed world, on positive reports about how things were done in the developed world, on news about successful Chinese projects modeled after similar projects in the developed world, and on commentary by experts from the developed world.[6] Commodities and brand names produced by companies from developed countries were perceived to be of higher quality than those produced by Chinese companies. Many of the fanciest department stores, supermarkets, malls, hotels, and restaurants in China were built at least partly with foreign investment. In China, as in post-socialist countries such as Russia and Nicaragua,[7] developed countries' currencies were valuable because of their stability

and high exchange value, because of their association with an allur-
ing world of foreign wealth, and because of the legal and economic
obstacles that kept them out of the hands of ordinary people. As in
many other developing countries,[8] individuals in China who were
fluent in the developed countries' languages or had returned from
study abroad often got better jobs than they could have obtained
with a comparable Chinese education.

Images of affluence exerted a halo effect on all aspects of developed countries. As Kalman Applbaum observed, in their effort to create new markets for their products, transnational corporations were
"grounded in a classifying framework in which local people's life
situations (demographic characteristics, mentality, and political environment) are evaluated, classified, and incorporated into the Western hierarchy of values for the purposes of making sales" to people
worldwide who "can be reached and appealed to with the message of
the objective superiority of Company X's products, 'brought to you
by' the civilization that made them possible."[9] Many Chinese citizens
accepted this hierarchy and lamented that life in China fell woefully
short by its standards. My US citizenship probably made Chinese
citizens more likely to talk about comparisons between China and
developed countries around me than they would normally. I could
tell, based on what I saw in the Chinese media, Internet discussion
groups, and conversations between strangers on the streets, however, that they also frequently made such comparisons even when
they did not know that someone with US citizenship was around.
Even strangers in buses and shops who did not know I was Chinese
American talked to each other about how "Chinese people are so
poor, unlike foreigners" and lamented that "this is Chinese people's
lot" (*zhongguoren jiu shi zhe ge ming*).

Increasing access to international media narratives that assumed,
enacted, or proclaimed developed countries' superiority over China
while exposing China's problems caused many Chinese citizens to
perceive China as backward. The Chinese media were free to broad-
cast news about events, ideas, and people in other parts of the world
that had no overt relation to Chinese problems. Music, movies, and
television shows from abroad were widely circulated in China, either
through official trade channels or through an illegal but ubiquitous
trade in pirated video compact discs. Although not explicitly critical
of China, global flows of supposedly apolitical information produced
yearnings for the lifestyles and opportunities available abroad and

dissatisfaction with the unavailability of those lifestyles and opportunities in China.[10]

Before going abroad, Chinese citizens in my study got most of their knowledge about life abroad from television, newspapers, magazines, movies, textbooks, and the Internet. Negative views of life abroad were therefore less common among them than among the residents of southern China that Andrea Louie studied, who had more information from friends and relatives who had lived or were living abroad and could tell them about the lives of unsuccessful as well as successful migrants abroad.[11]

Choosing a Country in Which to Study

According to the 256 transnational students who responded to my fill-in-the-blank 2008–2010 survey question "Which places outside of mainland China have you lived in for at least six months," 42 percent had lived in Japan, 15 percent in Ireland, 7 percent in Australia, 8 percent in Britain, 8 percent in the United States, 7 percent in New Zealand, 8 percent in other geographically European countries besides Britain and Ireland, 7 percent in Canada, 6 percent in Singapore, and 2 percent in the Republic of Korea.[12] No other countries were named. The countries in which the transnational students in my study ended up reflects a combination of their personal preferences and the willingness or unwillingness of various countries' embassies to grant and renew their visas. Most transnational students in my study were unable to obtain visas to enter their top-choice countries (usually the United States, Canada, Britain, or Australia). Some applied for many different kinds of visas from many different developed countries before finally being granted a visa by one of them—often one they ranked at the bottom of their list of preferences, such as Japan or Ireland. The opportunities, advantages, and disadvantages that each country offered Chinese citizens varied from year to year. Here I describe how transnational students in my study perceived the countries they were considering as study-abroad destinations between 2000 and 2010, the decade during which most of them went abroad for the first time.

Japan was the country in which the largest proportion of transnational students in my study had lived for at least 6 months. This was due partly to the close (albeit troubled) economic and cultural relationship between Japan and China, and especially between

Japan and Dalian, which had been under Japanese colonial rule from 1905 to 1945.[13] There were many Japanese businesses in China and even more in Dalian than in most other Chinese cities as a result of Dalian's geographic proximity to Japan and its history as Japan's former colony. Chinese citizens proficient in Japanese language and culture therefore had significant advantages once they returned to China (especially Dalian) to find work. Japan is only 2 hours away from Dalian by plane and Japan is one of only three foreign countries with direct commercial airline connections to Dalian (the others being the Republic of Korea and the Democratic People's Republic of Korea). Japan often granted student visas to Chinese citizens who knew no Japanese. On the other hand, Canada, Australia, and the United States required that student visa applicants demonstrate that they could enroll in college or graduate school programs as soon as they arrived or after just a few years of language-school instruction by providing college or graduate school admission letters, passing scores on standardized tests (e.g., the International English Language Testing System [IELTS] or Test of English as a Foreign Language [TOEFL]), or interviews with embassy officials.

Japanese higher education was considered respectable, although its credentials were less universally transferable than those of Anglophone countries. Japan also had more low-skill job opportunities for Chinese students than most other developed countries. It had one of the highest life expectancies and lowest fertility rates in the world and thus an especially rapidly aging population. But Japan was even less likely than most other developed countries to grant permanent residency rights or legal citizenship to foreigners who might otherwise fill the low-skill job niche filled by immigrants in other developed countries. Japan therefore needed a constant supply of temporarily resident young foreign migrants to fill the jobs at the bottom of its socioeconomic hierarchy. Chinese citizens on student or work visas helped fill that need. Japan was the only developed country that allowed its companies to get work visas for Chinese citizens who were living in China and did not already have special skills or credentials but wanted to work in Japan. Because most of the Chinese citizens in my study had studied little or no Japanese language in China, even those who went to Japan on work visas often had to take language classes there to gain proficiency in Japanese.[14]

Most graduate programs and four-year college programs in China required that students demonstrate proficiency in a foreign language before they could graduate, and a foreign language was one of the three core subjects (along with math and Chinese language) tested by China's national college entrance exam and the high school entrance exams given in most Chinese cities, including Dalian. Most Chinese citizens born after 1978 have studied at least several years of a foreign language, and some with especially ambitious parents have studied a foreign language every year since they were in preschool. China's national college entrance exam and many Chinese cities' high school entrance exams allowed students to choose between English, Japanese, and Russian as the language on which they would be tested. But most Chinese junior high and high schools offered instruction only in English. Only a minority of Chinese schools offered Japanese as an alternative language track, and Russian was even rarer. Some Chinese citizens born before the 1970s had studied Russian and remembered looking up to the "Soviet Union" (*sulian*). The Soviet Union had been portrayed as China's more modern "older brother" during the 1950s. The "Russia" (*eluosi*) of the twenty-first century, however, was ignored because it seemed to rank lower than China in the global neoliberal system. English was perceived to be more versatile, useful, and prestigious than Japanese and Russian, and students worried that choosing non-English foreign-language tracks would narrow the range of their future educational opportunities by making them ineligible for the many high school and college programs that accepted only students who had been on the English track.

Because it was historically, geographically, and economically close to Japan, Dalian had more schools offering Japanese-language classes and more students taking these classes than most other Chinese cities. Still, students who wanted to study Japanese were in the minority because Japanese was useful only to those who traveled to Japan or worked with Japanese employers, trade partners and customers. English, on the other hand, was useful for dealing with people from an array of Anglophone countries and could also be used as an international lingua franca because even people from non-Anglophone societies (including Japan) were likely to have studied English. Chinese citizens attending college in Japan often had to study English as well, because most Japanese college programs required their students to become proficient in English. Many academic departments in Japan (especially those in scientific and technical fields) required that students be able to read English-language textbooks and journal articles because Anglophone countries' researchers were producing the most advanced research in those fields and no Japanese translations of their latest work had been published. Many Japanese employers, in China as well as Japan, also preferred to hire employees proficient in English and Japanese, because many of the materials and communications from other countries that Japanese businesses dealt with were in English. Chinese citizens therefore did not see Japanese as a language that could entirely replace English as a key to the developed world. Most studied Japanese as a third language, in college or in private extracurricular, non-degree-granting language programs, after spending many years studying English in junior high school and high school. Among my 2010 survey respondents who answered my language study question, 97 percent ($N = 679$) had studied English and 38 percent ($N = 690$) had studied Japanese, but only 1 percent ($N = 679$) had studied Japanese but not English.

Although Japan was considered the most convenient, lowest cost, and easiest option, it was usually not the top-choice destination for Chinese citizens in my study hoping to study abroad. Many of them had been taken on school field trips to historical museums that featured documentation of the atrocities committed by Japan against Chinese citizens. They grew up watching movies about the Sino-Japanese War, most of which portrayed Japanese soldiers as brutal, sadistic murderers, rapists, and torturers. Even though Chinese leaders wanted peaceful relations with Japan and hoped for increased trade with and investment from Japan, they also condoned suspicion of Japan's geopolitical motives, and this suspicion was reflected in Chinese news broadcasts about Sino-Japanese relations. Many Chinese politics and history textbooks and teachers also portrayed Japan as a former enemy and currently untrustworthy rival. Most Japanese employers offered higher wages and better working conditions than their Chinese counterparts, but Japanese employers were also said to pay less and to offer worse working conditions than Western employers while also demanding more work, longer hours, and stricter physical and personal discipline. Japanese attitudes toward Chinese people were also colored by historical and cultural biases and by discrimination based on perceptions of Chinese citizens as being poorer, less educated, and less well-mannered than Japanese citizens, although anti-Chinese sentiments were not as strong or commonplace among Japanese citizens as anti-Japanese sentiments were among Chinese citizens. Many Japanese politicians emphasized their intention to defend Japan from being overwhelmed by the crime and competition associated with Chinese immigration and by the military and economic threat China could potentially pose. By the mid-2000s, a combination of worsening economic conditions and political discourses associating immigration with criminality led to the tightening of policies that governed the granting and renewal of visas to Chinese students and workers, and fewer Chinese citizens in my study were able to go to or stay in Japan than in earlier years.

After Japan, Ireland was the next most likely country to have transnational students who responded to my survey in residence for at least 6 months. In the 1990s and early 2000s, Ireland had the least restrictive visa policies and the most low-skill job opportunities for Chinese students among all the Anglophone developed countries. Ireland's rapid economic growth during that period created large numbers of low-skill job opportunities for foreign sojourners, including transnational students from China. Chinese citizens learned from study-abroad brokers in China that Ireland was the Anglophone developed country most likely to have lenient enough visa laws and plentiful enough job opportunities to enable them to earn enough from low-skill service jobs to support themselves, pay language-school tuitions, and accumulate enough savings to pay for college tuition. Unlike Australia, Canada, and the United States, which were reluctant to grant student visas to Chinese citizens who could not prove that they had enough English-language proficiency to enroll in higher education programs soon after they arrived, Ireland often granted student visas even to Chinese citizens who knew little English.

Although most Chinese citizens in my study considered Ireland preferable to Japan as a place to study, Ireland was not their top choice either. Many knew nothing about Ireland until a study-abroad broker or friend or relative told them about it after their initial hopes of studying in other Anglophone countries were dashed. Ireland did not have many migrants from any country until its economic boom began in the 1990s. The first large wave of transnational migrants who arrived in Ireland then helped to create a market for services that encouraged further transnational migration, such as private ESOL (English for speakers of other languages) schools, Internet cafes, homestay programs, and study-abroad brokers. Chinese citizens considered Ireland's previous lack of immigrants an advantage, because it meant that there would be less competition for low-skill jobs. But Ireland was still considered less economically powerful and academically prestigious than the United States, Britain, Canada, or Australia. Ireland was also less likely than those countries to enable foreign students to eventually obtain permanent residency rights or legal citizenship after completing their degrees. Like Japan, Ireland began tightening its policies toward the granting and renewal of visas to Chinese citizens in the mid-2000s because of a combination of political pressures and worsening economic conditions.

Britain was seen as one of the most desirable places to study. It was Anglophone, seen as among the economically strongest and educationally and culturally most prestigious countries in the world, and respected for its history as a former superpower. It was also easier to get a student visa to enter Britain than it was to get a student visa to enter the United States, Canada, or Australia. Because of the exchange rate between the Chinese yuan and the British pound, however, the costs of living and tuition for Chinese citizens were even higher in Britain than in other developed countries. Britain also had immigration policies that resembled those of Japan and Ireland. It was harder for transnational students in my study to find jobs in Britain than it was in Japan and Ireland, because Britain's low-skill job market was already saturated with transnational migrants from Britain's former colonies.

Although it was harder to get a visa to enter Australia than it was to get a visa to enter Japan, Ireland, or Britain, Australia was one of the two Anglophone developed countries with the most lenient immigration policies for transnational students who wanted to become permanent residents or legal citizens (the other being New Zealand). Australia was therefore a top choice for those who hoped to immigrate. It was also preferred because it was Anglophone, known for its natural beauty and warm weather, and had a higher education system that was considered respectable, though not as prestigious as those of the United States, Britain, or Canada. Australia was more sparsely populated than most other developed countries, so there was less competition for jobs. But it also had fewer jobs, and most Chinese citizens in my study thought that Australia was less economically developed and therefore less likely to offer them good career opportunities than the United States, Britain, or Canada.

The United States was the top-choice destination for most Chinese citizens in my study, because it was Anglophone and also considered the most educationally, economically, culturally, and geopolitically powerful country in the world. The United States was also more likely than Britain, Ireland, or Japan (though less likely than Australia, Canada, and New Zealand) to allow transnational students to eventually become permanent residents or legal citizens. But the United States had stricter visa requirements than any other developed country, especially after September 11, 2001; thus only the wealthiest or highest achieving Chinese citizens in my study and those who already had parents in the United States had a chance of being able to study there. US visa-granting policies became more lenient in the late 2000s, but the United States was still considered the most difficult country for Chinese citizens to enter.

Canada was often a second or third choice after the United States, because it was perceived as similar to (though somewhat colder, less powerful and prestigious, and less economically developed than) the United States. Canada was also somewhat more lenient than the United States (though less lenient than Japan, Ireland, Britain, and Australia) with regard to the granting of visas, permanent residency rights, and legal citizenship to Chinese citizens.

Singapore granted visas, permanent residency rights, and citizenship as easily as Australia did and was also considered easier for Chinese citizens to adjust to, because Mandarin Chinese was one of its official languages and the second most commonly spoken language after English. Although most Singaporean college classes were offered in English, many classmates and instructors could offer explanations in Chinese, as could many other people throughout Singaporean society. Singapore's higher education system was considered respectable, but Singapore was too small to be deemed likely to offer many economic opportunities to Chinese citizens, many of whom considered it too similar to Chinese cities to be worth the effort and expense of study abroad.

New Zealand granted permanent residency rights and citizenship as easily as Australia did and granted visas even more easily than Australia did. But New Zealand was considered less educationally prestigious and less likely to offer economic opportunities than most other developed countries. As an Anglophone country with close geopolitical ties to Australia, New Zealand was considered a smaller, less developed version of Australia and sometimes a stepping-stone to Australia.

Some non-Anglophone Western European countries, such as France and Germany, were seen as desirable destinations because they offered a tuition-free university education to anyone who could qualify for university admissions, even Chinese citizens. Many Chinese citizens admired the cultures, economies, and historical accomplishments of these Western European countries. Permanent residency rights or legal citizenship in any European Union (EU) country could also allow one to have similar social and legal rights in all the other EU countries. But most Chinese citizens in my study were unable or unwilling to go to non-Anglophone European countries because they had not studied any European languages besides English and found the likelihood that they would have to learn a new language daunting. In addition, those countries were not seen as able to offer many opportunities for Chinese citizens to make money or acquire permanent residency rights or citizenship, and the university credentials they offered, while respectable, were harder to transfer to other parts of the developed world than the university credentials offered by Anglophone countries. Citizens of those countries also did not do much business in China, and most who did were proficient in English, so Chinese citizens considered proficiency in their languages less useful than proficiency in English or Japanese.

The Republic of Korea had laxer visa standards than most other developed countries and offered the advantages of being geographically and economically close to China without the historical animosities that existed between China and Japan. But most Chinese citizens in my study still did not consider it an acceptable study-abroad destination because it required knowledge of a language that was rarely taught in China and seemed unlikely to offer opportunities for immigration, economic advancement, or prestigious education that were much better than those that could be found in China.

Imagining Global Hierarchies

Chinese citizens told me that Dalian, as a relatively prosperous northeastern city, ranked above most places in China but still below larger, more prosperous places such as Shanghai, Beijing, and cities in the faster-developing south (e.g., Shenzhen and Guangzhou). Those who migrated from poorer places in China to Dalian told me that they once perceived Dalian the way Dalian people perceive developed countries. A 21-year-old singleton told me after she left Dalian to attend college in a smaller city, "I now know how you feel—because I'm from Dalian and my classmates would like to come to a wealthy city like Dalian, they treat me the way people here treat you, with both admiration and envy."

Like the rural Miao villagers whom Louisa Schein worked with, Chinese citizens in my study viewed the world as a hierarchy in which all places were ranked by their respective levels of development.[15] Schein observed that, when she attended an elaborate wedding ritual in a village of Miao (a minority ethnic group within China), many participants made reflexive comments to her such as, "We Miao people are just this way," "This is the way we minority nationalities drink," and "This is our minority nationality custom— what do you think?" They asked her to evaluate the wedding and "assess whether it was good or bad."[16] Teenagers and parents in Dalian often said the same things to me, substituting "Chinese" for "Miao." The same rhetoric that Miao people used to distinguish their own practices from those of the Han Chinese majority (and a Chinese state representing modernization) was used by the Han majority in Dalian to distinguish Chinese practices from those of developed countries. But in both Schein's study and mine, our interlocutors' reflexivity also positioned them as modern observers able to objectify their own society even as they were trapped within it.

Stacey Pigg observed that in Nepal "the question, for many, is how to bring modernity here, and whether it is possible to be 'here' in Nepal and be 'modern'" because Nepalese citizens believed that "modernity is somewhere else—India, perhaps, or China." She cited a Nepalese Internet discussant's claim that "compared to the advanced countries of the world, we are lagging about a half to a full century."[17] Ironically, I frequently heard people in Dalian make similar statements about the length of China's lag behind "advanced countries." But it would give Chinese citizens little comfort to know that their country was seen as a location of modernity in Nepalese eyes, because the existence of less developed countries like Nepal seldom impinged on their consciousness.

English-language textbooks provided glimpses of the developed world that fueled the dreams of teenagers like Liu Ying, a high school student I tutored in China. When she came across the phrase "the American Dream" in her textbook, she asked me what it referred to. "The American dream of being middle class and having a house and a car in a nice suburb," I answered.

"But that's not just an American dream. That's my dream too!" she said.

"Don't Chinese people prefer to live in the city rather than the suburbs?" I asked.

"Of course, because the suburbs are backward and remote in China," she replied. "But it's my dream to live in a nice suburb in America!"

Liu Ying was unable to get a visa to study in the United States after she graduated from high school, so she went to Ireland to attend college instead. She returned to China after finishing college in Ireland because she was unable to find an employer who could sponsor her for a work visa in Ireland. She told me that Ireland had disappointed her. "Ireland will not develop, because Irish people depend on foreigners to give them what they need," she said. "I didn't like Ireland. I thought it was boring. In Ireland, people's quality was too low, and you couldn't find very high class people anywhere." But she still dreams about eventually finding a way to immigrate to the United States. "The US is the best place, and even Irish people want to immigrate to the US," she said.

Filial Nationalism

Despite their admiration for developed countries, Chinese youth in my study retained a strong sense of loyalty to China based not on the idea of an imagined community but on the idea of an imagined family in which China was identified with a long-suffering parent who deserved the filial devotion of her children, despite her flaws.[18] Like their love for their parents, their love for their country was a matter of subjective loyalty that could not be nullified by what they believed was an objective understanding of China's status as a developing country. Ironically, their dissatisfaction with China arose from their generation's role as a critical force of modernization in their families and society, a role encouraged by their parents and the Chinese state.

For all its power, the dream of emigration was an ambivalent and problematic one. Many Chinese youth told me that their greatest dream was for China to become as wealthy and powerful as any of the developed countries. They hoped that their own efforts to join the developed world would not only bring greater well-being to themselves and their families but also eventually help to redefine China itself as part of the developed world. Transnational students in my study often presented their quests for developed world citizenship not just as a way to bring themselves into the paradise they imagined the developed world to be but also to make China part of that paradise by bringing social, cultural, and economic capital from the developed countries back to China.

A desire to emigrate and never return was sometimes seen as selfish and disloyal. Willingness to contribute to China's development by turning down opportunities to go abroad or by returning to China from abroad was praised as noble, though also sometimes self-sacrificing. Many transnational students in my study emphasized to everyone they knew in China and abroad that they intended to return to China eventually. They often talked about the analogy between filial duty and the duty of those who study abroad to return to China with skills, credentials, and connections that would aid in China's integration with the global economy. Many told me that, even if they stayed abroad, they would use their positions in developed countries to channel investment, trade, and knowledge back to China.

Some Chinese citizens said it was a "Chinese tragedy" that so many young Chinese citizens wanted to go abroad. Chinese civic education was much more strongly focused on the responsibility to remain loyal to the Chinese state than on the rights of the individual citizen.[19] Most of the Chinese citizens in my study took their patriotic responsibility seriously and felt uncomfortable when others accused them of betraying it. Some who were trying to get visas to study abroad emphasized to their friends and family members that they intended to return, but they were often met with cynicism and disbelief.

"I want to go abroad to learn the most advanced science, and come back to make China strong and prosperous," a 19-year-old singleton told her college classmate while the three of us were conversing about her study-abroad plans as we took a walk around her Chinese college campus.

"You're just blowing hot air," he scoffed. "I'd better say goodbye to you forever at the airport, because once you're living the good life abroad, you'll never want to come back."

Another 19-year-old singleton who was attending a Chinese college and who was among the most nationalistic Chinese citizens I have known sought me out for advice on ways to study abroad. He frequently complained about China's poverty, backwardness, and corruption. But he also sang patriotic songs during karaoke sessions, spoke with pride about the return of Hong Kong and Macao to China, joined student protests against NATO's bombing of the

Chinese embassy in Belgrade, rejoiced at seeing the televised parade of military equipment in Tiananmen Square during the October 1, 1999, celebration of the fiftieth anniversary of China, and vowed that if he became wealthy abroad, he would use his wealth to build schools in China. When I asked him how he reconciled his patriotism with his dissatisfaction with China, he replied, "I love China because China is my motherland, not because I think China is better than other countries. China is poorer and more backward than other countries, but my parents are also poorer and more backward than many other people's parents. I can't renounce my motherland any more than I can renounce my parents."

I was frequently reminded that filial obligations to China applied to me as well. When I first started doing research in China, I was dismayed that just about everyone I met complained incessantly about China's inferiority to developed countries. My dismay arose partly from my ethnic identification as a Chinese American and partly from my identification with an anthropological tradition that is skeptical of Western hegemony and appreciative of other societies. I countered complaints by emphasizing that China was wealthier than many other countries in the world, that developed countries had their own share of problems, such as poverty, loneliness, violence, crime, racism, family instability, and overcommodification, and that Chinese life had many advantages missing in developed countries, such as stronger ties of kinship and friendship and the excitement and opportunities that came with rapid social change. Chinese citizens who heard my arguments dismissed as irrelevant the existence of poorer countries that made China look more developed by comparison; they argued that the problems of developed countries were natural and inconsequential compared to Chinese problems, claimed that what I considered Chinese advantages were actually Chinese problems, and redoubled their condemnation of China. Eventually, I grew tired of arguing with them and started joking and complaining about China's problems the same way they did. To my surprise, they responded with indignation. Many started out complaining about China's problems, but as soon as I concurred, they switched to passionately defending China and saying that the problems they had complained about were inevitable because of historical and economic circumstances, not the fault of the Chinese government or people, likely to be overcome soon, and similar to or less serious than problems in many other societies, including the United States.

Many reminded me, "You, too, are a descendant of Emperors Yan and Huang, and you can't forget China any more than you can forget your parents."

My semiforeign status made Chinese citizens especially anxious to defend China to me, but I also saw them defend China to each other. Many who complained about China and praised developed countries on some occasions reprimanded others for doing the same thing on other occasions. An 18-year-old Chinese singleton I was tutoring in English complained to me, "China is too poor, and Chinese people have low quality and low education. I want to go abroad and be among well-educated, high-quality people." Her father overheard and responded angrily, "Don't speak that way about your motherland! I only had a primary school education. Does that mean you don't want to be around me?" To leave China was to leave one's parents, both literally and figuratively. As much as the young Chinese citizens in my study longed to leave both their country and their parents to pursue their dreams, they were still bound by their filial duty.

Chinese citizens living in China after studying abroad were often pressured to demonstrate that they were still patriotic. A 24-year-old Chinese singleton working for a Japanese-owned company in Dalian who had returned to China after spending four years completing a college degree in Japan came to a class reunion I organized, with 11 of his former junior high school classmates, none of whom had ever been abroad. He bowed to me as soon as he saw me, in a way that was distinctively Japanese. His former classmates burst into laughter. He told us about how polite and high-quality Japanese people were and how his professors in Japan had asked him to tell Chinese people that Japanese people were not the evil enemies many Chinese people believed they were. His classmates teased him and called him a missionary (*chuanjiaoshi*) for Japan. He insisted that he was "patriotic" (*aiguo*, which literally means "love the country").

"Which country?" a classmate asked teasingly.

"The People's Republic of China!" he replied with a salute.

Although most parents encouraged their children's transnational ambitions, some expressed ambivalence about the apparent lack of patriotism that sometimes accompanied such ambitions. This ambivalence was apparent when I had dinner at the home of Ye Yumei, a Communist Party member, and her 16-year-old son, Hu Jun.[20] When we talked about the 1997 return of Hong Kong from British to Chinese rule, Hu Jun expressed skepticism about the benefits for Hong Kong.

"Hong Kong is too good, so it's not worth it for them," he said. "Our government is poor and corrupt. I wish Britain had colonized all of China, and not just Hong Kong. Then we'd be as good as Hong Kong."

"How can you say that?" Ye Yumei protested. "That's slave mentality! Don't say that at school, or you'll get into fights. I haven't taught you well. We should love our country." Ye Yumei later told me that she found Hu Jun's statements disturbing but that it was partly her own fault for telling him all his life that she planned to send him to college in Britain. Although she considered herself highly patriotic and often tried to temper Hu Jun's complaints about China, she had also inundated him with English-language tutors, movies, and reading materials to prepare him for study abroad. She told me that she believed this approach caused Hu Jun to "worship foreigners" and to speak "as if he were an Englishman and not Chinese." She worried that his attitude would get him in trouble with more patriotic teachers and classmates. His disdain for the Chinese state and admiration of Britain were unusual. Most of his peers praised developed countries and complained about China but also condemned colonialism and strongly supported China's claims to Hong Kong, Taiwan, and Macao. Ye Yumei also worried that her son would be disappointed once he actually went to Britain, because it could not possibly be as wonderful as he imagined it would be.

Chinese intellectuals who promoted nationalism at the dawn of the twentieth century feared that Chinese people were too focused on their filial duty to their lineages to devote their loyalties to an imagined national community. In their effort to supplant the lineage and the family as the focus of loyalty, Maoist state leaders actively denounced Confucianism and encouraged youth to rebel against their elders. Ironically, however, it was the analogy of filial duty that served as the most effective basis for nationalism in the globalized neoliberal environment of the twenty-first century.

In addition to promoting filial nationalism, state leaders also tried to promote nationalism based on admiration of China for its culture, government policies, geographic beauty, and successful modernization. The state-controlled educational system encouraged nationalism with politics classes that required students to understand and memorize state policies and their rationales. State-run work units often required that their employees attend meetings to promote admiration and support for particular state policies. The state-controlled Chinese media presented news, editorials, movies, shows, and music that praised the Chinese nation and state. Much state propaganda focused on making Chinese people proud that, as then Chinese president Jiang Zemin proclaimed in 2002, "For more than 5,000 years, the Chinese nation has evolved a great national spirit centering on patriotism and featuring unity and solidarity, love of peace, industry, courage and ceaseless self-improvement."[21]

Yet young Chinese citizens in my study identified far more with invocations of filial nationalism than with efforts to portray China as particularly admirable. Like German Democratic Republic readers who told Dominic Boyer that they felt distant from the texts produced by their Communist state because such texts fitted poorly with the realities of their lives,[22] many young Chinese citizens in my study told me that they considered the material in their politics classes boring (*wuliao*) and unrealistic (*bu shiji*). Only 27 percent of 1999 survey respondents (*N* = 2,196) indicated that politics was among their favorite academic subjects, whereas each of the other subjects (chemistry, Chinese, foreign languages, history, math, and physics) was named as a favorite subject by 42–50 percent of respondents. When students in a high school homeroom I observed were required to write essays praising China (in commemoration of October 1, 1999, the fiftieth anniversary of the founding of China), 21 of the 45 students failed to do so by the school's deadline. The teacher told those who had not written the essay to stand up and then asked a top student, who had on other occasions spoken eloquently about her desire to contribute to China's development, why she had not written the essay. She burst into tears and said, "If I knew how to write this essay, I would have!" Some of her classmates applauded. Several students later told me that they also could not think of anything sincere to write in praise of their nation-state.

Although the Chinese government sometimes tried to promote a discourse of nationalism based on loyalty to one's hometown, this discourse was not highly salient for Chinese citizens in my study, most of whom were children or grandchildren of migrants from poorer areas of China.[23] Among my 1999 survey respondents, 7 percent (*N* = 2,123) had at least one parent born in the countryside, 92 percent (*N* = 2,109) had at least one parent who had lived in the countryside, 43 percent (*N* = 1,769) had at least one grandparent who had worked as a farmer, and 66 percent (*N* = 2,165) indicated that their *jiguan* (paternal grandfather's hometown) was not Dalian city or any of its surrounding rural counties. They acknowledged that

Dalian was "a good place," but young Chinese citizens in my study were more concerned with their belief that there were even better places elsewhere. Because of their high ambitions, they often identified themselves as already belonging to that superior "elsewhere."

Nor did Chinese citizens in my study express great admiration for an imagined Chinese or Confucian community of "East Asia" or "Greater China." Aihwa Ong saw possibilities for Asian resistance to Western hegemony in the way transnational narratives of Confucian culture produced a distinctively "East Asian model of modernization."[24] Chinese officials sometimes invoked this model in their efforts to promote nationalism, but Chinese citizens in my study viewed it with ambivalence. On the one hand, they pointed to the accomplishments of overseas Chinese as evidence that Chinese people were intelligent (*congming*). They took comfort in such evidence because it gave them hope that China could eventually become a developed country. However, many of them also said that Chinese people were mean (*huai*). This meanness referred to the jealousy, unfairness, competitiveness, corruption, and elitism that often accompanied the complex system of social obligations characteristic of the East Asian model of modernization. Some Chinese singletons told me that their dream of emigration resulted not only from a desire for affluence but also from a desire to get away from the problems of meanness they associated with Chinese culture. They said that if they went abroad, they would try to avoid these problems by avoiding other Chinese and associating primarily with non-Chinese.

Yet, although they did not consider China particularly admirable, young Chinese citizens in my study professed a deep love for China that was reminiscent of the love they felt for their parents. Some cited the propaganda slogan "Study hard to repay the motherland" (*haohao xuexi, baoxiao zuguo*) when discussing their desire for further education, whether in China or abroad. "I want to get a bachelor's degree, master's degree, and Ph.D. abroad and then work a few years abroad so I can make some money and get experience, and let people know that I can succeed anywhere," an 18-year-old singleton told me a year before she went to Japan to attend college. "But eventually, I'll return to China," she added. "China is my motherland, and my parents are here. Ever since primary school, my teachers have been saying that we should study hard so that we can repay the motherland, and I still believe that."

Chinese citizens in my study were especially passionate about defending China's status in the world. When it came to issues related to China's status on the world stage, many of them sincerely and adamantly shared the perspective of the Chinese government, and sometimes the fervor of their nationalistic passion even made government officials uneasy. As Yongnian Zheng observed, "Nationalism could become a dangerous Pandora's Box," unleashing demands for more political participation than the government allowed.[25] The Chinese government therefore tried to exercise restraint even when trying to use nationalism to bolster its own legitimacy, as Zheng described in the case of the government's campaign against Western "anti-China theories." The popular response to NATO's bombing of the Chinese embassy in Belgrade on May 8, 1999, demonstrated both the power and the danger of nationalistic sentiments to Chinese leaders, who at first fanned the flames of popular indignation with heavy and strongly negative media coverage of the bombing and granted official permission for student demonstrations against the bombing. However, they quickly shifted to nationally televised appeals for restraint, nonviolence, and stability after some demonstrations led to violence. Many Chinese citizens were angry that their government showed too much restraint in its response to the bombing. After Chinese officials declared that students should stop protesting, a 19-year-old student at a Chinese college fumed to her classmates and me, "If China doesn't do anything about this, it just shows that our country is weak and doomed. But what can we do? China is so poor and backward that we can't fight back."

Filial nationalism could also be seen in musical tastes. Karaoke singing was one of the most popular recreational activities in China. People could choose from a wide variety of music videos for karaoke sessions in restaurants, hotels, karaoke bars, and their own homes. Chinese citizens born before the 1970s were more likely to favor folk songs and nostalgic songs from their own youth (many of which included exaggerated praise of the Chinese government that their children found laughable), whereas those born after the 1970s were more likely to favor songs about romance by pop stars from developed countries as well as China. Songs about familial love, however, seemed favored by people of all ages, as were certain kinds of nationalistic songs that emphasized love for the Chinese people rather than praise of the Chinese nation-state. Like their parents, young Chinese citizens in my study strongly identified with the sentiments expressed in such nationalistic songs as "China My Home" and "My Chinese Heart." A common favorite was the music video "Chinese People," which was sung on top of the Great Wall by the Hong Kong superstar Liu Dehua (Andy Lau).[26] Clad in the kind of traditional gown worn by prerevolutionary Chinese scholar-officials, Liu Dehua was surrounded by Qing dynasty (1644–1911) banners, a troop of solemn Chinese men in traditional gowns standing in formation and waving red banners bearing the words "Chinese people," and a crowd of smiling Chinese children wearing red kerchiefs that signified their membership in the Young Pioneers, a children's organization sponsored by the Chinese Communist Party. Amid all this, Liu Dehua sang:

> Five thousand years of wind and rain have brought forth so
>   many dreams.
> Yellow faces, black eyes; it is the smiles that are unchanging.
> Eight thousand *li* of mountains and rivers are like a song:
> It doesn't matter where you came from, or where you will go in
>   the future.
> The same tears, the same pain;
> The suffering of the past we have kept in our hearts.
> The same blood, the same race;
> There are still dreams in the future, let us develop them together!
> Hand in hand, not distinguishing between you and me, striding
>   forward together;
> Let the world know we are all Chinese!

Young Chinese citizens in my study told me that they found Liu Dehua's song more appealing than songs that contained effusive praise of the Chinese nation-state because, rather than claiming that there was anything particularly admirable about China, Liu Dehua's song focused on the empathy and loyalty that he (and by extension people of Hong Kong and Chinese people everywhere) felt toward other Chinese people because of their shared history and ancestry. Overseas Chinese nationalists were often critical or ambivalent about Chinese living conditions, cultural traditions, and state policies, even as they expressed love and empathy for the Chinese people. Helen Siu observed that the same group of Hong Kong professionals and performers who raised $75 million for Chinese flood victims in 1991 had also raised $1.5 million for students who protested against the Chinese government in 1989.[27] Andrea Louie found that many Chinese American youth who traveled to China to participate in a "Roots" program were moved by their Chinese hosts' appeal to their sense of kinship but were uncomfortable with the poverty they found.[28] Regardless of whether they had ever gone abroad, young Chinese citizens in my study espoused a kind of filial nationalism similar to that of overseas Chinese.

As in other societies with strong lineages,[29] nationalism based on an analogy with filial devotion may have seemed problematic in early and mid-twentieth century China, when lineage-based loyalties were seen as threatening to the national unity necessary for the building of a modern nation-state. By the end of the twentieth century, however, the bulk of the lineages' power had been usurped by the state, China's existence as an imagined community and a geopolitically recognized entity was secure, and the main threat it faced was not fragmentation or foreign conquest but rather its low rank in the global neoliberal system, which could only be overcome through infusions of capital and knowledge from developed countries. Under these conditions, youth, parents, and even the Chinese government perceived filial nationalism as an appropriate attitude for youth who had been designated by their state, society, and parents—and by the global neoliberal system—as the generation with the resources and ambition to transform China into a developed country.

Although ideas of Chinese "race" and "culturalism" were unifying themes for the prerevolutionary Chinese empire,[30] the idea of the Chinese nation as the kind of imagined community described by Benedict Anderson[31] did not emerge until the late nineteenth century. At that time, a growing number of Chinese intellectuals became aware of the capitalist world system, were distressed by China's low position within it, and became convinced that China needed nationalism to avoid falling victim to conquest and colonization. These intellectuals believed that Chinese people needed to unite against foreign domination by imagining themselves as belonging to China rather than to regional and lineage-based groups and needed to avoid dangerous complacency by recognizing that China was merely "one nation among many" rather than the Confucian center of an infinitely civilizable world.[32] Chinese people who were living or had lived abroad were key contributors to as well as targets of this new discourse of nationalism.[33] Many of the most influential Chinese political and intellectual leaders of the twentieth century (including Chiang Kai-Shek, Deng Xiaoping, Hu Shi, Lu Xun, Sun Yat-Sen, and Zhou Enlai) had studied abroad.

China was first dragged into the capitalist world system during the Opium Wars (1839–1842 and 1856–1860). After its defeat in those wars, the imperial Chinese government made concessions of territory, sovereignty, money, and trade rights to a variety of foreign countries, including Austria, England, France, Germany, Italy, Japan, Russia, Spain, and the United States. Problems caused by these concessions contributed to the replacement of the Qing dynasty with a revolutionary nationalist government in 1911. That government was in turn replaced in 1949 by a Communist government led by Mao Zedong after a bitter civil war. Under the Maoist government, China was briefly allied with the Soviet bloc, which tried to establish a socialist world system separate from the capitalist world system. Despite its Marxist-Leninist ideology, however, the socialist world system bore many similarities to its capitalist counterpart, including a hierarchy based on levels of development. After relations between China and the Soviet Union cooled in the 1960s, the Maoist Chinese government promoted autarky in an attempt to remove China from all world systems. This attempt ultimately failed because the Maoist state was itself based on a desire to catch up to the military and industrial standards of the developed countries (a desire that led to tragedies such as the Great Leap Forward famine of 1958–1960). After Mao Zedong died in 1976, the Chinese government stopped trying to keep China from integrating into the capitalist world system, which by then was becoming a global neoliberal system. Instead, it sought to raise China's position within this system by developing the same kind of low fertility, high educational levels, and neoliberal political economy that had enabled the developed countries to rise to the top.[34]

To enlist youth in its struggle to replace family- and lineage-based centers of power, the Maoist government (1949–1976) denounced Confucian values and encouraged children to rebel against their parents and elders.[35] Many Chinese citizens born before the 1970s told me that they had observed or participated in criticism, denunciation, and violence against authority figures such as teachers, officials, and even their own parents during the Cultural Revolution (1966–1976), although most of them also told me that they themselves had felt ambivalent about Maoist attempts to replace loyalty to the family with loyalty to the state. Unlike the prerevolutionary Confucian rhetoric that encouraged subjects to obey their emperor as sons obeyed fathers, Maoist rhetoric promoted an egalitarian imagined community in which everyone could be called comrade, authority figures lived in fear of being denounced and tortured by disgruntled employees, students, and even younger family members, and individuals were expected to have greater loyalty to the state than to their own families. Beginning in the late 1970s, post-Mao leaders moved away from such violently egalitarian rhetoric because it did not fit well with their new emphasis on order and stability. Yet they would have strained their credibility if they had simply reverted to the rhetoric of prerevolutionary authoritarianism that had been so recently denounced. Therefore, instead of demanding the submission associated with Confucian patriarchy, post-Mao leaders emphasized sentimental bonds of filial devotion that could apply simultaneously to the family, the Chinese state, and China.

The filial devotion of the twenty-first century was based less on Confucian discourses about ritual attitudes, patrilineal continuity, and ancestor worship[36] than on the deeply felt sentiments of love and loyalty associated with Margery Wolf's model of the "uterine family."[37] As with many other nationalisms based on familial idioms[38] that portrayed the nation as a "collective individual,"[39] China was identified with a loving mother who deserved the lifelong devotion of her children. To celebrate the return of the Portuguese colony Macao to Chinese rule on December 20, 1999, Dalian's government put up a billboard that featured a little girl running to the outstretched arms of her mother, with the caption "Mama, I'm returning." Behind the toddler were the ruins of St. Paul's Cathedral (Macao's emblematic monument), and behind the mother was Tiananmen Square, a symbol of the Chinese state. Another billboard put up by Dalian's government featured the caption "The Return of Macao"; it showed a chubby baby's hand labeled "Macao" tenderly held by a slender feminine hand labeled "People's Republic of China." Such explicit analogies between mothers and the motherland were designed to bolster Chinese nationalism by identifying it with filial devotion, a highly salient component of Chinese moral sentiments that remained powerful through all the revolutions that transformed twentieth-century China. Although they had grown up with anti-Confucian Maoist discourses, Chinese citizens born before the 1970s spoke frequently about the importance of filial devotion in reference to both what they owed their own parents and what they expected from their children. Chinese citizens born after the 1970s also spoke about the importance of filial devotion. Like their parents, they conceived of filial devotion not as a tenet of Confucianism per se but rather as a tenet of basic human decency. When discussing their motivations for working hard in school, young Chinese citizens in my study often talked about their dream of making their parents proud and of having enough money to enable their parents to retire in affluent comfort. Successful students pointed to filial devotion as one of their greatest motivations for academic achievement, whereas unsuccessful students pointed to their parents' disappointment as their deepest regret.

Most Chinese citizens in my study[40] conceptualized their nationalism in terms of the same kind of autochthony, historical precedence, and homogeneity at the heart of many European nationalisms.[41] Chinese citizens born before and after the 1970s shared this concept of nationalism, but relationships between national and personal identity were marked by generational differences. Having grown up in an autarkic, propaganda-saturated Maoist political culture that had limited access to the world outside China while encouraging Chinese people to identify with and take pride in their nation-state, many Chinese citizens born before the 1970s expressed sentiments that resembled the "personal nationalism" that Anthony Cohen found among Scots. Cohen said, "I substantiate the otherwise vacuous national label in terms of my own experience, my reading of history, my perception of the landscape, and my reading of Scotland's literature and music, so that when I 'see' the nation, I am looking at myself."[42] Their sentiments also resembled the "defensive" nationalism that Stuart Hall found in England: "When you know what everybody else is, then you are what they are not."[43] Unlike their parents, however, Chinese citizens born after the 1970s were raised with widespread access to a global neoliberal system that inundated them with discourses proclaiming the superiority and desirability of the developed world. They were therefore less likely than their parents to believe that their culture, nation, hometown, or state was particularly congenial to their own values, desires, and personalities. Rather, their nationalistic sentiments resembled the anthropological empathy that Virginia Dominguez called "the kind of love we feel for family members, tough love at times but never disengagement or hagiography."[44] Although they lived in China, they often spoke critically and reflexively about their country, as if they were already the developed world citizens they hoped to become. At the same time, they believed they had a duty to bring China into the imagined community of the developed world to which they felt they belonged.

Conclusion: Their Parents' Children

Francis Fukuyama and Michael Mandelbaum argued that national-ism has been declining as the global triumph of liberalism and free markets have rendered national differences increasingly irrelevant.[45] Samuel Huntington argued that, on the contrary, the "clash of civi-lizations" is becoming more important as post–Cold War politics are increasingly driven by people's convictions about the superiority of their own respective national cultures.[46] Thomas Friedman and Benjamin Barber maintained that some particularly wealthy, mobile groups are increasingly motivated by globalizing forces that erode nationalism, even while others around them are involved in increas-ingly powerful clashes of civilizations.[47] What all these perspectives have in common are their assumptions about globalization's ten-dency to erode nationalism and the extent to which nationalism is based on a belief in the superiority of one's own national culture. The filial nationalism I observed in Dalian, however, suggests that it is possible for a powerful sense of nationalism and a powerful sense of identification with the imagined community of the global neoliberal system to coexist and that nationalism does not necessarily depend on a belief in the superiority of one's own national culture.

Despite their identification with developed countries, young Chi-nese citizens in my study had made an uneasy truce with China's flaws as part of what Michael Herzfeld calls cultural intimacy. As Herzfeld argued, "If the nation is credibly represented as a family, people are loyal to it because they know that families are flawed—that is part of love—and so they rally to the defense of its compro-mising but warmly familiar intimacy."[48] Although the students in my study complained about China's backwardness, they also excused it as a result of China's poverty and said that they owed it to their "motherland" to bring modernizations that would alleviate that poverty, just as they had a duty to bring their parents out of poverty by getting high-income work, in China or abroad. Like their parents, the Chinese state supported their dream of studying abroad despite concern about losing them. The dream of becoming part of the devel-oped world was shared by state leaders and those they governed, just as it was shared by parents and children. Those born under China's fertility limitation policies were raised with the expectation that their generation would modernize their country, whether by building a modern political economy within China or by going abroad and channeling developed countries' social, cultural, and economic capital into China. There was always the risk that those who went abroad would never return or do anything to benefit the parents and motherland they left behind, but Chinese state leaders, like most parents, had enough faith in the filial devotion of emigrants to take that risk.

Filial nationalism and dissatisfaction with China could coexist because such nationalism was quite unlike the "personal nationalism" that could allow a Scottish person to claim that "when I 'see' the nation, I am looking at myself."[49] Chinese youth in my study did not define China as themselves writ large. On the contrary, they saw themselves as modern individuals who were just unfortunate enough to be born in China, an environment that they considered a disadvantage in their quest for developed world citizenship. Well educated and raised on developed countries' images and brand names, they thought that they did not resemble the backwardness they associated with their motherland any more than they resembled their long-suffering, poorly educated parents. Yet Chinese youth shared with their elders a powerful sense of nationalism based on the belief that they could no more cease to be "people of China" than they could cease to be their parents' children. When Chinese youth in my study saw the Chinese nation, they were looking at their parents; when they expressed devotion to their nation, they recalled their devotion to their parents with the uneasy combination of love, ambivalence, frustration, and duty that filial devotion entails.

CHAPTER 3

Choosing the Road Less Traveled

How and Why Chinese Citizens Decide to Study Abroad

THE FINANCIAL BURDEN of tuition and living expenses in developed countries was onerous for parents of students who could not earn enough to pay for their own tuition and living expenses while abroad. Even some relatively well-off families had to go into debt to support their children abroad. Parents risked losing all the money they put into the startup costs of study abroad if, after going abroad, their children could not get into college, pass their college classes, or earn enough income to become self-supporting and had to return to China empty-handed. Such a risky investment was especially dangerous for poorer parents who used their life savings to send their children abroad and would not be able to come up with more money to tide their children over if their children could not find enough work to become self-supporting immediately after leaving China. It was no surprise, then, that children of the urban Chinese middle class (here defined as those whose parents had worked as managers, professionals, or owners of businesses with more than two employees) were more likely than children of workers, farmers, and small business owners to have studied abroad by 2008–2010.[1] Among the 336 2008–2010 survey respondents who had two middle-class parents, 30 percent had studied abroad; among the 347 who had one middle-class parent, 18 percent had studied abroad; and among the 456 who had no middle-class parents, only 13 percent had studied abroad.

Still, some of those who ended up studying abroad were among those I had thought were least likely to do so, based on their limited financial resources, lack of knowledge about study-abroad opportunities, and/or relatively low interest in going abroad. At the same time, some of those who had seemed the most likely to study abroad (based on their affluence, the detailed plans for study abroad they described to me, and their strong desire to study abroad) when I first met them have not yet gone abroad, either because their desire to study abroad eventually waned or because they had not yet found any study-abroad opportunities that seemed better than opportunities they already had in China.

In this chapter I explore the combination of systematic and idiosyncratic factors that led some singletons to study abroad and others to remain in China. My survey data suggest that those with middle-class parents were especially likely to study abroad. At the individual level, however, I found that random events and subjective emotions of the moment were the most important factors in determining who studied abroad and who did not.

A Generation Born and Raised for the Developed World

Chinese citizens born under the economic reforms and the fertility limitation policies that began in the 1970s were socialized to desire developed world citizenship more strongly than older Chinese citizens who had been socialized under the Maoist government, which had tried to withdraw China from all global systems.

Most Chinese citizens in my study who were born before the 1970s considered going abroad not only difficult and impractical but also undesirable. They grew up during the Cultural Revolution, when the teaching of foreign languages was prohibited at many schools. By the 1990s, when foreign languages were taught at most Chinese junior high schools, college prep high schools, and colleges and universities, those born before the 1970s had already completed their education and thought they were too old to learn new languages. They lacked the skills and education necessary for finding work or study opportunities abroad. Even many of those who identified with the developed world and criticized China still felt that they belonged in China. They joked that they would starve to death abroad, because they could never get full on foreign food, which they assumed was like the expensive small portions from McDonald's and Kentucky Fried Chicken that their children craved.[2] Pierre Bourdieu argued that "generation conflicts oppose not age-classes separated by natural properties, but habitus which have been produced by different modes of generation, that is, by conditions of existence which, in imposing different definitions of the impossible, the possible, and the probable, cause one group to experience as natural or reasonable practices or aspirations which another group finds unthinkable or scandalous, or vice versa."[3] Those who grew up in the autarkic political culture of the Cultural Revolution (1966–1976) felt too socially, emotionally, and culturally bound to China to consider going abroad a desirable option, even when they agreed with their children that life was better abroad. Parents pinned their yearnings to become part of the developed world onto children born into an era of post-Mao globalization, fertility decline, and intensifying integration into the global neoliberal system. Unlike their parents, children born into this era believed it would be natural and reasonable for them to study abroad.

Parents encouraged their children to study abroad as part of a broader strategy of upward mobility. Many parents born before the 1970s thought that they themselves had little potential for upward mobility. Among 2,173 respondents to a parental employment question on my 1999 survey, 34 percent indicated that at least one parent had been laid off or had retired even though that year the average age of survey respondents' mothers ($N = 2,091$) was 43 and the average age of their fathers ($N = 2,093$) was 45. Survey respondents' parents' were vulnerable to layoffs and compulsory early retirement even as early as their 40s, and some of those who had jobs were considered too old and poorly educated to get promotions or better jobs. Their salaries and pensions had not kept up with inflation and in some cases had even decreased because of the financial difficulties experienced by many employers in the state sector, which had employed most urban parents of their generation before they were laid off or retired.

Youth born in the 1980s, however, had great potential for upward mobility. Even if their parents became unemployed and unemployable, those born in the 1980s were able to find work in rapidly expanding, high-paying service sector fields such as tourism, hospitality, education, commerce, catering, finance, trade, business, and communications. These fields often favored youth who were proficient in the languages and cultures of developed countries. The Chinese higher education system also prioritized foreign-language proficiency, with many college and graduate programs making passage of a foreign-language test a requirement for all students regardless of their major.

Chinese state leaders promulgated a two-child policy beginning in 1970 and a one-child policy beginning in 1979 to produce children with consumption and education levels similar to those enjoyed by their counterparts in the developed world.[4] Having only one child encouraged parents to concentrate all their resources on providing that child with the best that money could buy. Consequently, children born under the fertility limitation policies often had the high expectations, consumption patterns, and educational attainment characteristic of developed world citizens. As Ann Anagnost observed, "The child's body becomes the repository of expended value, presumably justified by its heightened 'quality,' which compensates for the loss of more reproduction."[5]

The singleton generation had much more education than their parents and grandparents. Most respondents to my survey surpassed their grandparents' educational attainments after just a few years of primary school, and they were also likely to surpass their parents' educational attainment as soon as they graduated from their high schools. Respondents to my 2008–2010 survey indicated in 1999 that 76 percent ($N = 959$) of them had no parents with any kind of college degree, 55 percent of their mothers ($N = 959$) and 49 percent of their fathers ($N = 954$) had no more than a junior high school degree, and 40 percent of their maternal grandmothers ($N = 819$), 42 percent of their paternal grandmothers ($N = 815$), 11 percent of their maternal grandfathers ($N = 810$), and 13 percent of their paternal grandfathers ($N = 801$) were illiterate.[6] But statistics kept by Dalian city's government indicated that, by 2000, almost all urban Dalian teenagers attended primary school, junior high school, and high school, and the majority attended college as well.[7] By 2008–2010, 81 percent of my 990 survey respondents (including 96 percent of the 385 from the college prep high school, 63 percent of the 218 from the vocational high school, and 78 percent of the 387 from the junior high school) had some kind of college degree. Frequently told by their parents and state officials that they were the generation with the education, resources, and ambition to bring their families and country into the developed world, many young Chinese citizens spoke as though they themselves were already cultural citizens of the developed world but just unfortunate enough to lack social and legal citizenship in that world. As a 14-year-old singleton Chinese citizen told me about his desire for the luxurious American lifestyles he observed while watching the situation comedy *Growing Pains*, "It's just my bad luck to be born in China."

Chinese singletons hoped that this problem would be resolved by the transformation of China into a developed country, but they were not sure whether such a transformation would occur within their lifetime. Therefore many of them wanted to gain the developed world citizenship they saw as the birthright of their generation by learning developed countries' languages, by working for developed world employers, and in some cases by migrating to a developed country, which they hoped would complete their transformation into full cultural, social, and possibly legal citizens of the developed world.

The stakes for their generation are especially high because when singletons lose out in the competition for elite status, parents have no other children to rely on for support, and a singleton who falls into poverty will have no siblings to turn to for help. China's fertility limitation policies have produced a society in which every child is expected to be a winner, regardless of gender, ability, or socioeconomic status. China's rapidly intensifying engagement with the global neoliberal system has caused increases in inequality, unemployment, and the costs and standards of health care and a comfortable lifestyle, even as neoliberal cost shifting from the state to the family makes the stakes of success especially high for the singleton generation. Unlike children of the large families common in China in previous generations, who had many siblings to share the costs of supporting parents and grandparents, singletons need jobs with developed-world-level incomes to cover the rapidly inflating costs of providing education, medical care, and respectable lifestyles for themselves and their children as well as the medical and nursing care and comfortable retirement some of them will be expected to provide to their parents, grandparents, and parents-in-law.

China's socioeconomic stratification system has little room at the top.[8] But Chinese singletons in my study were too ambitious to accept relegation to the bottom, even when that was where their exam scores and their parents' socioeconomic status placed them. When they were denied prestigious education and high-paying careers in China, they saw study abroad as an alternative means of attaining developed world citizenship, despite their lack of academic achievement and family wealth. Increasing numbers of their generation are now studying abroad because, as only children who are their parents' only hope for the future, they were socialized to aspire to developed world citizenship regardless of their abilities and their parents' ability to pay for their education and career opportunities. The same quest for development that led to the one-child policy also led to policies that enabled Chinese incomes and housing prices to rise to the point where even ordinary urban parents can access enough money to send their children abroad, even if they have to sell their homes and borrow money from friends and relatives to do so. With only one child, parents could invest an unprecedented amount on their children's education, which they saw as a source of capabilities that could provide more long-term security than any other financial investment could. As a Chinese company manager told me a year before his 26-year-old son received a college degree in Britain, "If you put money in the bank, it deflates quickly and you lose a lot. . . . If I didn't invest in my son's education, I would be investing in something else, like a factory or business, and those are not as good as an education, because if they failed, my money would be gone, whereas with an education my son will always be able to make more money even if he loses all his money in the short run."

Unlike their parents, Chinese citizens born in the 1980s had never known a time when the lifestyles of the developed world were anything but desirable and ubiquitous. They blamed China's failure to become part of the developed world on a wide array of problems attributed to "Chinese backwardness," such as poverty, corruption, laziness, jealousy, meanness, low quality, treachery, and the need to use and be used by social connections to get anything done. Many of these problems were the same ones condemned during the May Fourth Movement of the 1910s and 1920s by young Chinese activists, including Mao Zedong and Zhou Enlai.[9] The vision of foreign superiority held up in the 2000s as a rebuke of Chinese backwardness remained similar to that constructed by those activists. But unlike their early-twentieth-century predecessors, some of whom saw socialism as an alternative model of modernization that would enable China to leapfrog over developed countries in the Marxist scheme of social evolution, Chinese citizens in my study saw intensification of their own participation in the global neoliberal system as the only possible means for achieving upward mobility for themselves, their families, and their nation. They told me that they would like to see China develop the admirable qualities they attributed to the developed world and that they hoped to help transfer to China the knowledge, resources, capital, and connections from developed countries necessary to bring China into the developed world. In the meantime, though, they hoped that study abroad would enable them to become citizens of the developed world even if China itself was not yet a developed country.

Study Abroad as an Alternative Path to Developed World Citizenship

Born into an era of global neoliberalism, Chinese singletons grew up admiring images of developed countries, which sometimes looked like paradise in the media, advertisements, and descriptions and photographs provided by others who had returned from study abroad. These images made them yearn to become part of the developed world. As children of the one-child policy, raised with the kind of expectations, competitiveness, and parental investment common in the low-fertility families of the developed world, they had the means and motivation to launch themselves into that world and resented being stuck in the developing world.

Many of them hoped that study abroad would enable them to leapfrog over those who had been more successful in the Chinese educational system, which they saw as an oppressively competitive, narrow path to social and cultural citizenship in the developed world. Access to higher education increased during the 1990s and 2000s as college programs expanded to accommodate the singleton generation's rapidly rising demand and ability to pay for higher education. Yet the kind of education that could qualify them for white-collar work remained elusive because of the equally rapid inflation of diplomas, expectations, and consumption demands.[10] Every year's graduates found themselves qualified for less desirable jobs than those with similar academic credentials would have qualified for just a few years earlier. Many Chinese singletons were dissatisfied with their incomes, work conditions, and advancement opportunities, which always seemed less than what they thought they were qualified for. As in other societies, Chinese youth considered incongruities between the status they expected and the status they attained a major source of stress.[11]

Many told me that they wanted to study abroad because they had failed to get into a sufficiently prestigious college program in China. Standards for the kind of education that would have been prestigious enough to keep them in China varied widely. Some were unable to get into any Chinese college at all; others had been accepted to Chinese three-year college programs (*zhuanke*) but failed to get into Chinese four-year college programs (*benke*), and still others were graduates of relatively prestigious Chinese four-year college programs who nevertheless thought that their degrees were still not prestigious enough to make them full social and cultural citizens of the developed world. All of them seemed to believe that their future happiness would depend on getting education and work that would enable them to enjoy developed world levels of prestige, purchasing power, security, and mobility. They thought that, although a prestigious college education was the only path to developed world citizenship if one remained in China, ways to become part of the developed world were more plentiful and diverse for those who studied abroad.

Obstacles to Going Abroad

The autarkic policies of the Maoist government had made it difficult for Chinese citizens to go abroad between 1949 and 1978. After 1978, however, post-Mao Chinese leaders recognized that overseas Chinese and Chinese citizens who returned to China after sojourns abroad were important sources of the capital and expertise necessary for China's economic growth.[12] By the early 2000s, the Chinese government had removed most of the bureaucratic obstacles that used to make it hard for Chinese citizens to get passports to go abroad,[13] and some state-owned schools and work units even provided funds for top students and employees to visit or study abroad.

Developed countries, however, continued to be reluctant to grant visas to Chinese citizens who did not already have enough wealth, credentials, professional status, family members abroad, and previous transnational travel experiences to qualify them as social and cultural citizens of the developed world. Fearing illegal immigration, their embassy officials often rejected Chinese citizens' visa applications.[14] Foreign embassies in China granted visas for work, business, or immigration in developed countries only to Chinese citizens with family members abroad or those with prestigious credentials, skills in high-demand fields (e.g., engineering, science, and computer programming), or high positions in businesses or government bureaus that sponsored them to go abroad. Tourist and student visas required proof of either a full scholarship or significant savings and family income, and student visas also required acceptance letters and in some cases evidence that tuition had already been prepaid from a school in the country granting the visa. I even knew some Chinese citizens living in Ireland, Britain, Japan, and Australia with valid student visas who had their tourist visa applications rejected by the US embassy, and I knew Chinese citizens with valid student visas living in the United States who experienced prohibitively troublesome hassles and delays when they tried to get visas to enter other developed countries on short notice.

Most of the Chinese citizens in my study were not willing to enter or stay in any country illegally. As singletons whose parents had spared them from most household chores, they were unwilling to work at the mostly dirty, unpleasant, unsafe, and underpaid kinds of jobs available to undocumented immigrants. They had heard from the Chinese and international media that undocumented immigrants in developed countries worked for less than minimum wage, lived in fear of deportation, lacked access to health care, education, and other social programs, had little protection from abuse by employers, landlords, and criminals who took advantage of their fear of law enforcement, and were unable to return unless they were willing to return permanently to China, where they would face fines and probably never again be able to get a visa to go abroad. Illegal immigration would be counterproductive to their goal of acquiring flexible developed world citizenship that would enable them to shuttle freely and easily between China and developed countries. Even though transnational migration was becoming common among their generation, it was extremely rare among older generations and thus not yet perceived as a normal or necessary means to upward mobility. Unlike undocumented immigrants from historically transnational areas of southern China, such as those studied by Frank Pieke, Pal Nyiri, and their collaborators, where "emigration is a normal, indeed an almost inevitable act,"[15] Chinese citizens in my study saw emigration as merely one of several possible means to upward mobility and thus considered the legal, economic, and psychological problems associated with illegal immigration too high a price to pay.

Among the 287 who responded to my 2008–2010 survey question about the visas they used to go abroad, 35 percent used student visas, 31 percent used tourist visas, 24 percent used work visas, 4 percent used family visit visas, 3 percent used immigration visas, 6 percent used business visas, 1 percent used spousal visas, and 1 percent used other kinds of visas.[16] Emigration brokers (*zhongjie*) became ubiquitous in southern China by the 1990s[17] and in northeastern cities like Dalian by the early 2000s. Brokers recruited applicants through newspaper ads, Internet websites, and connections with Chinese school administrators as well as through word of mouth. Brokers matched applicants with countries, schools, and homestay families abroad, handled financial transactions for expenses such as tuition, room, board, and transportation that had to be paid in advance, helped applicants prepare their visa application packages, delivered the visa applications to the appropriate embassies, and helped the applicants purchase plane tickets suitable for their itineraries. Brokers also gave applicants advice about which countries currently had the least stringent visa requirements for those of the applicant's background, what kinds of work, education, and immigration opportunities were available in those countries, how to answer visa application and interview questions in ways that would attract the least suspicion, and in some cases how to get fake or exaggerated documentation of assets and family income. Transnational students in my study paid broker's fees ranging from 3,000 to 60,000 yuan (US$381–US$7,614) (in addition to the tuition, room, board, transportation, and visa application fees charged by third parties) to facilitate their visa applications. The lowest fees were charged by newer brokers without established reputations (some of whom had just returned from study abroad themselves); the highest fees were charged either by brokers who offered illegal or semilegal ways to get visas or by well-known established brokers who had good reputations with applicants, embassy officials, and schools abroad and offered a wide range of services both before and during the sojourn.

Brokers usually matched applicants with schools and homestay families with which the broker already had connections and sometimes received kickbacks from them for each student recruited. Many Chinese citizens distrusted brokers even before they went abroad. And their distrust was often validated. After they went abroad, many learned that their brokers had charged them fees that were much higher than what other brokers had charged other Chinese students for the same services, charged exorbitant fees for simple services they could have done themselves, and charged room, board, and tuition fees that were much higher than what they could find on their own. Worst of all, some transnational Chinese students learned that their brokers had lied to them about the availability of opportunities for work, education, and immigration in the countries in which they studied. Still, most were initially so unfamiliar with visa application and study-abroad processes that they believed they needed to hire brokers if they were to have any chance at success.

Obtaining a visa required the expenditure of significant time, energy, and economic and social capital. Visa application processes sometimes took more than a year because developed countries' embassies in China were understaffed and had difficulty processing the large volume of applications they received. Because the number of Chinese citizens who applied for visas exceeded developed countries' embassies' quotas for Chinese citizens, visa applications were often rejected. Rejection most often occurred when the applicants had questionable supporting documents (such as documents that seemed to exaggerate family incomes, savings account deposits that were really loans from relatives or loan businesses, or letters of acceptance from language schools abroad that had reputations for focusing more on enabling foreign students to qualify for visas than on actual education) or when they gave responses in interviews that seemed untruthful, inadequately fluent, or suggestive of "immigration intent" (*yimin qingxiang*, a nebulous reason for visa denial that was subjectively defined by the embassy officer who evaluated a particular application). Even visa applications that did not actually have these problems were frequently denied for arousing embassy officers' suspicions of such problems. The degree of scrutiny that applicants received varied widely, depending not only on the applicants' own background and application materials but also on the attitude, experience, and judgment of the particular embassy official assigned to each application. I heard of several cases in which one Chinese citizen was denied a visa while his or her friend or relative was granted one, even though both of them had nearly identical credentials and submitted nearly identical visa applications to the same embassy at the same time.

Even a Chinese citizen who shopped around for the cheapest possible options in the country with the lowest costs for study abroad (usually Ireland or Japan at the time of my study), who planned to work enough hours to become fully self-supporting immediately after arriving in a developed country, and who took out a loan from a private company to fund the savings account that would provide the proof of assets required for visa applications, had to prepay at least 3,000 yuan (US$381) for the loan, another 3,000 yuan for study-abroad broker fees, 2,700 yuan (US$343) to 7,000 yuan (US$888) for plane and sometimes train tickets, 5,000 yuan (US$635) for the first term at a language school, and another 5,000 yuan for the first month of room and board with a host family abroad. Even such an inexpensive route to study abroad cost more than the average factory worker's annual salary.[18] Such a low-budget visa application package was also likely to arouse the suspicion of embassy officials, who preferred to grant visas to Chinese citizens who could afford more prestigious and expensive foreign-language programs, or better yet college programs, and had enough income and assets to provide authentic documentation without relying on loans.

A Chinese citizen who went through a prestigious broker with a reputation for reliability, or alternatively a broker willing to provide illegal documents and services, could pay as much as 60,000 yuan (US$7,614) just for the broker fees. A Chinese citizen who wanted to attend a university in one of the more expensive countries (Britain, Canada, and the United States at the time of my study) could pay more than 200,000 yuan (US$25,381) for just one year of tuition. Even the wealthiest Chinese citizens in my study would take many years to earn that much in China.

Children of factory workers who went abroad often had to use their parents' entire life savings and proceeds from sales of their family homes in addition to loans from aunts, uncles, and friends just to pay for the startup costs of study abroad. To pay for their children's education, whether in China or abroad, parents were often willing to sell their homes and use their life savings, which they had planned to use for their own retirement or their children's neolocal marital housing. In addition to feeling so desperate about their children's prospects without further education that they were willing to sacrifice anything they had to ensure that their children received more education, parents assumed that investing in their children's education could have a bigger payoff in the long run than any other financial investment they could make. Because many of their parents had many siblings, each of whom had only one child, it was also possible for a singleton to get loans from many relatives to fund the startup costs of study abroad. Such loans put a lot of pressure on the transnational student to earn enough money abroad to pay back those loans as soon as possible.

The rapid inflation of housing prices close to city centers increased the wealth of urban Chinese citizens, most of whom had state-assigned apartments that they were allowed to purchase for low prices as soon as the housing market was privatized in the late 1990s.

Some middle-class families purchased several apartments as soon as the housing market was privatized, both as investments and in preparation for the day their children would marry and need neolocal housing. Their investments paid off, as housing prices doubled every few years in the 2000s. By 2010, apartments near the center of cities like Dalian were worth 10,000–30,000 yuan (US$1,471–US$4,412) per square meter—more than 10 times what they had been worth when housing first became privatized in the 1990s. Urban housing prices were driven up by rising incomes and the influx of rural migrants to urban areas.[19] As rural Chinese youth sought greater access to developed world citizenship by migrating to Chinese cities, they provided urban families with rental income and home sale profits that helped enable urban youth to migrate to developed countries. Housing near the city center was often double or triple the prices of housing in the rural or semirural areas an hour's drive away from the city center, so it was possible even for relatively poor factory worker parents to make large profits by renting or selling their apartments in the city center and moving to apartments in semirural areas or by renting or selling extra apartments they had inherited. Retired parents who no longer needed to work in the city center sometimes rented or sold their centrally located housing and moved into more remote housing to get profits that would fund their children's study abroad, although they considered it a great sacrifice because it entailed moving away from conveniently located neighborhoods where they had spent most of their lives. Those who had purchased several apartments as investments when housing prices were much lower were able to make even more profit by renting or selling their extra apartments. These profits enabled their children to study abroad even though the costs of doing so were often much higher than what their parents earned from a lifetime of work.

Some countries (such as Japan and Ireland during the late 1990s and early 2000s) were less careful than others (such as Australia, Canada, and the United States,[20] particularly after September 11, 2001) about verifying that the money in savings accounts had not been borrowed, that the applicant did not constitute a security risk, that applicants' families really had enough income to support their study abroad, and that the applicant did not have "immigration intent." Yet windows of opportunity for easy visa application approvals were brief. By the mid-2000s, the embassies of Japan and Ireland were making it harder for Chinese citizens to obtain visas because their citizens were becoming increasingly concerned about cultural, political, and economic problems that might be caused by rising immigration.

Some Chinese citizens had their visa applications rejected by several countries before they finally received a visa (usually from a country to which they had not previously applied, because applications with histories of previous rejections by the same embassy were subject to extra scrutiny). A successful visa application was therefore considered a rare, precious opportunity that may not come again if one passed it up.

Study Abroad as an Activity Best Suited to Youth

Study abroad was seen as an especially high-risk, high-reward kind of opportunity that was open primarily to youth. A 24-year-old singleton Chinese citizen who had left China at age 20 to study at an Australian university told me, "I thought that if I didn't go abroad when I was young, I might never have another chance."

Unlike the kind of emigrant from Fujian villages described by Frank Pieke and his collaborators, whose "core objective is to generate savings and remittances for his or her natal or nuclear family, or both,"[21] the transnational students in my study considered their own personal transformation into developed world citizens their core objective. Making money was merely one of several possible means to that objective. Other means, such as paying tuition to attend college or graduate school abroad, might actually cause them to lose money, at least in the short run. Even those who hoped to save enough money to start businesses in China focused on the implications this would have for their own upward mobility. Few of the transnational students in my study managed to earn enough abroad to send remittances to their families in China, and some actually depended on remittances from their parents to fund their lives and education abroad. Although they hoped that their own upward mobility would also bring upward mobility to their parents, it was clear to the whole family that upward mobility for the individual studying abroad, not the immediate earning of money that could be sent as remittances for those left behind in China, was the main purpose of study abroad. Unlike nonstudent transnational migrants from China and elsewhere who have been described in previous studies,[22] most of the transnational students in my study had no dependents to support and were singletons used to being the main focus of their family's financial and emotional investments.[23] They and their parents hoped that their transformation into developed world citizens would improve their parents' lives as well as their own in the long term, but they and their parents agreed that it would be shortsighted for them to do extra work, at the expense of their studies, to send remittances to improve their parents' lives in the short term.

Those I met in Dalian considered their youth a precious, fleeting window of opportunity to become part of the developed world, in China or abroad. They often talked about their fear that upward mobility would become increasingly difficult to attain once the strength, energy, attractiveness, and good health of youth faded and they had to take on the responsibilities that would come with marriage, childbearing, child rearing, and the increasing age and infirmity of their parents and grandparents. They referred to youth as a "rainy season" (*yuji*) during which seeds of future success could be planted, and they considered dead-end jobs ways to "waste the springtime of youth" (*langfei qingchun*). They often spoke about the importance of using their teens and 20s to seize fleeting opportunities for education and upward mobility. Those who wasted their youth on dead-end jobs were said to be "eating spring rice" (*chi qingchun fan*), which would be depleted as they aged.[24]

Chinese families and developed countries' embassy officials alike considered study abroad most appropriate for young, single, childless high school or college graduates. Parents were reluctant to send children younger than 18 abroad, for fear that they would get into trouble without parental supervision. Developed countries' embassies rarely granted visas to individuals under 18 without evidence that they would be supervised by family members or boarding schools, which most Chinese citizens in my study could not afford. Sending children abroad before they finished high school would also mean that these children would not finish acquiring the basic credentials and skills (especially in Chinese language) expected by most Chinese colleges and employers and thus that they would have difficulty getting any kind of higher education or white-collar work in China if they failed to get into college abroad. Children under 18 would also have difficulty getting jobs that would allow them to support themselves abroad. The level of wealth and tolerance for risk necessary for Chinese parents to send "parachute children" abroad when they were under 18 was out of reach for most families in my study.[25]

At the other end of the age spectrum, embassy officials were more likely to deny student visas to Chinese citizens who were past their mid-20s or had spouses and/or children, because they did not fit the traditional student profile and seemed likely to focus on other things (such as work or immigration) that student visas were not meant to facilitate. Married Chinese citizens were also reluctant to study abroad or let their spouses study abroad, because it could entail prolonged separation that could destroy their marriage. The same fear of long-term family separation also made those in China who were preparing to study abroad reluctant to marry, much less have children, while in China. None of the 126 transnational student survey respondents who were asked about the year they first went abroad were married or had children before that year.[26] Unlike transnational migrants from areas with stronger emigration traditions and more pathways to work and business abroad,[27] Chinese citizens in my study considered having children before study abroad too risky, because they had no idea how long it might actually take to realize their goals abroad or how much money they could earn while maintaining student statuses abroad. In addition, it was so difficult to get and renew visas that it was unlikely for spouses to each get and keep legal residency rights in the same country.

Many Chinese citizens in my study dreamed of studying abroad but abandoned that dream as they ran out of time to experiment with life's possibilities, acquired adult responsibilities, and became more risk averse. An 18-year-old singleton Chinese citizen told me right after he graduated from a vocational high school, "I want to go abroad now, while I'm still young, so that even if I learn once abroad that I made a mistake, I'll still have time to recover from the mistake and get on with what I should do in my life." He was the only child of poor factory workers. He hoped to enter an Anglophone developed country as an ESOL student, eventually acquire enough English skills and save enough from low-skill jobs to pay for college in that country, and then get a white-collar job and permanent residency rights in that country. He spent four years taking private English lessons, working as a security guard, and applying for student visas from the embassies of the United States, Canada, Australia, Britain, and Ireland, but his applications were rejected by all of them. At age 22 he decided that he needed to move on with his life in China and entered a three-year adult education college program. After graduating with a degree from that program at age 25, he got a clerical job with more long-term potential for promotion than his security guard job and married a co-worker. By the time he was 27, his wife was pregnant and he had completely abandoned his dream of going abroad. "I'm not a child anymore, and I can't just think of myself," he explained to me. "I just want a stable life now, so I can do right by my family."

Gendered Risks and Opportunities Associated with Study Abroad

Women's parents were more likely than men's parents to worry about their children's ability to remain safe and chaste while abroad. In addition, women faced a shorter biological clock than their male counterparts (both in terms of the period in which they would be fertile and in terms of the period in which they would be considered young and attractive enough to attract a suitable spouse), which made the postponement of marriage and childbearing that was often necessary when studying abroad more risky for women than for men. Dating and marrying foreigners was more likely and desirable for Chinese women than for Chinese men because of foreign and Chinese expectations of female hypergamy and Western and Chinese associations of Asian cultures with femininity and Western cultures with masculinity.[28] Such factors might eventually make Chinese women who go abroad more likely to stay abroad than their male counterparts. But no one in my study told me that a desire to date or marry foreigners was at all important either in motivating them to study abroad or in facilitating their transnational migration. Unlike some older, less educationally focused transnational migrants in other studies,[29] for whom marriage and romance were important reasons and means for transnational migration, most Chinese citizens in my study did not know any foreigners well enough to even consider dating or marrying them before going abroad, did not think that the benefits of going abroad would be worth the stigma and risks associated with trying to find lovers or spouses through transnational online dating, and considered themselves too young to be seriously considering marriage. Only 35 percent of the 589 women and 24 percent of the 536 men who responded to the marriage question on my 2008–2010 survey had ever married.

Among those who had never been abroad, 68 percent of the 325 women and 60 percent of the 294 men indicated on the most recent survey they completed between 2008 and 2010 that they wanted to live abroad someday.[30] On average, the 1,321 female survey respondents scored higher than their 952 male classmates who took the same foreign-language tests in grades 8–12 in 1999. Among those who indicated their college major on my 2008–2010 survey, 14 percent of the 401 women and 5 percent of the 403 men had foreign-language-related majors in college. But male respondents were slightly more likely than female respondents to actually go abroad. Among the 637 men who responded to my 2008–2010 survey, 34 percent had been abroad (including the 22 percent who had studied abroad); among their 728 female counterparts, 29 percent had been abroad (including the 18 percent who had studied abroad).[31] This may have been because parents (the main source of initial funding for study abroad) perceived study abroad as somewhat riskier for women than for men.

Although desires and opportunities for study abroad varied somewhat by gender, the variation was remarkably small. My survey respondents were born after China's one-child policy, which created many sonless families that treated daughters the same way they would have treated sons.[32] The socialization and parental investment males and females had were fairly similar while they were single, childless students, and they consequently had similar aspirations and opportunities to go abroad. Unlike researchers who studied migrants who viewed transnational migration partly as a way to escape the gender inequality prevalent in their homelands,[33] I did not find any large, systematic gender differences in my quantitative or qualitative analysis of Chinese transnational citizens' study-abroad decisions, experiences, or trajectories.

Where Roads Diverge

So far I have discussed factors that shaped possibilities for and constraints on study abroad. What such a discussion cannot reveal, however, are the idiosyncratic factors that caused one Chinese citizen to study abroad while a demographically and socioeconomically similar friend, neighbor, cousin, or classmate did not. In the remainder of this chapter I look at the experiences of two Chinese citizens who ended up studying abroad and two who did not. These four youths were from the same neighborhood in Dalian. What I hope to show with these examples is the extent to which unpredictable, random events and emotions precipitated or prevented study abroad. Looking at patterns in quantitative data, it is tempting to argue that particular socioeconomic and demographic factors determined who studied abroad and who did not. But, although such factors affected the likelihood of study abroad for those with particular characteristics, they did not ultimately determine who actually studied abroad and who did not. Rather, at the individual level, such determinations were often made in moments of emotional turmoil, in response to random and unexpected events.

"The Only Way Out"

When Wang Jun was a senior at a college prep high school in China, he did not seem very interested in English or study abroad. He was an academic underachiever who sat in the back of the classroom and often slept or chatted with friends instead of studying. He rushed out to the dirt field outside his school building to play soccer whenever he had a spare moment—sometimes even during the brief 20-minute break between afternoon and evening classes. He scored near the bottom of his class on practice exams.

Wang Jun was the only child of factory worker parents who fretted over his low scores. They lacked the money and connections to provide him with a safety net if he failed to get into college. But Wang Jun did not seem as worried as his parents were. He was unusually talented at soccer and hoped to get into a local university through a special athletic admissions program that would accept talented soccer players even if they had relatively low scores. He dreamed of becoming a professional soccer player. His dream was not entirely unrealistic, because he sometimes ranked near the top of high school soccer contests in Dalian, a city known for producing top-notch soccer players.

When he took the college entrance exam, Wang Jun did not score nearly high enough to get into college through regular admissions processes. Wang Jun hoped that his soccer skills could get him into a Dalian university with a good soccer program, but he was dismayed when the only university that admitted him through a special athletic admissions program was one in a poor, faraway province with a soccer program that was not as good as the soccer programs available in Dalian. Wang Jun's parents wanted him to enroll, but Wang Jun did not want to waste his time. "Who wants to go to such a remote place?" he scoffed. His parents scolded him for having passed up his one chance at attending a university.

Wang Jun spent three years after high school practicing and test-ing to get into a professional soccer training program in Dalian while working as a cook and cashier at a fast-food outlet for spending money. When he failed to perform well enough in soccer contests to get into the professional soccer training program, however, he became desperate about his future. "I have no way out," he told me. He was certain that he would score even lower if he retook the college entrance exam, because he had forgotten what little he had managed to learn in high school. Even during his senior year of high school (when he was most prepared to take the college entrance exam), he had scored so low on that exam that he would not have been admit-ted into any university without the help of a special athletic admis-sions program, which was no longer open to him now that he had graduated from high school. His parents were factory workers who lacked the money, connections, and power to help him start a busi-ness or get him a white-collar job despite his lack of a college degree. Without professional soccer training or a college degree, he seemed headed toward a life of low-level service or factory jobs, which he considered intolerable. He envied his high school classmates, most of whom were almost finished with college.

One of his high school classmates, however, had also not yet started college. Liu Peng, Wang Jun's best friend from high school, had left for Britain the year after he failed to get into any prestigious four-year Chinese university. Liu Peng was attending an ESOL school in Britain, trying to gain enough English proficiency to enter a Brit-ish university. Unlike Wang Jun, Liu Peng had a father who was a wealthy company manager. He managed to pay for Liu Peng's tuition and living expenses abroad by selling one of the condos he owned. Liu Peng occasionally worked at fast-food restaurants in Brit-ain for extra spending money, but he did not have to work to support himself. Liu Peng often talked to Wang Jun by phone and e-mail and told him about how carefree his life was in Britain, away from paren-tal supervision and the judgments of peers and relatives in China.

Wang Jun knew that his life abroad would not be as carefree as Liu Peng's because he could not depend on his parents for financial support and would have to earn enough money from low-wage jobs to pay for his own tuition and living expenses. Still, at age 21, he applied for a visa to study in Britain. He was elated when his visa application was granted by the British embassy four months later. "I thought soccer would be my way out, but after I failed at that, going abroad was the only way out," Wang Jun told me. "In China I would have been a worker all my life, but abroad I can develop myself."

A Road Not Taken

Liu Nian was the same age as Wang Jun and lived just a few blocks away. When I first met him, he was a senior at a keypoint college prep high school. He was the only child of white-collar office workers. Although he studied a lot, his performance on practice exams was erratic, and his parents often complained that he was lazy. Liu Nian admitted that he did not always study as much as he should. On several practice tests, he had ranked among the top 10 students in his homeroom; on other practice tests, however, he ranked in the middle or even at the bottom of his class.

After he took his college entrance exam, Liu Nian was uncertain how he had performed because he could not remember what answers he had put down. Unable to estimate his score, he and his parents agonized over which schools he should make his top choices. In the end, his parents told him to gamble on assuming that he had scored high enough to get into a top-ranked college. They lost their gamble. Liu Nian scored below the cutoffs of all his top-choice colleges.

Liu Nian was admitted to a low-ranked junior college, but neither he nor his parents thought it would be worthwhile for him to enroll. Liu Nian told his parents that he was sick of the Chinese educational system and wanted to study abroad. Liu Nian's parents wanted him to spend another year in high school and then retake the entrance exam. Liu Nian refused. "I'll kill myself before I go through that hell for another year!" he told them. His parents scolded him and pleaded with him, but they eventually gave up. They reluctantly agreed to send him abroad. He enrolled in private English classes and went to study-abroad brokers to figure out his options. At first, Liu Nian was glad to be free of the sleepless, high-pressure schedule he kept during high school. But he regretted having done so poorly on his college entrance exam and felt guilty about his desire to study abroad despite his parents' reluctance to send him.

Liu Nian's guilt intensified when his father fell down the stairs of his apartment building, breaking his leg. Two weeks later, his mother was hospitalized with a respiratory infection, which Liu Nian attributed to the stress of taking care of his father. "I'm sad," Liu Nian told me. "It was all because I was arguing with him, and I got him so angry that he didn't look where he was going! He could have died in that fall. If he had died, I would have killed myself. I didn't realize how much I loved my parents until they ended up in the hospital. Now I think about how they're getting old, and how they won't be here forever. I've resolved to stop fighting with them. They're good people, and I'll miss them after they die. If I keep fighting with them, then after they die, I'll regret not having been a good son while they were still alive."

The day his mother went to the hospital, Liu Nian decided that study abroad would not be worth the deprivation it would cause his parents. "They'd be happier if I attend a good college in China, because I'd be nearby, and they wouldn't have to pay so much money to support me," he told me. "Yet they're willing to use all their savings to satisfy my desire to go abroad, because they really care for me. Would I be doing right by them if I go?"

Liu Nian's parents were happy when Liu Nian told them that he had changed his mind and would retake the college entrance exam rather than study abroad. He scored much higher when he retook the exam the following year and was accepted by a university that was respectable, though still not as prestigious as the ones his parents wanted him to attend. After he graduated, he got a job as a clerk in the state-owned work unit. He still works there and married a co-worker. Although he sometimes still talks about going abroad for study or work, he now sees it more as a distant fantasy than an actual possibility.

Following a Cousin Abroad

Dai Shuping attended the same college prep high school Wang Jun attended. She was the only child of factory worker parents and one of the top students in her class. She told me that her greatest dream was to go to a good college in China and get a job that paid a developed-world-level salary in China. "Many people think the moon is rounder abroad and are willing to sacrifice anything to leave our country, but I don't think it's worth it," Dai Shuping told me when she was 19.

When she took the college entrance exam at age 20, however, Dai Shuping scored only high enough to get into a little-known junior college. While Dai Shuping was at college, her older cousin Lin Tao went to Dublin, Ireland, where he attended an ESOL school while working full-time as a busboy at a bar. When he returned to China to visit his family, he had enough money to treat friends and relatives to meals at expensive restaurants for lunch as well as dinner every day. He threw out the old pots and pans his parents had used for decades and bought new ones for them. His parents were delighted, but they complained about how much water he used when showering and washing dishes, because water was expensive in Dalian. Lin Tao told his relatives, "In Ireland, water is free, and I can use as much as I want—now I don't feel clean unless I shower every day." He showed Dai Shuping and other relatives the photos he took of the pristine, unpolluted beaches of Ireland. Dai Shuping envied the life Lin Tao had in Ireland, and she started talking about wanting to go there as well.

Dai Shuping made her decision one day in 2002 during her winter vacation, when she was working at a part-time job selling frozen dumplings at a market. She had to stand all day next to a freezer in an area of the market with little heat. Her hands were frostbitten from handling the frozen dumplings, and her feet and back ached. She worked from 9 am to 8 pm, with only an hour for lunch, and she received only 200 yuan (US$24) for her 10 hours of work. "As I stood there in the cold, I decided I would definitely have to go abroad," Dai Shuping told me. "At the very worst, I might get a job like this abroad that makes my whole body ache, but then at least I would be paid 10 times as much! Why experience such misery in China for so little money?"

Two months later, at age 23, Dai Shuping hand-delivered her passport and application to the Irish embassy in Beijing and waited for a reply. Four months later, she graduated from college and got a job as a teacher at a private foreign-language school in Dalian that paid her 1,000 yuan (US$121) per month. She thought her salary was too low, and she was becoming dissatisfied with China. "My cousin makes twice as much in an hour as a busboy in Ireland than I make in a day as a teacher in China!" she told me. "China's too poor and backward. Maybe there's no future for me here."

She got to know many students who were hoping to study abroad, and their excitement made her even more eager to follow suit. The private school she worked for offered little job security and often made her work overtime for no pay. She avoided looking for better, more permanent jobs that would require her to sign contracts with financial penalties for quitting, because she thought she might have to drop everything to go abroad at any moment. For the same reason, she avoided dating, despite her mother's frequent nagging about the need for her to find a husband before she got too old.

At age 25, two years after she submitted her application, she received a rejection letter from the Irish embassy. Disappointed and dejected, she considered giving up her dream of study abroad. "Maybe I should just get a stable job, get married, have a child, and live my life in China," she told me.

Yet it was hard to give up. "I've already started walking this road, and told everyone I would try to go abroad," she told me. "If I give up now, everyone will laugh at me, the sacrifices I made would have been for nothing, and I'll always wonder if my life could have been different." She went to several different study-abroad agencies and asked about possibilities for studying in Britain, Denmark, Australia, or the United States. She found that all these other countries were too expensive and difficult to get into, so she reapplied to the Irish embassy, which by this time had streamlined its application procedures to decrease the kinds of delays that Dai Shuping had previously experienced. Four months later, Dai Shuping received a student visa. She took a few weeks to pack and say goodbye to her friends and family and got on the plane to Ireland.

Trying to Follow a Friend Abroad and Giving Up

As Dai Shuping started talking about study abroad, her excitement inspired her childhood friend Chen Kefei, who, like Dai Shuping, was also the only child of factory workers. Dai Shuping and Chen Kefei lived just a block apart and had been close friends since they attended the same junior high school together, even though Chen Kefei went on to a vocational high school while Dai Shuping went on to a college prep high school. Chen Kefei had been working as a salesclerk since graduating from vocational high school. Although her academic credentials were not impressive, Chen Kefei was beautiful, and her beauty helped her to get unusually high-paying salesclerk positions. Chen Kefei's salesclerk job paid her a base salary of about 1,000 yuan (US$121) per month, the same as what Dai Shuping made as a private school English-language teacher, but Chen Kefei sometimes earned up to 2,000 yuan ($242) per month because of bonuses she received when she was successful in making sales. Chen Kefei was fairly content with her life. However, when Dai Shuping started talking about her cousin's stories of life in Ireland, Chen Kefei decided that she wanted to go with Dai Shuping to Ireland. The life that Chen Kefei had previously considered satisfactory seemed boring in comparison to the life that study abroad could open up. "Life at home is so dull," Chen Kefei told me. "I just work all day. It's not fun. I want a different environment."

Chen Kefei also thought that having her close friend Dai Shuping as a companion would make study abroad more fun and less lonely than it might otherwise be. Dai Shuping liked the idea of having Chen Kefei as a companion on her journey abroad but also worried about causing her friend to embark too hastily on a risky, life-changing journey. "I can't make the decision for you," Dai Shuping told Chen Kefei. "I can only give you information."

Chen Kefei insisted, however, that she was just as determined to study abroad as Dai Shuping was. Chen Kefei submitted her application for a visa to study in Ireland at the same time Dai Shuping did—when both of them were 23. While she was waiting for a reply, she was introduced to a man a few years older than her, with a high-paying job in international trade. After a year of dating, he asked her to marry him, and she happily agreed. By the time Chen Kefei received news that her visa application had been declined by the Irish embassy (at the same time that Dai Shuping did—two years after they first submitted their visa applications), Chen Kefei's desire to study abroad had waned. Her fiancé had no desire to live abroad, and she did not want to leave him. "It's my fate to stay in China," Chen Kefei told me. Unlike Dai Shuping, Chen Kefei did not want to try again. A year after Dai Shuping went to Ireland, Chen Kefei got married. Chen Kefei only regretted that Dai Shuping could not be in China for the wedding, for Chen Kefei and Dai Shuping had agreed when they were teenagers that whoever married first would invite the other to be her maid of honor.

Conclusion: Who Studied Abroad and Why?

Chinese citizens told me that wealthier parents were more likely than poorer parents to send their children abroad and that failure to attain a satisfactory education or career in China was the main motivation for studying abroad. Such explanations were corroborated by my survey data and illustrated by the experiences of many Chinese citizens in my study. But such explanations could not account for why one went abroad and another did not, even though they had almost identical socioeconomic backgrounds and experiences of educational or professional failure. Chinese transnational students proposed such explanations for the study-abroad phenomenon in general, not for their own motivations and experiences in particular. When explaining their own decisions, they suggested that they ended up studying abroad or not because of a more complex confluence of factors, the most important of which seemed to be unpredictable events and emotionally driven decisions. They found themselves at particular crossroads in their lives, with study in a particular developed country as one possible path, and made their decisions in response to events such as a parent's illness, a marriage proposal, the comments of a friend, acquaintance, or relative, or an unpleasant day at work. Many described themselves as having made their decision to study abroad based not on a careful consideration of advantages and disadvantages but rather on a gamble they made without adequate information.[34]

Even after making the decision to study in a particular country, some found that their visa applications were denied for unpredictable, incomprehensible reasons. Some, like Chen Kefei, gave up after a visa denial and moved on with their lives in China. Others, like Dai Shuping, however, decided to reapply for a visa to enter the same country or to apply for a visa to a different country. Such decisions were again based more on subjective reactions to the circumstances of particular moments than on careful planning or calculations. Most of those who ended up studying abroad explained their ultimate paths as the result of their subjective responses to a series of unpredictable events (such as Wang Jun's failure to get into a soccer training program or Dai Shuping's unpleasant work experiences) and not as the culmination of long-held goals, plans, traits, and resources. Likewise, those who had made but then abandoned plans to study abroad also attributed those decisions to unpredictable events, such as Liu Nian's father's injury and mother's illness (which made Liu Nian rethink whether study abroad was worth the cost to his parents) or the marriage proposal that made Chen Kefei reluctant to leave China.

This was in contrast to their explanations for taking more conventional paths to education, careers, marriage, and childbearing in China. As in many other countries,[35] youth in China had clear ideas of dominant cultural scripts for these paths and perceived themselves as following them more or less well. Although they sometimes talked about luck as having led them to the particular high school, university, job, spouse, and child they ended up with, most youth I knew in Dalian talked about their decision to pursue secondary and tertiary education, seek employment, marry, and have a child as predictable phases of long-term plans based on well-established road maps.

Study abroad, on the other hand, was seen as an unexpected path that they had not prepared to take. Whether they ended up taking it depended on a series of unpredictable events that led them onto or off that path. They could envision the broad parameters of their life course if they stayed in China, pursuing education, work, marriage, and childbearing in the same ways that many others around them were doing and had done for decades, but they knew little about what would happen if they studied abroad.

Study abroad may have been a predictable part of a life plan based on established road maps for members of southern Chinese communities with long transgenerational histories of emigration,[36] but it was not for those in my study. Most of them had no relatives abroad; if they knew anyone abroad (other than me), it was likely to be a friend or cousin who had gone abroad only a few years earlier. Opportunities to study abroad were so rare, poorly understood, difficult to come by, and risky that it was considered foolish to plan on them. Decisions about study abroad could be perceived only as shots in the dark that seemed to make sense in a moment of desperation or exuberance. Therefore, even though almost everyone I knew in Dalian talked about studying abroad, few seriously considered it part of their life plan until the moment they actually went. The combination of experiences of failure with enough family wealth to have a shot at getting student visas caused many of the youth I met in Dalian to become interested in study abroad, but whether they actually ended up abroad and which country they ended up in depended more on a series of unpredictable events.

Although children of middle-class parents had more opportunities to study abroad, the relationship between socioeconomic status and study abroad was far from clear-cut. Some of those who studied abroad (such as Dai Shuping and Wang Jun) were of much lower socioeconomic status than their friends, neighbors, former classmates, and relatives who did not study abroad. The desire to live abroad seemed similarly common among respondents of different socioeconomic backgrounds.[37] Countering the tendency of low socioeconomic status to discourage Chinese citizens from going abroad was the fact that failure to attain a satisfactory education or career in China was often a key motivation for Chinese citizens to study abroad. Definitions of failure were subjective. Some told me that they studied abroad because of their failure to get into any college or failure to get any white-collar job at all, but others told me that they studied abroad because they "failed" to get into a Chinese university even more prestigious than the prestigious Chinese university that did accept them or because they "failed" to get a job even more high-paying and prestigious than the high-paying and prestigious job they did get.

When I started my research in China in the late 1990s, I had assumed that study abroad would be reserved for those who had unusually wealthy parents or enough academic qualifications to win full scholarships from foreign universities. However, I was surprised at how many of the academically and socioeconomically average or below-average singletons in my study also ended up studying abroad, even though it often meant they had to use up their parents' entire life savings and all the profits from the homes their parents sold and accept loans and gifts from friends and relatives. Raised with high aspirations based on comparisons to friends, classmates, and relatives of even higher socioeconomic status and feeling that they had just enough wealth and education to launch them into the upper class if they were lucky and determined enough, yet lacking the advantages that truly upper-class status could confer, Chinese youth in my study were reluctant to accept their "failure" to reach the high educational and career goals to which they and their families aspired and saw study abroad as a way around that "failure."

When one looks at the big picture of "migration systems,"[38] it may seem that migration trajectories are determined primarily by socioeconomic factors. Research about large-scale migration trends often assumes that people make migration decisions for rational, predictable reasons that are discernible through quantitative analysis.[39] A quantitative analysis of my survey data does indeed suggest that children of professionals, managers, and large business owners were more likely to study abroad. But qualitative analysis of my ethnographic data suggests that this was not the most important reason for migration decisions at the individual level. When I asked transnational Chinese students why they studied abroad, even those in the socioeconomic group most likely to study abroad talked about particular events and idiosyncratic reactions that led them to do so rather than a belief that everyone of their socioeconomic status could or should study abroad. Many were surprised that they ended up studying abroad. At the individual level, migration decisions were based not on a rational analysis of the costs and benefits of migration but rather on subjective responses to events that seemed unpredictable to those who experienced them.

CHAPTER 4

The Floating Life

Dilemmas of Education, Work, and Marriage Abroad

CHINESE CITIZENS in my study went abroad hoping to become part of the developed world by getting citizenship or permanent residency rights in a developed country, earning enough money from work abroad to start lucrative businesses in China, and/or earning developed world college degrees that could help them win prestigious, high-paying jobs in China or a developed country. Some hoped that they could eventually get legal citizenship or permanent residency rights in a developed country by securing white-collar jobs with employers in that country who were willing to sponsor them for such rights, and they hoped to live the rest of their lives in that country. Others hoped that they would be able to return to China with useful skills, prestigious degrees, and large amounts of money that would enable them to live as social and cultural citizens of the developed world even though they remained legal citizens and residents of China. Still others hoped to spend the rest of their lives in China even after they secured permanent residency rights or legal citizenship in a developed country, or they hoped to get work that would allow them to travel frequently between China and one or more developed countries. Most vacillated between all these possible paths from year to year, month to month, and sometimes moment to moment.

Unlike the mostly rural emigrants described by Frank Pieke, who "come to Europe with one overriding motive: making money,"[1] most of the transnational students in my study were ambivalent about the relative importance of making money, getting college degrees, and getting legal citizenship or permanent residency rights. They paid a high price for their ambivalence, because it sometimes prevented them from succeeding at any one of their goals. The availability of diverse possible paths to developed world citizenship was one of the main advantages of study abroad, but transnational Chinese students also found it hard to choose between these paths and agonized over which path would lead to the greatest happiness with the least risk and sacrifice. Many hoped to combine all these paths. For most, however, these paths were mutually contradictory. Spending too much time working and too little money on education could hinder efforts to earn a degree that could enable them to get a prestigious, high-paying job in China or abroad and thus also reduce the likelihood that they would be allowed to stay long enough in a developed country to attain legal citizenship or permanent residency rights. Spending too much time and money on education could hinder efforts to accumulate enough savings to start a business after returning to China, and all the money spent on education could be wasted if they failed to complete a degree abroad (which could easily happen if they failed too many classes, ran out of money to pay tuition, or were denied a visa renewal). Petitioning for political asylum, marrying a legal citizen of a developed country, bearing a child in that country, or illegally overstaying a visa could take time and energy away from work and study or cause them to lose many aspects of Chinese citizenship as well as developed world citizenship. Wasting too many years of their fleeting youth abroad on low-skilled work in developed countries could reduce the amount of time they had to establish a career in China (where those trying to build careers later in life encountered significant age discrimination) and could delay marriage and childbearing, which increased the risk of infertility, high-risk pregnancies, and inability to find a suitable spouse.

Even those who started out wanting only to make a lot of money and return to China once they had done so were tempted to get university degrees, white-collar jobs, and permanent residency rights or legal citizenship abroad. On the other hand, even those who started out wanting only a college or graduate degree from a developed country were also tempted to try to immigrate or make money while abroad. Those who started out wanting to gain legal citizenship or permanent residency rights in a developed country also had second thoughts once they were living abroad and realized how much they would have to sacrifice to immigrate. The clear goals many had started out with became murky as they found themselves in unanticipated situations and started redefining themselves and what would make them happier in the long run.

Even as their absence from China eroded their Chinese social and cultural citizenship, most of the transnational students in my study had difficulty attaining social, cultural, or legal citizenship in developed countries. Because they were not legal citizens of those countries, they lacked access to many of the social welfare benefits enjoyed by legal citizens, such as public housing, poverty relief stipends, free or subsidized education, and free or subsidized health care. Those on student visas had to limit their work hours to the amount allowed by the terms of their visas, or they worked extra hours illegally for employers who sometimes felt free to exploit them. They also had to stay enrolled in school full-time, getting passing grades and meeting school attendance standards, to avoid deportation. In many cases, limited proficiency in the local language, fear of threats to their visa status, and lack of understanding about the legal system prevented them from taking advantage of even the limited legal protections and social welfare benefits that were available to them. Recognizing that most transnational students lacked the knowledge and political and financial security to file complaints or lawsuits, some landlords and employers cheated them of money or mistreated them in illegal ways. Many transnational Chinese students told me that their landlords had illegally raised their rents, evicted them, refused to make repairs or improve poor housing conditions, or kept their rental deposits; they also told me that their employers ignored laws that guaranteed workers minimum wages, decent working conditions, and overtime pay. They also said that challenging such landlords and employers through the legal system was too difficult to be worth the risk, expense, and stress involved.

Transnational Chinese students often described their sojourns in developed countries as conditions of floating (*piao*), a concept associated with instability, transience, uncertainty, and lack of rootedness. Terms associated with floating have long been used in Chinese discourses about the unstable nature of life in general and of the lives of travelers and migrants in particular. The term *floating population* (*liudong renkou*) has become a semi-official category used by the Chinese government and scholars worldwide to describe rural-to-urban migrants in China.[2] Shen Fu, an eighteenth-century Chinese government clerk, wrote about his hobbies, travels, work, romances, and marriage, much of which was characterized by both joy and impermanence, in a classic autobiographical novel he titled *Six Records of a Floating Life* (*fu sheng liu ji*).[3] The classic Tang dynasty poet Li Bai (701–762) wrote in a poem, "Now the heavens and earth are the hostels of creation; and time has seen a full hundred generations. Ah, this floating life, like a dream. . . . True happiness is so rare!"[4] The 1990s saw the release of the film *Floating Life* (by and about migrants from Hong Kong to Australia) and of a popular Chinese song sung from the perspective of a Chinese migrant meeting an old hometown neighbor in another Chinese town and asking, "Are you used to the floating life?"[5] In the context of these discourses, the concept of floating had connotations that were usually negative, or at best neutral, rather than positive.

Goals for Upward Mobility

Although some transnational students in my study were motivated more by a desire to acquire developed world skills, credentials, and cultural capital than by a desire to make money abroad in the short run, just about all of them were also motivated to go abroad at least partly by a desire for the higher incomes, greater consumption power, and upward mobility that transnational migration could bring them in the long run. Many told me of their desire for developed-world-level incomes, which could be both a means to and an indicator of social, cultural, and legal citizenship in the developed world. They often lamented about how much lower Chinese incomes were than the incomes available in developed countries. The US federal government's official poverty line for an American family of three was US$13,880 in 1999 and US$18,310 in 2009.[6] Yet, according to Chinese government estimates, the average annual salary in Chinese cities and towns was 8,346 yuan (US$1,008) in 1999 and 29,229 yuan (US$4,181) in 2008.[7]

The cheapest food available cost many times less in China than in developed countries, and most Chinese citizens could at least live in the old, small apartments that they, their parents, or their grandparents had been assigned before housing was privatized in the 1990s. Thus few urban Chinese citizens were actually at risk of the starvation and homelessness that would befall someone who earned an average Chinese salary while living in a developed country. Yet many luxury goods and services available in China—such as plane tickets, automobiles, electronics, household appliances, clothing with developed world brand names, lodging in developed world hotels and in luxurious new, private condominiums in the center of the city, meals at eateries run by developed world corporations such as Pizza Hut, Starbucks, McDonald's, and Kentucky Fried Chicken, and enrollment at elite private schools (or top public schools for which one could not qualify based on entrance exam scores alone)—cost as much in China as in developed countries.

Even relatively disadvantaged workers of developed countries were sometimes perceived as more advantaged than most Chinese citizens. In 2002, when I asked a 16-year-old high school student why he wanted to go abroad, he told me, "My cousin in Ireland is a dishwasher, which is the worst job you can get, but he still made over €1,000 [US$1,000] a month, and he had enough money to buy a car just a few months after he started working in Ireland. If I get a really good job in China, as a white-collar office worker, I might make 1,000 yuan [US$121] a month, but you can't buy anything with 1,000 yuan." The gap between Chinese and developed world purchasing power had not been so troubling under the autarkic, isolationist policies of the Maoist government (1949–1976), but it was painful in the global neoliberal system in which the transnational students in my study were socialized.

In addition to yearning for luxury goods that could be purchased only with developed-world-level incomes, Chinese citizens also yearned for the prestige associated with developed countries. Goods produced by companies based in developed countries were perceived to be of higher quality than those produced by Chinese companies, and even those that were not of higher quality basked in the halo effect of those that were. Chinese businesses often put the flags, maps, place names, and historical figures of developed countries on their advertisements and products regardless of whether they actually sold products from those countries. Some Chinese citizens told me that they bought brands from the developed world rather than brands from China whenever possible, even though the foreign brands were more expensive. A 21-year-old Chinese singleton attending college in China told me that she sometimes went with her friends to Pizza Hut even though she did not like the taste of pizza and did not feel comfortable spending as much on one meal there as they would spend for a week's worth of meals at Chinese restaurants. When I asked why she kept eating at Pizza Hut even though she did not like its food or prices, she replied, "I like the environment. There are many wealthy people and foreigners, and when I'm there, it feels like I'm abroad."

Chinese citizens often complained about how incomes in China were much lower than incomes for comparable work in developed countries even though many luxury goods and services cost as much in China as they did in developed countries. A Chinese income could buy enough food, clothes, and shelter to survive, but only a developed world income could allow one to enjoy world-class cars, planes, electronics, clothes, hotels, restaurants, housing, medical treatments, and education. When transnational students in my study first started working in developed countries, even those who worked at low-skill minimum-wage jobs were thrilled to find that they could earn enough to buy luxuries that only white-collar workers could afford in China. A 22-year-old singleton told me a year after he left China to attend an ESOL school and work at fast-food restaurants in Britain, "In China my parents worked all their lives and still can't afford a car, but here I could afford a car after less than a year of work."

Because incomes in developed countries were many times higher than incomes from comparable work in China, those who returned to China with savings they accumulated after years of work in developed countries were wealthy by Chinese standards, as were those who received remittances from family members who were working in developed countries. Chinese citizens working for foreign-owned companies or in fields such as shipping, trade, travel, translation, and tourism also had higher salaries than their counterparts who were working for Chinese employers who did not deal with developed countries and their citizens. Many Chinese citizens in my study therefore wanted to work for or with citizens of developed countries. "I want to work for a foreign company [in China], or go abroad," a 17-year-old Chinese singleton told me in 2000. "There's no future in Chinese work units. They have no money, so they can't pay a good salary even if you work very hard for them. Besides, after China joins the WTO [World Trade Organization], all the Chinese work units will go bankrupt, because their technology and management methods are not as advanced as those abroad, and they won't be able to compete."

Foreign companies and Chinese employers who had to deal with foreigners often preferred to hire Chinese citizens who had studied in developed countries. "If you have a foreign degree, it means you have advanced foreign knowledge and also that you managed to survive on your own abroad, [whereas if] you just have experience living in China, you have only the same experience that all Chinese people have," a 29-year-old manager told me six years after he returned to China with a college degree from Japan. "And [if you've studied abroad] you know how to deal with foreigners, so whenever there are foreigners around for a visit, or at international meetings, you can go and talk with them, and you speak their language. It gives your employers face."

Parents often cited the possibility of enabling their children to earn much higher incomes in the long term as an important reason for their desire to send their children to developed countries. Although parents expressed great love and protectiveness toward their children, their desire to keep their singletons close by was often overridden by their desire to help their children gain developed world citizenship by studying abroad. "I don't want my son to have a life like mine," the father of 15-year-old singleton Gao Qiang told me. "I have a good job in an office, a white-collar job, and yet I'm always thinking of how to save money. You just can't make a lot of money in a Chinese work unit. I want him to be just like foreigners and be able to have whatever he wants, and not have to worry about money."

Gao Qiang's parents hoped to send him abroad for college. They had been sending him to expensive private English classes since he was a toddler, and they often bought him English-language tapes, books, and movies on video compact discs (VCDs). "I want him to go abroad to study and stay there if he can get a good job," Gao Qiang's mother told me in 1999. "Or, at the very worst, he can just get a college degree abroad, and let the foreign enterprises fight over him when he comes back to China. In those enterprises, he can make at least 4,000 yuan [US$483] a month for doing the same work as people in Chinese work units who make 1,000 yuan [US$121] a month."

Upward Mobility as a Means to Fulfill Social Obligations

Despite their great expectations and hard work, many Chinese singletons still could not get the prestigious Chinese university degrees that could qualify them for high-paying careers. Study abroad was attractive because it offered an alternative path to upward mobility for them, their parents, and their future children.

Many singletons in my study told me that they wanted to study abroad partly because they wanted to eventually make enough money to enable their parents to spend their old age in carefree comfort. A 24-year-old singleton junior college graduate who earned only about 1,000 yuan (US$121) per month at her office job in China in 2004 told me as we looked over US and Canadian college brochures in the cramped one-room apartment she shared with her parents, who were selling snacks on the street below their apartment, "I want to be affluent too, but even more, I want my parents to be affluent. They have sacrificed so much for me. My Ma can't bear to buy herself food and clothes, because she saves all her money for me." She told me that she hoped to get a bachelor's degree from the United States or Canada so that she could get a high-paying job in China or abroad, buy her parents a large condo in China, and "let them play, be happy, and be able to buy anything they want without having to think about money."

Some men in my study hoped that study abroad would make them worthy suitors for current or potential girlfriends of higher socioeconomic status. A low-level office worker with a junior college degree, whose parents owned a small business, told me that he felt he had to try to study abroad when, at age 25, his wealthier and better educated girlfriend's parents told him that they would not allow him to marry his girlfriend because he had less income, education, and family wealth than she did. Similarly, a 23-year-old salesclerk whose parents were factory workers told me that he made up his mind to try to study abroad the day his girlfriend's mother yelled at him for not having career prospects that would enable him to be a good husband for her daughter. Both men ended up studying in Europe, where they were later joined by their girlfriends (whose parents then grudgingly considered the men worthy suitors because they were studying abroad).

Some Chinese citizens told me about their hope that study abroad would enable them to give their future children better opportunities. A few weeks before he left China for Japan, a 23-year-old singleton security guard told me, "My grandparents were farmers in Shandong, but they came to Dalian so their descendants could get a better future. I have to thank them for doing that; otherwise my father and I would have been born on their farm and spent our lives staring at yellow earth. So I want to do even better for my future child by going abroad, so that my future child can have even more opportunities than I've had."

A 19-year-old singleton junior college student told me a month before he left China to attend an ESOL school in New Zealand, "My family background is poor, and I felt a lot of pressure to do well in school because I knew my parents couldn't help me. My parents always worked and had no money. I don't want to be like that. I want my child to be affluent from childhood onwards, and not feel the burdens I felt. I want my child to have foreign citizenship, which will make it easy get a good, free education abroad instead of having to struggle for it as I do."

Higher Education in Developed Countries

Among those in my study who began studying abroad after finishing high school in China, some applied to and were accepted at foreign colleges before they even graduated and did not even take the Chinese college entrance exam. Among those who did take that exam, some were unable to get into any Chinese college program at all, some were accepted by Chinese college programs that they thought were not prestigious enough to be worth attending, and some were accepted by Chinese college programs that they thought were prestigious enough but chose to attend college abroad anyway for other reasons.

Some decided to study abroad as soon as they learned that they had not gotten into a Chinese college program they felt was worth attending. Those with the greatest wealth and foreign-language proficiency enrolled in college abroad immediately after leaving China; those who were less proficient or less wealthy went abroad on student, tourist, work, family visit, or business visas and spent several years working at low-skilled jobs while attending foreign-language schools (which were less expensive than college and did not demand any particular level of foreign-language proficiency before admission), hoping to eventually acquire enough savings and foreign-language proficiency to qualify for college abroad. Others spent several years after high school working, taking private foreign-language classes, or studying foreign-language books on their own at home in China while waiting for a developed country's embassy to grant them a visa; in some cases they experienced visa denials from several developed countries' embassies before finally succeeding.

Some Chinese citizens in my study attended Chinese college programs for a year or two before dropping out of those programs to attend college abroad. Some of them had initially been willing to finish the Chinese college programs to which they had been admitted but changed their minds while attending those programs. Others started applying for student visas from developed countries as soon as they received their admissions from Chinese college programs they considered inadequate, but they attended those programs while waiting for developed countries' embassies to respond to their student visa applications. That way they would at least have a Chinese college degree in case their plans for study abroad failed. Some attended Chinese college programs that included a semester or year of study in a developed country that counted toward both a Chinese college degree and a degree from a college in a developed country. A few who did unusually well in Chinese higher education programs were admitted to graduate programs abroad directly from China; others attended college or foreign-language schools abroad before attending graduate programs abroad.

Some Chinese citizens in my study never attended college in China but spent several years after high school working and/or attending private foreign-language classes in China before going abroad to attend college. Others received college degrees in China and worked for several years but then went abroad to attend a language school or graduate school because they were dissatisfied with their prospects in China. Still others attended college in developed countries even though they already had Chinese college degrees; they believed that a degree from a college in a developed country would enable them to get a better job (in China or abroad) than they could get with a Chinese college degree. Some who earned a less prestigious three-year college degree (*dazhuan*, which is similar to an associate's degree) in China went abroad to get a more prestigious bachelor's degree.

Unlike Chinese college and graduate programs, all of which were at least somewhat selective, some undergraduate and even graduate programs in developed countries accepted all students who were willing and able to pay tuition and able to pass a basic test of proficiency in the language in which those programs were taught. It was thus possible for Chinese citizens who had been unable to get into any higher education program in China to get into such a program abroad. Some of the transnational students in my study (particularly those who had graduated from vocational or technical high schools, which did not prepare them for college entrance exams) chose to study abroad partly because they thought it was the only way they could get a college or graduate degree, which seemed increasingly necessary for any kind of professional career in China or abroad. A 24-year-old college student in Ireland who had graduated from a vocational high school in China and found herself unable to get into any Chinese college program (even in the adult education system) told me, "In China I couldn't even get a steady job as a salesclerk with my vocational high school degree, so I came to Ireland because it was the only way I could get into college. Now a college degree is like a junior high school degree was for our parents—everyone has one, so you can't get a job without one."

However, many transnational Chinese college students learned to their chagrin that passing enough classes and in some cases writing a thesis to get a college or graduate degree in a developed country was much harder than they had anticipated. Most had studied English every year of junior high school and high school, and some had studied English during primary school and college as well. Some had studied Japanese instead of English during high school, and others had studied Japanese in private after-school classes or during college. But their junior high school and high school foreign-language classes focused on preparation for the grammar, vocabulary, and reading comprehension questions that constituted the bulk of the foreign-language test questions on the Chinese college and high school entrance exams, not on speaking, listening, or writing skills. Consequently, even top students who had studied a foreign language for many years in China had trouble writing university-level papers and exam essays in that language abroad. Lower-achieving students also had great difficulty understanding and communicating with instructors and participating in class discussions abroad. Higher education was even more difficult for those who had studied English only in China but then studied in non-Anglophone countries.

Some had to drop out or took much longer than the three or four years they had anticipated to finish their college or graduate programs. The reasons included needing to take remedial foreign-language classes, losing their jobs and not being able to find others, working so many hours that they did not have enough time to study to pass their classes, or running out of money (either their own or their parents') to support their higher education because of changes in tuition rates, their parents' financial circumstances, their expectations about standards of living, the cost of living in the country in which they studied, or the exchange rate between that country and China. Spending too much time working to earn money to pay tuition often backfired. It caused students to fail their classes, and sometimes students had to pay even more to retake those classes than they had earned from the jobs that prevented them from passing in the first place.

Some transnational students in my study had to change schools or even countries because of changing financial circumstances. Sun Na's parents assumed that they had enough savings in Chinese yuan to pay for all her tuition and living expenses in British pounds when they first sent her to Britain to attend a college prep program and then college in 2001, when she was 17. Soon after she got to Britain, however, the US budget deficit began increasing. This caused the devaluation of the US dollar against the British pound, which in turn caused the devaluation of Chinese yuan against the British pound (because the Chinese yuan was pegged to the US dollar by the Chinese government's monetary policy). That in turn caused the devaluation of Sun Na's parents' purchasing power in the British education market. Even after Sun Na's parents sold one of the two condos they owned and started new businesses to pay for Sun Na's escalating tuition and living expenses, they still could not keep up with the rising costs of living and tuition in Britain, and they told her she would soon have to get a job because they were running out of money. But Sun Na could not find any suitable job in her small British college town. She also feared that she would fail her classes if she spent too much time working instead of studying. She heard from a former classmate who was studying in Australia that the costs of living and tuition in Australia were lower than they were in Britain, that there were more work opportunities in his large Australian city than there were in her small British college town, and that his Australian city was more fun and had better weather. So after two years of study in Britain, Sun Na applied for and received a visa to study in Australia. The costs of living and college there were indeed a lot less than in Britain, and she was able to find jobs as a waitress and as a babysitter soon after she arrived in Australia, but the process of changing countries meant that she lost the college credits she had earned in Britain and had to start over in a college prep program and then college in Australia.

Many transnational Chinese students told me that they were surprised that the cost of living abroad was much higher than they anticipated. Some had been given overly low standard-of-living estimates by study-abroad brokers hoping to earn more money by enticing students to study abroad even if they were likely to have trouble affording it. Other transnational Chinese students underestimated the cost of living abroad because of outdated information from friends, relatives, and the Internet that did not account for inflation or changing currency exchange rates, or they failed to consider costs besides those of food, housing, and tuition. A 27-year-old graduate student in Singapore told me nine years after she left China in 2001 to attend college in that island nation that "Singapore offered a scholarship that would pay for half my tuition, so I would only have to pay 25,000 yuan [US$3,023] per year in tuition, and my parents could afford that. So I thought if I went to Singapore, I could focus on studying and not have to work. But I didn't know the cost of living would be so high! The first year I came to Singapore, I spent 120,000 yuan [US$14,510] and ran out of money after paying my second semester school fee. So I had to spend much of my time working at a tea shop for about 20 yuan [US$2.42] per hour."

Many transnational students in my study also did not realize how much their own expectations for a minimum acceptable standard of living, and thus the cost of meeting those expectations, would rise once they were living abroad and interacting with developed world citizens with much higher standards of living than what they had considered acceptable in China. For instance, it was common for four to eight college students to share a single dorm room in China, so many Chinese citizens estimated their likely rent abroad based on the assumption that they would share a bedroom with a similar number of students. Once abroad, however, they learned that the norm was for each college student to have his/her own bedroom or at most share it with one close friend or romantic partner, so this became their expectation as well, and they justified it as necessary for enabling them to concentrate enough on their studies to pass their college classes.

Some transnational Chinese students failed at least some of their college classes because they had low proficiency in the language of the country in which they studied, inadequate preparation for college-level classes in subjects that had been taught differently or not at all in China, and/or not enough time to write papers and study for exams. They had insufficient time to study because they had to work many hours to pay for their college education, got distracted by nonacademic aspects of life in the absence of the heavy supervision from teachers and parents they had been used to, or maintained the same poor time management habits that prevented them from studying enough to get into college in China. They then had to spend additional time and money to retake classes they had failed, which made it even more likely that they would run out of money before they got their degrees. A 22-year-old singleton who left China at age 18 to attend an Australian university told me after he failed a class there, "I only spend a few hours a day in class, but I feel more pressure than I did in high school. I can only understand half of what my teachers say, and they're impatient if I ask for help after class. I think the teachers want us to fail so we'll have to pay more tuition. It takes me so long just to read and understand the textbook, and I don't have enough time because I have to work. My classmates who were worse students than me in high school are now doing better than me in college in China—they're not worried about failing classes, and even if they do, it doesn't cost so much to retake them."

Most scholarships offered by colleges and other organizations in developed countries were reserved for citizens or permanent residents of those countries. The few scholarships available for transnational students in developed countries were extremely selective or available only to students admitted to extremely selective programs. Most Chinese citizens in my study lacked the academic preparation and foreign-language proficiency necessary to win those scholarships. With only a few exceptions (such as those of France and Germany), public universities in developed countries charged foreign students much more than they charged their own citizens. Transnational students in my study complained about how the education of wealthier developed countries' citizens was subsidized by tuition from students from poorer countries like China.[8]

Some transnational students in my study who had been offered admission by relatively selective four-year universities in China chose to decline those offers and attend similarly selective universities in developed countries instead, partly because they believed that degrees from universities in developed countries would be considered more prestigious and valuable by future employers in China and abroad than comparably selective universities in China. They had heard about older relatives and acquaintances who received college or graduate degrees from universities of average or below-average selectivity in developed countries but who were favored in hiring and promotion processes over those who had gotten degrees from universities of similar or better selectivity in China. Proficiency in the cultures and languages of developed countries was considered a valuable asset by transnational corporations and by Chinese businesses and government offices that frequently worked with foreigners; therefore those who had such proficiency (as demonstrated by a college degree from a selective university in a developed country) were more likely than their counterparts with college degrees from Chinese universities to get desirable jobs and promotions. A college degree from a developed country also opened doors to employment abroad that were usually closed to those with Chinese college degrees.

"I've Wasted My Youth"

Most transnational students who completed higher education degrees in developed countries did get employment and promotion opportunities in China and abroad that were not available to their former high school classmates who never left China. But some told me that they were disappointed to find that the differences between the salaries, prestige, quality, and quantity of jobs available to them and those available to their former classmates who never left China were not as great as they had imagined they would be. Foreign education could even be disadvantageous for those applying for Chinese civil service jobs for which personal connections, an understanding of local culture and practices, and political trustworthiness and Communist Party membership were especially important.

Because the process of transnational migration often entailed several years of waiting for visas, learning the language of the destination country, working to save enough money to pay for college tuition in that country, or transferring between universities and even countries when plans went awry, many transnational students finished college degrees abroad years later than their former classmates who stayed in China for college. Consequently, many transnational students who returned to China in their late 20s to begin their professional careers found that, although their starting salaries were higher than those that their former classmates who never studied abroad received at age 22, those former classmates now had higher salaries and more prestigious jobs because they had begun their professional careers immediately after graduating from college at age 22 or a master's program at age 25 and because they had received promotions and pay raises every year or used their work experience to get even better jobs. Meanwhile, the transnational students in my study were more likely to have started their professional careers in their mid-20s or late 20s because it took longer for them to earn college or graduate degrees abroad.

Some Chinese citizens who attended college or graduate school in developed countries also found to their dismay that degrees from average or below-average colleges and universities in developed countries not only did not qualify them for middle-class jobs in developed countries but also did not necessarily give them as much of an advantage over graduates of Chinese universities as they had imagined and in some cases gave them no advantages at all. Some of them remained unemployed for years after returning to China. Although they could have gotten the same jobs that most Chinese college graduates were able to get, they were unwilling to settle for such jobs and chose to remain unemployed while trying to get better jobs in China or while preparing to get visas to go abroad again for study, work, or business. Their parents scolded them for having wasted their families' money by studying abroad, and their relatives and friends criticized them for being "unable to get what's high, unwilling to settle for what's low" (*gao bu cheng, di bu jiu*).

"I really regret studying abroad," a 25-year-old told me while we ate lunch at his parents' home in Dalian in 2009 after he returned to China with a Japanese college degree. He was staying at home, unemployed, because he still could not find a job in China that paid much more than the 2,000 yuan (US$294) per month received by most of his former classmates who had graduated from the Chinese college whose admission offer he had turned down when he chose to attend college in Japan. "[The Japanese college I attended] isn't very famous, and nowadays people only recognize brand name colleges, in China or abroad. Japanese look down on Chinese, especially those who didn't go to brand name colleges, so I had to return to China to find a job. But I went abroad right during 'study abroad fever,' when too many people studied abroad just because they couldn't get into any college in China, so now Chinese people think I'm just one of the 'study abroad trash.' I've wasted my youth and all my parents' money, and if I settle for a low-paying job, I may never earn back what they paid for me to study abroad."[9]

Many Chinese citizens told me before they left China that they believed that higher education in developed countries could teach them more useful, accurate, and up-to-date knowledge and skills in a more interesting and less boring and stressful way. They believed that it would be easier for them to get a higher education in a developed country than in China because university admissions standards abroad were less competitive than those in China, that even degrees from less selective universities in developed countries would be more prestigious and useful than degrees from comparably less selective Chinese universities, and/or that the higher education available in developed countries would be more interesting, practical, useful, flexible, high quality, and stress-free than the kind of education offered in China. They believed that they would have more freedom abroad to explore and choose classes and majors they enjoyed and were good at than they would in China, where they had to choose a college major the summer before they started college. The choice of a major in a Chinese college program was often based more on their own, their parents,' and their teachers' guesses about which majors at which schools would have lower college entrance score requirements and which majors were more likely to qualify them for higher-paying jobs, rather than on their own interest in the major. In addition, in a Chinese college program the students were unlikely to be allowed to switch majors once they enrolled; they would be locked into a rigid curriculum specific to their major, with few electives, and then would be limited to related graduate programs, which also allowed few electives.[10]

Once abroad, many transnational students in my study told me that the content of their higher education abroad was indeed more useful, accurate, interesting, and up-to-date than what they had learned in their Chinese high schools and what they believed they would have learned from higher education in China. But some also complained that their college or graduate school instructors abroad were not as caring or as good at teaching as the high school, college, or graduate school instructors in China. Many actually had no firsthand knowledge of college or graduate school instruction in China and were just comparing their classes abroad with their high school education in China and with what they were told by their former classmates about college and graduate school classes in China. I also heard many college students in China make similar comparisons between their higher education and high school education, so it is possible that what transnational students complained about was due more to differences between higher education and high school education than to differences between China and developed countries. In any case, it was clear that many transnational students in my study thought that their college classes abroad were not as good as what they had expected when they first decided to study abroad.

Many who pursued higher education in developed countries were also disappointed at how little freedom they actually had to choose college majors and classes even in the higher education systems of developed countries. Although college and graduate programs in developed countries were far less restrictive than their Chinese counterparts with regard to choice of a major, the ability to switch majors, and the classes required to graduate with a particular major, transnational Chinese students found that their educational choices were still heavily restricted by their limited proficiency in the languages of developed countries and by the high stakes attached to their educational decisions. These factors made them afraid to choose majors or classes that seemed likely to be difficult for them or unlikely to give them advantages in the job market. Even transnational students in my study who had enjoyed and excelled at the social sciences and humanities in China were afraid to major in those fields in developed countries because those fields required a higher level of foreign-language proficiency than math, science, computer programming, technology, engineering, finance, economics, business, and accounting. Also, because Chinese K–12 schools devoted much more time to math and science than most K–12 schools in Australia, Europe, New Zealand, and North America, many transnational students in my study who attended K–12 schools in China had better quantitative skills than natives of Western countries. They also found that the quantitative knowledge and skills they had learned in China were the same ones that colleges and universities taught in developed countries, whereas much of the qualitative knowledge and skills they had learned in China were useless in colleges and graduate schools in developed countries, which taught qualitative social science and humanities knowledge and skills that were different from those taught in China. Quantitative fields also seemed likely to offer more and better professional job opportunities in China as well as abroad. Most transnational college and graduate students in my study, even those who disliked math, science, and engineering, therefore felt compelled to choose majors in quantitative fields, which were deemed most likely to lead to good jobs in China as well as abroad. Transnational Chinese students in those fields did not have to learn as much in new knowledge and skills as the humanities and qualitative social sciences would require in a developed country.

Although the freedom to choose majors and classes was among the incentives for transnational students in my study to attend college or graduate school in developed countries, once abroad these students found that they still had to choose majors and classes primarily on the basis of how well they were likely to do in them and how likely they were to open up opportunities to gain legal citizenship or permanent residency rights in a developed country and to work in high-paying, prestigious fields in China or abroad. How much they enjoyed a particular major was at most a secondary consideration and was often irrelevant. A 20-year-old singleton Chinese citizen told me when she chose to major in accounting at an Australian university, "Math always gave me a headache or made me fall asleep, and I can't stand work that's repetitive and detailed, so I know I'll hate accounting. But I have no other way. I'd rather study art, but it's too risky to study a field with no job opportunities. Maybe someday when I have money and P.R. [permanent residency rights] I'll study art."

Foreign-Language Schools: Stepping-Stone or Trap?

Some transnational Chinese students who had work, business, tourist, family visit, or immigration visas rather than student visas could spend their time abroad working full-time while attending foreign-language classes or job-training classes part-time. Life was less stressful for them than for those on student visas, because their visas did not depend on constant full-time school enrollment. They could focus most of their time on work and only had to spend as much time and money on school as they could afford. Other transnational Chinese students already had college or graduate degrees from Chinese schools they considered respectable but went abroad just to improve their foreign-language skills and become more cosmopolitan. Those who only wanted to attain enough proficiency in the language and culture of a developed country to get a better job in China than they would have gotten had they not studied abroad faced relatively little pressure, so long as they avoided the temptation to try to get permanent residency or legal citizenship in a developed country or to save enough money to pursue higher education abroad or start a business in China. Language schools were far less expensive than higher education and also did not require that students spend as much time studying as they would in college or graduate school programs; therefore their students usually had no trouble supporting themselves with part-time work, and they even found it easier to do so than when they attended college in China, where the gap between college tuition and wages from part-time work was far greater. "When I attended college in China, I couldn't find enough work to support myself, so I felt a lot of pressure because I was asking my parents for money even though they were poor and couldn't bear to spend any money on themselves," a 23-year-old woman told me a year after she graduated from college in China and went to Japan to attend Japanese-language classes while working as a waitress. "Now that I'm in Japan, I can earn enough to support my own studies, without asking my parents for any money. How free I am!"

Some transnational students just wanted to earn enough money abroad to start a business in China but went abroad on student visas because it was easier to acquire such visas than it was to acquire work or business visas, not because they had a strong desire to improve their foreign-language proficiency, pursue higher education abroad, or gain permanent residency rights or legal citizenship in a developed country. They enrolled in the least time-consuming, most inexpensive foreign-language courses possible (often far below their actual level of proficiency in the language studied), so that they could minimize expenses and maximize the amount of time they could spend on employment (usually in low-skill minimum-wage jobs because of their limited proficiency in the language of the developed country and sometimes partly illegally when they exceeded the number of hours their student visas allowed them to work). "I'm here to work, not study," 22-year-old Chen Weiwen told me as we ate dinner together in the cramped two-bedroom apartment he shared with 11 other Chinese citizens, a year after he left China on a student visa to work as a waiter in Ireland while attending an ESOL school to maintain his student visa status. "Service [sector] jobs were all I could get in China, so I felt that if I had to do that kind of work, I might as well do it abroad, where I can make a lot more money. Once I have enough money, I'll start my own business in China."

I knew many transnational Chinese students, however, who had started out with goals similar to Chen Weiwen's but later changed their minds and decided that they wanted to attend college or pursue permanent residency rights or legal citizenship in a developed country after all. Most transnational students in my study eventually became uncertain about their goals, even if they started out with clear goals in mind. Chen Weiwen himself went through periods of indecisiveness about whether he should use his hard-earned savings for college abroad rather than use it to start a business in China. He ultimately found that he did not have enough English proficiency to get into any Irish college, and therefore he returned to China after four years in Ireland.

Language students who hoped to eventually pursue higher education abroad or get permanent residency rights or legal citizenship from a developed country faced a lot more pressure. Even some of those who already had degrees from Chinese college programs started their sojourns abroad by attending foreign-language schools because they lacked enough money to pay for higher education abroad, did not have enough foreign-language proficiency to qualify for college or graduate school when they first left China, or both. Some entered a developed country on a work, business, family visit, or tourist visa but hoped to use their time in that country to become proficient enough in that country's language to qualify for college or graduate school there. Regardless of their visa status, most of those whose parents could not afford to support them abroad had to spend most of their time working instead of studying. They started out with low proficiency in the languages of the countries in which they studied, so the only jobs they could get were ones that required little language proficiency and did not give them many opportunities to practice their foreign-language skills. Consequently, they had difficulty acquiring enough foreign-language proficiency to gain admission to a university in a developed country and pass enough classes to get a degree from that university. They often had to miss classes in order to work enough hours to support themselves, save money for tuition, and repay loans they had taken from family members and friends to pay for the startup costs of study abroad. Some of them ended up spending far more time and money in foreign-language schools than they had intended because they could not save enough money to pay for college tuition or get their foreign-language proficiency to college level while spending most of their time working for close to minimum wage.

Students, teachers, and administrators at some of the least expensive foreign-language schools in developed countries recognized that the primary purpose of these schools was to enable international students to secure and maintain valid student visas, so these schools provided low-quality instruction in exchange for low tuition rates. Transnational students referred to the tuition they paid these schools as a way to "buy a visa" (*mai qianzheng*). Those who missed too many classes risked having their student visa renewal applications denied.

Chinese students in Malta, Ireland, and Britain told me that, during periods of heightened concern about rising numbers of foreign students, government inspectors sometimes paid surprise visits to their ESOL schools to ensure that their attendance records actually matched the number of students who showed up for class. Schools that were deemed too lax were forced to shut down, and even students with good attendance records at those schools lost the tuition they had paid and risked nonrenewal of their student visas as a result of suspicions about their attendance records.

Government crackdowns sometimes even targeted students who had missed classes for legitimate reasons, such as injuries or illness. A 28-year-old Chinese citizen attending an ESOL school in Malta, for instance, was threatened with visa nonrenewal because she had missed just one day of class (she had actually arrived at school earlier that day but had to go home early after spraining her ankle while walking from one class to another) on the day an immigration law enforcement officer made a surprise visit to her school; the officer made a list of all the students who were enrolled at the school but happened to be absent at the time he visited and put that information in the students' permanent records. The injured student eventually got her visa renewed (after a teacher testified that he had seen her sprain her ankle and given her a ride home), but some other students at her ESOL school who were absent that day did not.

Transnational students in my study worried constantly about failing to get a visa renewal before they were ready to return to China. "All my friends in China are working in offices now," a 26-year-old singleton Chinese citizen attending an ESOL school in Ireland told me as I walked with her from her school to the office building where she worked as a janitor. "I don't want to be stuck doing manual labor all my life. I can't get a better job without a degree, but I can't afford college here. And I don't even know how long they'll keep renewing my visa. What will I do if I have to go back to China, with no career and no family, but too old to start over? I don't know what price I'll be paying for the special life I'm living here."

Visa renewal application denials could happen at any time, whether because of transnational students' violations of the terms of their visas, changes in visa policies, or even the seemingly random whims of immigration officials. The consequences of getting a visa denial before one had accomplished enough to make study abroad worthwhile could be devastating, as Yang Guolin, who left China to take English classes in Britain when he was 20, learned when severe back pain forced him to return to China three years later.[11] Yang Guolin had gone to Britain hoping to save enough money and acquire enough English proficiency to eventually attend college there. He spent two years in Britain taking English classes and working in a variety of low-skilled labor fields, including food service and factory assembly lines, before severe back pain, which he attributed to the heavy lifting and frequent bending he had to do in his job as an assembly-line worker, caused him to miss so many English classes that he was unable to renew his student visa. He stayed in Britain illegally for an additional year, trying to make as much money as he could from his dishwashing job in Britain before returning to China. "Now that I've become illegal, I'll never be able to go abroad again once I return to China," Yang Guolin told me. "I don't care, because I don't like life abroad, and I'd return to China right now if I could. But I need to earn enough money to make what I've sacrificed worthwhile."

Yang Guolin returned to China at age 23. He used the money he had earned in Britain to open a snack bar in China. He told me that, although his backaches were becoming less severe as a result of the Chinese and Western medicines and acupuncture he had been given in Chinese hospitals, he and his parents still regretted his having gone abroad because it had ruined his health and his chance at getting a higher education. "I earned some money, but I lost my health, and health is more important than money," Yang Guolin told me. "My English is better, but what use is that without a college degree? I've forgotten everything I learned in high school, and I could never pass the college entrance exam again. I feel like an old man already. I've wasted the best time of my life."

Developed countries' immigration laws aim to return sojourners with failing health to their homelands before they can burden developed countries' health care systems. Transnational students hoping to immigrate thus have to race against time to attain permanent residency rights in developed countries before their youth and health run out, as they did for Yang Guolin. But taking time off or returning to China for personal or family emergencies could threaten their work or student visa status; they could be fired from their jobs, not save enough money to pay for tuition, or not attend enough classes to qualify for student visa renewals.

Low-Skilled Jobs Abroad

Most Chinese citizens who had not earned college degrees in developed countries could qualify for only low-skilled jobs abroad. A few who had special skills or opportunities managed to find higher paid work as translators, masseurs, teaching assistants, elder care aides, or Chinese, math, or musical instrument tutors. Most, however, could get only minimum-wage jobs that offered enough flexibility to accommodate their school schedules and did not require much language proficiency as, for example, cashiers, salesclerks, housekeepers, hotel staff, bar staff, waitstaff, cleaners, cooks, food servers or deliverers, babysitters, and factory assembly line workers.

Many went abroad with little money and started looking for work as soon as they left the airport. As I waited with her in an Irish city for the bus that would take her to her ESOL class, a 26-year-old singleton who had graduated from a three-year college program in China told me about how hard it had been to find enough work to support herself the first month after she arrived a year ago. "I spent all day outside looking for a job, but didn't eat anything, because I was afraid to spend money, since I wasn't earning money and I had very little left," she told me. "One day I went at 5 AM to a store, only to learn that the store had no openings—the person who told me the store had openings had given me incorrect information. The store manager gave me the address of another branch of the same chain and said maybe they would have openings since they just opened. I went there that night after getting out of class, but they said they didn't have openings either—a few days ago they did, but now their openings were all filled and everyone had already been trained. I felt so desperate and asked, 'What should I do?' The Chinese supervisor at the store was sympathetic and asked if I had eaten that day. I said I hadn't eaten all day. I was beyond caring about face by then. He asked one of the workers to make a chicken sandwich for me. I said, 'How much does it cost?' He said he would give it to me for free, as he remembered how hard it was to be looking for a job without money when he first arrived. I took it, because I was really hungry. But I felt so bad. I had truly become a beggar, begging for food. But I was on my way to my night cleaning job, and it would have been hard to work on an empty stomach. So I ate the chicken sandwich they gave me, though I had tears in my eyes and could hardly bear the shame."

Those who did get work often found it unpleasant. A 22-year-old singleton Chinese citizen attending college in Australia told me when I asked about the scars on her hands that her hands were allergic to the detergents she had to use to wash dishes, tables, and floors when she started working in Australia as a dishwasher and waitress to pay for her college tuition. "My Ma used to spoil me and never even let me do the dishes, so my skin was delicate and started bleeding soon after I started working," she told me. "Even when I wore gloves, the hot water made my skin peel off with the gloves when I took them off. My hands hurt so much I couldn't write or type, so I failed my classes. Sometimes I wept while cleaning, and my tears fell on the table that I just mopped, so I had to mop again."

Hand injuries were common among those who took cleaning or cooking jobs, which were among the few kinds of jobs available to those with limited foreign-language proficiency. "My hands are not like a woman's hands anymore," a 23-year-old singleton Chinese citizen working as a cleaner while taking Japanese-language classes in Japan told me. "They are full of scars and peeling skin. The cleansers dry my skin out, and I keep cutting my hands when I clean and knock them against sharp edges. Next time I get my wages, I'll buy some gloves and Vaseline. I used to wear gloves, but I stopped because the skin on my hands got infected."

Many Chinese transnational students told me about how work-related injuries made it harder for them to attend school and complete their assignments. A 22-year-old singleton who left China at age 18 to attend college in Britain told me that he failed an exam because he could not write fast enough after he burned his right hand while working as a cook: "My Ma scolded me because she thought I failed because I hadn't studied enough, but I didn't dare tell her it was because I had burned my hand, because it would be too hard for her to bear."

Some transnational Chinese students were so exhausted after work that they just wanted to play computer games, have instant messenger chats with friends in China, or watch Chinese movies and shows on VCDs and DVDs they had brought with them, leaving even less time for studying. Many had gone abroad hoping to find better opportunities after they failed to gain admission to top Chinese college programs. Often, however, the factors that prevented them from getting into such programs in China also prevented them from getting better opportunities abroad. They lacked the extraordinary discipline, time management, concentration, and other study skills that were necessary for getting high entrance exam scores in China, acquiring foreign-language proficiency, and earning (and saving) enough money to pay for college tuition abroad. Many studied even less abroad than in China, because they were far from the parental supervision that had helped them focus on their studies and resist temptations to spend their time and money on leisure.

Some had worried a lot less about money in China than they did abroad. They needed to live frugally to save enough money to pay tuition abroad. But many of those whose families were relatively well off in China could not get used to living like the poor students they became once abroad. They were tempted to spend their hard-earned money on electronics, fashionable clothes, tourism, and good food rather than save it for tuition. They were also unhappy about working at low-paying, nonprestigious, unpleasant, and exhausting jobs that they would never have taken in China. A 21-year-old singleton Chinese citizen attending college in Australia and working as a waitress to help support her studies lamented to me, "Did I spend all my parents' money just to work as a waitress? I thought life would be easier abroad, but I still feel so much pressure to study hard so I can graduate, and now I have to work as well. I've seen the world now, and the moon is not rounder abroad. It's the same everywhere."

The Limits of Cosmopolitanism:
Seeking Housemates Abroad

Most transnational students in my study lived in crowded housing while abroad. A minority lived alone in dorm rooms or studio apartments because they were wealthier, were in areas with inexpensive housing, or feared that housemates would distract them from their studies. The majority, however, tried to save money by living with as many housemates as possible, sometimes by putting two to six bunk beds in each room.

Most of their housemates were friends or relatives from China or Chinese transnational students they had met at work or school abroad. Many told me that they would have preferred to live with citizens of the country in which they studied so that they could practice their foreign-language skills, get practical advice about life in that country, and better integrate into the local society, but they did not know any local citizens well enough to ask them to share housing. The few local citizens they did know were often reluctant to live in overcrowded housing to save money. Some Chinese transnational students who preferred to live alone or with non-Chinese housemates were also pressured into sharing their housing with newly arrived friends or relatives from China who could not afford to live alone and did not know anyone else well enough to room with them. "I prefer not to have Chinese housemates, but I felt sorry for my classmates when they couldn't find anywhere else to live and asked to live with me, so I let them come," a 24-year-old singleton Chinese citizen told me five years after she left China to attend college in the United States. "I came so far and worked so hard, so I don't want to just speak Chinese all the time. I tried to get foreigners to come here as our housemates, but when they came to see our house they didn't like it because it was too old and crowded."

Some Chinese transnational students started out living in the homes of local citizens participating in homestay programs coordinated by their schools or study-abroad brokers, but most of them eventually moved out because they could find much cheaper, more conveniently located, and more comfortable housing on their own. Some found local citizen housemates on their own, but misunderstandings caused by language barriers and cultural differences and exacerbated by crowded conditions often drove them or their housemates to move out. Misunderstandings were even more common when Chinese and non-Chinese transnational students shared housing, because they could only communicate in a local language that none of them spoke well. When I lived in the homes of Chinese students in Australia, Britain, Ireland, Japan, and the United States, I was sometimes asked to translate between Chinese and non-Chinese housemates, and I shared their frustrations when trying to communicate with those who spoke no Chinese and could barely speak English. A 25-year-old Chinese singleton who roomed in Britain with Indian, Kenyan, and Korean classmates from his ESOL school when he first arrived from China four years earlier told me, "I thought it would be good to live with people who couldn't speak Chinese, because it would force me to practice English. But after awhile I couldn't stand it. We fought over who would use the kitchen at what times and couldn't stand the smell of each other's food. It took hours just to figure out the simplest things, such as who should do which chores and how much each should pay for electricity and Internet service. We went our separate ways as soon as our lease was up, and I've lived with Chinese friends ever since."

Intimate Contingencies: Dating, Marriage, and Childbearing Abroad

Most transnational students in my study dated other transnational students from China. Many of them met and started dating before they went abroad. The most fortunate couples went abroad at the same time to the same place. Their relationships tended to be strong, because they relied heavily on each other for love, companionship, and practical assistance. As a 21-year-old singleton Chinese citizen attending a university in Australia told me about her relationship with her 22-year-old boyfriend, a classmate who had come to Australia with her from China two years earlier, "Our love is getting deeper and deeper because we don't know anyone else and can only depend on each other."

Less fortunate couples were unable to get visas to enter the same country at the same time. They were separated when one went abroad while the other stayed in China or when they went to different countries at the same time, hoping to reunite after they married and one could sponsor the other for a spousal visa. Many of these couples broke up after a few years of separation, either because one or both of them started dating others or because one or both of them felt that their erstwhile goal of eventually reuniting in one location was too costly in terms of the time and money they would lose in the process of trying to transfer from one school and country to another. A 26-year-old singleton Chinese citizen studying at a university in Japan told me, "My girlfriend and I had hoped we could study in Japan together, but her visa application was denied, so she went to college in New Zealand instead. She wants to try to get me to New Zealand, but I don't want to struggle so much for an uncertain future. I worked so hard to learn Japanese, and I've forgotten all my English, so if I go to New Zealand, I'll have to start all over again. We've only seen each other for a few weeks in the past three years, and we've both changed so much. I don't know if we'll still love each other after such a long time apart." Soon afterward, he broke up with his girlfriend and began dating another Chinese citizen he met at his university in Japan.

Transnational students in my study who were eager to marry at the same time as their peers in China were marrying were particularly frustrated by the dearth of marriage-minded prospects among those they met abroad, even those who were also Chinese citizens. A 23-year-old female Chinese citizen studying at a university in the United States told me, "I don't want to date my classmates, because they're too immature. I'm anxious to find someone I can marry, but none of them are even thinking of marriage."

Some complained that it was harder to find suitable spouses abroad than it would have been in China, where they could draw on gossip networks to figure out if there was anything problematic about a potential date or spouse. Those who refused to date non-Chinese also found that the pool of potential dating and marriage partners who fit their criteria for age, socioeconomic status, goals, and personality was much more limited abroad than it had been in China. A 29-year-old singleton Chinese citizen attending Japanese-language classes and working at a factory in Japan told me, "I don't want to marry a Japanese man, but I also don't want to marry someone else on a student visa. If we're both floating, how can we stay together? At any time, one of us might get a visa denial, go to another country, or return to China. I want to marry someone with a stable career, either here or in China, who knows what his future will be like. But it's hard for me to find someone like that here who will want me. All my friends in China are married now, but I don't even have a boyfriend. If I stay too much longer, I'll get too old and no one will want me."

Many transnational Chinese students ended up dating classmates, co-workers, and housemates. Those who started dating sometimes felt rushed into sexual relationships because they needed to room together to save money. Women were particularly concerned about how men in developed countries (Chinese and non-Chinese alike) often did not feel obligated to marry women with whom they had sex. A 22-year-old female Chinese citizen attending an ESOL school while working at a hotel in Ireland told me, "Chinese couples in Ireland are not as stable as in China. Here it seems a lot of couples are together just for convenience but wouldn't have chosen each other if they had more choices. And it's scary how it's expected that boyfriends and girlfriends always live together right away here. A girl could end up pregnant and have a baby with no one to take care of the baby. Or the girl could go back to China and others will hear about her having had sex with a man in Ireland, and she will have trouble finding a husband, or her husband will be mad at her after he finds out."

Most transnational students in my study had schedules and budgets that were too tight to enable them to comfortably raise small children as couples, let alone as single parents. They also worried that a child raised in a developed country would never acquire the linguistic, social, cultural, and academic skills necessary to compete in the Chinese educational system if they had to return to China, where schools were more competitive and taught more discipline and knowledge to children at earlier ages than most schools in developed countries, especially Western ones. This was less of a problem for children born in countries such as the United States and Canada, which offered birthright citizenship (legal citizenship that was granted to all children born in a country regardless of their parents' legal citizenship status), because they could live in those countries the rest of their lives if they could not get used to China.[12] The risks were far greater for transnational Chinese students' children who were born and raised in countries that did not offer birthright citizenship, such as Japan and most of the countries of Western Europe. If transnational Chinese students failed to get permanent residency rights in those countries, their children could be forced to return to China with them even if they could barely speak Chinese. Most transnational students in my study who were living in countries that did not offer birthright citizenship had no desire to give birth until they had either returned to China or were granted permanent residency rights in those countries. Even some of the students who became permanent residents of other countries hoped to send their children to live with their grandparents in China, both because they did not have time for child care and because they wanted their children to get enough of their education in China to enable them to compete in China's educational system and job market if they could not go abroad again.

On the other hand, in my study many transnational students who lived in countries that offered birthright citizenship hoped to eventually bear children in those countries, so that their children would have legal citizenship in a developed country without having to struggle for it and perhaps could even sponsor their parents' permanent residency rights applications. Most, however, would consider bearing children in those countries only after finishing college, establishing careers, and marrying; they believed that the drain on their time and budget resulting from childbearing and child rearing before then would not be worth the benefits of having a child with citizenship in a developed country. Nevertheless, some unmarried transnational students who accidentally became pregnant or got their girlfriends pregnant before they were ready for children ended up keeping the pregnancies, partly because the benefits of having a child with citizenship in a developed country balanced out some of the costs.

But immigration issues were contentious in developed countries, and their policies frequently changed in response to political pressures. Before 2003, for instance, the Republic of Ireland granted legal citizenship to every child born in its territory and granted noncitizen parents of legal citizens the right to live in Ireland. Irish citizens and political leaders became increasingly alarmed, however, when they saw Irish citizenship being granted to babies born to the large wave of foreign workers, refugees, and students who entered Ireland during the high-technology-fueled Irish economic boom of the 1990s. Public outcry about the dangers of Ireland becoming swamped by immigrants caused the Irish government to enact stricter laws and to tighten its enforcement of existing laws to reduce the number of hours foreign students could work, the length of time they could stay in Ireland on student visas, and the immigration opportunities available to them. On January 23, 2003, the Irish Supreme Court ruled that noncitizen parents of Irish citizens did not have the right to stay in Ireland; on June 11, 2004, Irish voters overwhelmingly approved a referendum to insert a clause into the Irish constitution that limited Irish citizenship to those who at the time of birth had at least one parent who was an Irish citizen or was entitled to become an Irish citizen.

This policy change had a devastating effect on Chinese citizens who became pregnant in Ireland. In some cases, pregnancies were initially accidents that became permanent because most abortions were illegal in the Republic of Ireland. In other cases, pregnancies had been planned, and the desire to acquire Irish citizenship for the children and possibly the parents was among the factors that led to the planning of the pregnancies.

Freed from the strict parental supervision and cultural prohibitions against premarital sex that restricted their sexual exploration in China, many transnational Chinese students had romantic and sexual relationships with each other while studying abroad. Liu Yang, for instance, was only 18 when she went to Ireland to attend an ESOL school and only 20 when she became pregnant after having sex with a 24-year-old housemate who had also recently arrived from China.[13] What little Liu Yang knew about sex and pregnancy she had picked up from gossip and the mass media. Chinese family planning policies ensured that contraception and abortions were inexpensive and readily available in China. At the same time, however, many Chinese teachers and parents assumed that unmarried teenagers would not have sex and therefore would not need sex education until they were engaged to be married. Liu Yang told me that she had not known much about contraception, much less how to obtain it in Ireland, before her pregnancy. She also had not known that abortion was illegal in Ireland.

An unintended consequence of Ireland's strict laws against abortion was that citizens of developing countries ended up having babies in Ireland as a result of unplanned pregnancies that they were not allowed to terminate. Unlike Irish citizens, most of whom could quickly and easily travel to other countries to have abortions if they wanted them, citizens of developing countries whose presence in Ireland was contingent on the maintenance of student visas were deterred from that strategy by their lack of money and fluency in European languages, their unfamiliarity with European health care systems, the difficulty that citizens of developing countries had in trying to get visas to enter other European countries on short notice, and the fact that sudden departures could jeopardize their finances, jobs, schooling, and visa status in Ireland.

Liu Yang was scared when she learned she was pregnant. Her boyfriend was also scared and encouraged her to have an abortion. Neither of them wanted to be parents, because they feared that parenthood would destroy their prospects for higher education and the upward mobility they were seeking. They did not want to marry because they had been arguing and did not feel their relationship could last.

By the time Liu Yang was pregnant, Ireland no longer offered birthright citizenship. Morning sickness caused her to cut back on her janitorial shifts, and she had not even saved enough money to pay for the next semester's tuition at her ESOL school. Her parents did not have enough savings left to subsidize her life in Ireland, and she was not sure whether they would even allow her to stay in Ireland to give birth once she told them she was pregnant.

Several months into her pregnancy, Liu Yang returned to China and got an abortion. She was unable to return to Ireland because she had been unable to get a reentry visa, as she had not saved enough money in Ireland to pay for the next semester's ESOL school tuition. Her parents were also afraid that she would get pregnant again if they let her go abroad once more. She told me that she regretted her decision to study abroad. She had lost her family's life savings, her education was now several years behind schedule, she had not significantly improved her English skills while in Ireland, she had wasted her virginity on a man she did not love deeply or have a future with, and she feared that her health, fertility, and reputation had been damaged by her premarital sex and abortion.

Dating and Marrying Non-Chinese

The rising prevalence of dating and marriage between Chinese women and non-Chinese men has been well documented in recent studies.[14] This phenomenon was also a frequent topic of conversation among Chinese citizens in my study, both in China and in developed countries. Yet actual dating and marriage between Chinese and non-Chinese were rare among Chinese citizens in my study and even among those who were studying abroad. Dating and marriage between Chinese citizens and legal citizens of other countries who were of Chinese descent were viewed as largely similar to dating and marriage between Chinese citizens, and in such cases legal citizenship in a developed country was perceived in the same way as other desirable assets, such as a high-paying career, wealthy parents, or a prestigious university degree. Chinese citizens who dated and married across ethnic lines, however, were viewed with more suspicion.

Although most of the transnational students in my study were part of the middle class in China, they were part of the lower class in the developed countries in which they studied. They had limited proficiency in the languages of those countries, and most of those who worked did so at low-wage jobs as salesclerks, cooks, waitstaff, and janitors while taking classes at language schools or low-prestige colleges. In addition to associating Asians with femininity and Westerners with masculinity, Western, Japanese, and Chinese gender ideologies deemed it more acceptable for lower status women to date or marry higher status men than vice versa.

Among the 71 male transnational students in my study who told me about their dating and marriage experiences, none told me that they had dated or married non-Chinese women. Among the 92 female transnational students in my study who told me about their dating and marriage experiences, 18 told me that they had dated non-Chinese men, and 5 of those 18 had married non-Chinese men.

I did hear some Chinese citizens speak, with varying degrees of bemusement, amusement, and admiration, about a few other male Chinese citizens (not those in my study) who dated or married non-Chinese women. Those male Chinese citizens seemed less likely to attract criticism than female Chinese citizens who dated or married non-Chinese men. Some Chinese citizens even praised male Chinese citizens they knew for having enough status, wealth, charm, and good looks to attract non-Chinese women, who were presumed to desire the same hypergamous relationships that Chinese women were presumed to desire.[15] Others predicted that their relationships would soon fall apart because of cultural differences. They described the couples as amusingly foolish romantics, fitting the kinds of stereotypes promoted by the 1990s Chinese soap opera *Foreign Babes in Beijing*, which focused on a romantically adventurous white American woman's seduction of a married Chinese man.[16]

Many male transnational students in my study told me that they would not even consider dating non-Chinese women. A 24-year-old singleton Chinese citizen attending an ESOL school in Ireland told me, "I would never date a foreign girl. There is no way that we could get along. Someone who did not grow up in China will have different habits and lifestyle. I could not fulfill an Irish girl's demands. Would I go out with an Irish girl to go dancing, jump and shout? Why would I want to do these things that I don't like? Would I make and eat my own Chinese meal, while she goes out and buys fast food?"

Obstacles to dating and marriage between Chinese and non-Chinese seemed much more severe for transnational students in my study than they seemed for Chinese people I knew outside my study. In my own US-based academic networks, I have known many male and female Chinese citizens who dated and married non-Chinese partners, and they did not seem to encounter criticisms from other Chinese citizens I knew outside my study that were as harsh or stereotypical as the criticisms that Chinese citizens in my study made about such couples. But most couples in my academic networks met at elite universities and workplaces, where cultural, socioeconomic, and linguistic differences between Chinese citizens and their non-Chinese romantic partners were not as great as they were in the less prestigious universities, colleges, ESOL schools, working-class neighborhoods, and low-skill jobs where transnational students in my study were likely to meet non-Chinese people.

The idea of marriage between Chinese and non-Chinese was not necessarily stigmatized per se, even by Chinese citizens in my study. I often heard them talk about how children of mixed blood (*hunxue*) were unusually beautiful and intelligent, and many transnational students in my study joked or fantasized about someday becoming the parent of a mixed-blood child.[17] I sometimes heard female (and, more rarely, male) Chinese citizens in China and abroad talking about wanting to marry non-Chinese citizens of developed countries. They were not necessarily reproached by other Chinese citizens for such talk. Some Chinese citizens asked me to introduce them to "Americans" of any ethnicity who might be interested in marrying them, their children, their relatives, or their friends. I also heard some Chinese citizens speak with approval and admiration of successful marriages between Chinese women and non-Chinese men that they knew or had heard of, and of the beauty and intelligence of their mixed-blood children. Mark "Dashan" Rowswell, a white Canadian famed throughout China for his televised comedy acts and English lessons, even made a cameo appearance with his Chinese wife and their child, along with other young Chinese celebrity couples, in a nationally televised performance of a song about family reunions in the Spring Festival variety show of 1999.[18] The performance implied that Rowswell and his wife were just another one of many admirable culturally Chinese couples visiting their parents (symbolized by two elderly Chinese couples).

Most of the Chinese citizens I knew in China and abroad considered dating and marriage between Chinese and non-Chinese acceptable so long as they followed the same cultural scripts that contemporary urban Chinese youth were supposed to follow when dating and marrying each other. These scripts required that the selection and courtship of a potential spouse would be the primary purpose of dating, that premarital chastity would be maintained (particularly by women but also to a lesser extent by men), that the age and socioeconomic differences between husband and wife would not be too great, that there would be enough personal compatibility between spouses to enable a companionate marriage, and that both spouses would be able to maintain ties to their natal families and fulfill their filial obligations. The problem faced by Chinese citizens I knew or heard of who dated or married non-Chinese, however, was that their practices could easily deviate from Chinese cultural scripts of ideal dating and marriage practices and were sometimes also misinterpreted by others as deviating from those scripts even when they did not.

Some female transnational students in my study were suspected by their fellow Chinese citizens of compromising their chastity to attract non-Chinese men, who were presumed to be more likely to demand premarital sex than Chinese men. I often heard non-Chinese and Chinese men and women criticize what they perceived as loveless, mercenary liaisons between non-Chinese men seeking young, submissive sexual partners and Chinese women seeking cultural, social, and legal citizenship in a developed country, particularly in cases where the men were much older than the women. As Nicole Constable and Karen Kelsky observed, negative stereotypes about romances between Asian women and Western men abounded both in the West and in Asia.[19] Western men in such romances were portrayed as shallow playboys, patriarchal oppressors, or besotted dupes, and their Asian female partners were shown as promiscuous mistresses, submissive victims, or calculating manipulators. Like Constable and Kelsky, I found that many individuals in such romances belied the stereotypes. However, even these individuals sometimes experienced shame and ostracism because of the stereotypes and those who believed in them. I also observed relationships between Chinese women and non-Chinese men that seemed to illustrate some of the conflicting expectations at the heart of the stereotypes. Although Chinese stereotypes of non-Chinese men's casual attitudes toward sex were exaggerated, they were also based on awareness of the real risks faced by some Chinese women who dated non-Chinese men. Because most of the transnational students in my study had limited English proficiency and most of the non-Chinese men they encountered knew little or no Chinese, the language barrier was a significant obstacle to successful relationships between them. Cultural differences and gender-based double standards also heightened opportunities for conflict and misunderstandings. Because most cultural norms of developed countries emphasized chastity less (particularly for men) than Chinese norms did and made marriage more optional than it is in China and because of their relatively secure position as citizens of their own societies, citizens of developed countries were more likely than the transnational students in my study to view dating, sex, and romance as enjoyable for their own sake and not necessarily as part of courtship that would lead to marriage. Citizens of developed countries were also more likely than transnational students in my study to disdain the idea of marriage as an instrumental means to such advantages as citizenship. On the other hand, transnational Chinese women students in my study were more likely than the non-Chinese men they dated to see the need to find someone to marry as the primary (and often the only) reason for dating—a perspective that reflected not only their desire to secure legal, social, and cultural citizenship in a developed country through marriage but also Chinese assumptions (and to a lesser extent, older Western, Christian, and Japanese assumptions) about the importance of women's chastity and about marriage as a milestone that all women and men must attain to qualify for full adult personhood. Chinese citizens were more likely to be comfortable with the idea of marriage as a means to socioeconomic advantages because of a Chinese cultural model of marriage that stressed social and economic factors over emotional ones. As 23-year-old Lin Yuan told me while she was dating a white Canadian man in China, "Of course I want to go to Canada, and that's part of why I like him, but it's not the only reason. When I was looking for a match, I was just like anyone else, looking for someone who had good conditions and who I also liked. My Ma married my Pa because his parents were poor farmers, so he could protect her [from political persecution resulting from her parents' classification as landlords] during the Cultural Revolution. Now people all say they want to marry those with good jobs and good education. So why is it different if I want to marry a Canadian?"

Lin Yuan was devastated when her white Canadian boyfriend broke up with her, claiming that he was not ready for marriage. Not only had her romance failed to gain her access to Canadian cultural, social, or legal citizenship, but it had also caused other Chinese citizens to suspect her of violating Chinese standards of patriotism and chastity. Although she had not discussed her sex life with me, some of her acquaintances told me that they had heard that she had sex with her white Canadian boyfriend, that many people assumed that she unpatriotically preferred Western men over Chinese men, and that any Chinese man would now be cautious about marrying her because he would assume that she was promiscuous and might leave him for a foreigner at the first opportunity. Lin Yuan's acquaintances' assumptions damaged her reputation. Moreover, because romances with non-Chinese were often seen as detrimental to the responsibilities of Chinese social and cultural citizenship, the gossip about Lin Yuan seemed even harsher than gossip about Chinese women who had premarital sex with Chinese men.

Many Chinese citizens I met in China spoke with disdain about Chinese women who spent a lot of time in bars and cafes in China that catered to foreigners and even likened such behavior to prostitution. Several Chinese citizens told me about Chinese female acquaintances who had been arrested for prostitution in Chinese hotels after spending the night there with their non-Chinese boyfriends. Others Chinese citizens told me that they had observed Chinese men hurling insults and stones at Chinese women and non-Chinese men who walked hand in hand down Chinese streets.

Many transnational students in my study also seemed to condemn Chinese women who dated non-Chinese men. When I lived in a house in Britain with three male and four female ESOL school students in their 20s who had recently arrived from China, I found that 25-year-old Ye Luzhu seemed to be disliked by many of her male and female housemates, who said she was "strange," had "problems," "doesn't respect herself," and "thinks she's better than us." She told me that her housemates' disdain toward her resulted from a combination of prejudice against non-Chinese and envy at the advantages she gained by dating British citizens. "Chinese people are envious," Ye Luzhu explained to me. "If you're lucky, Chinese people say 'Why are you so lucky when you're no better than me?' They say I'll have a bad result if I keep dating foreigners, but how do they know? They're just envious."

Even romances between Chinese and non-Chinese that did lead to marriage were suspect. Many transnational students in my study gossiped, often with disapproval, about Chinese women in their social networks who had married non-Chinese citizens of the developed countries in which they were studying. Gossipers seemed at least partly motivated by the envy Ye Luzhu complained about; they implied that women who used marriage as a shortcut to citizenship in a developed country were less deserving than those (like the gossipers themselves) who were trying to earn developed world citizenship through education and work. Their gossip also focused on the presumed mercenary nature of marriages between Chinese citizens and citizens of developed countries. Although they were more likely than citizens of developed countries to consider the pursuit of social and economic advantages an acceptable consideration in romance, Chinese citizens in my study still looked down on romances that seemed based solely on the exchange of youth and beauty for practical advantages, without any regard for interpersonal compatibility. Romances between Chinese women and much older citizens of developed countries were often placed in this category by many in the couple's Chinese and non-Chinese social networks. Even when no significant age differences were involved (as in the case of Ye Luzhu and the non-Chinese men she dated), cross-ethnic romances were still subject to much more suspicion of instrumental motives than intra-ethnic romances.

Chinese citizens' disapproval of romances between Chinese women and non-Chinese men also had a nationalistic component. Chinese citizens who refused to date or marry non-Chinese often linked their refusal to their sense of national identity. A 23-year-old singleton Chinese citizen attending an ESOL school in Ireland told me after expressing disapproval of a Chinese woman and white man holding hands across the street from us, "I want to stay in Ireland, but I don't want to marry an Irishman. I want to marry a Chinese man even in Ireland, because I am Chinese and will always be Chinese." Nationalistic disapproval was especially strong in Chinese citizens' discourses about female Chinese citizens who dated or married Japanese men. Many Chinese citizens continued to resent the invasion, colonization, and war crimes that Japan perpetrated against China during the Sino-Japanese War and to a lesser extent Japan's continuing role as China's economic and military rival. Chinese citizens who said anything positive about Japan or Japanese people were therefore subjected to much harsher criticism from their fellow Chinese citizens than Chinese citizens who said positive things about other developed countries and their citizens. I even heard a few Chinese citizens calling other Chinese citizens traitors (*hanjian*) because they had suggested that Japan or Japanese people were superior to China and Chinese people. I never heard that term applied to Chinese citizens who made similar claims about other developed countries and their people. Chinese women who dated or married Japanese men were targeted by such criticism, even when they claimed that their love was for the particular Japanese men they dated or married rather than for Japanese culture or the Japanese nation. Chinese discourses stereotyped Japanese men as more patriarchal and perverted than Chinese men and thus unlikely to be desirable partners for Chinese women based on their personal qualities alone. Consequently, Chinese citizens often assumed that marriage and dating between Chinese women and Japanese men were based on loveless, mercenary exchanges of Chinese women's youth, beauty, and submission for Japanese men's provision of money, resources, and permanent residency rights in Japan. Some Chinese citizens compared such exchanges to participation in Japan's sex industry. A 25-year-old male Chinese citizen working at a factory in Japan while taking Japanese-language classes told me, "Most Chinese women in Japan prostitute themselves. Some do it by marrying one Japanese man, while others do it by going out with many Japanese men, but it's the same principle." Japan had a flourishing sex industry and legal and cultural norms that were far more sexually permissive than China's. Chinese women living in Japan were often lured and sometimes coerced into sex work, to the extent that many Chinese women who lived in Japan were suspected by Japanese and Chinese citizens of having done sex work regardless of whether they actually had done it. Japan's sex industry offered work opportunities ranging from hostessing to stripping to prostitution to pornography, and this industry actively recruited impoverished Chinese women studying or working in Japan, offering them far higher incomes than they could earn in any other field. This contributed to Chinese stereotypes about Japanese people as sexually perverted. Some Chinese citizens in my study spoke with pity about Chinese sex workers in Japan, comparing them to the Chinese women who had been abducted by Japanese troops and forced to work as prostitutes for Japanese troops during the Sino-Japanese War. Others were harsher, referring to them as traitors (*hanjian*) who were perverted (*biantai*) and "didn't care about face" (*bu yao lian*).

Nationalistic critiques of dating and marriage between Chinese women and non-Chinese men seemed based partly on Chinese discourses of nationalism that associated foreign imperialism with the emasculation of Chinese men[20] and partly on the persisting significance of virilocal, patrilineal, androcentric Chinese kinship models that equated marriage with the bride's abandonment of her natal kin and absorption into her husband's lineage.[21] Although such kinship models were increasingly irrelevant among families in urban China that could live in close proximity to the parents of the wife and the husband,[22] they persisted in the Chinese countryside, partly because village exogamy, long distances between villages, and a lack of vehicles meant that married daughters tended to live too far away to maintain close relationships with their natal families. Chinese citizens studying abroad told me that they would face a similar problem if they married citizens of developed countries who had no interest in permanent residence in China. Geographic distance could make it difficult for Chinese citizens who married citizens of developed countries to maintain ties with their parents and homeland. Marrying a citizen of a developed country could entail a commitment to spend the rest of one's life in that country, with only occasional visits to China. Many transnational students were not ready to give up the option of settling permanently in China. A 27-year-old singleton Chinese citizen attending an ESOL school in Ireland lamented to me after she broke up with her white Irish boyfriend, "Sometimes I like foreigners, but how can I marry a foreigner when my parents are in China? Ireland may never let them come to live here, and even if it did, my parents are too old to get used to a new country. Maybe we could take time off from work to visit my parents in China once a year, but would that do right by them? They always ask when I'm going to marry so they can hold a grandchild, but if I marry a foreigner, they'll barely know their grandchild. They only have one child, and they've given so much to raise me to this age—I can't just abandon them."

Some transnational students in my study felt torn between their desire to marry citizens of developed countries and their desire to fulfill their obligations, as filial daughters, to eventually return to China to provide care and companionship to their parents in their old age. Although marriage to citizens of developed countries could bring them social, cultural, and legal citizenship in those countries, it could also entail a commitment to live the rest of their lives in those countries, with only brief, occasional visits to China, where their parents are likely to stay because of the legal, financial, and cultural obstacles that make it difficult for elderly Chinese parents to emigrate. Even though they could and sometimes did draw on older Chinese patrilineal ideologies that minimized women's filial obligations, they were also concerned about violating newer ideologies of female filiality that emerged after China's one-child policy. This policy had enabled them to grow up as brotherless daughters and experience the parental investment and expectations for old-age support formerly reserved for sons. Such ideologies were often the basis for the significant parental investment that enabled them to study abroad in the first place. Their decisions about whether to marry citizens of developed countries were based not only on considerations of their compatibility with those men and their desires for developed world citizenship but also on where they and their parents stood with regard to Chinese ideas about the relationship between gender and intergenerational contracts, their views about national identity, and how much they feared the stigmatizing gossip of those in their social networks who disapproved of such marriages.

Overstaying Visas or Petitioning for Asylum

Although transnational students in my study hoped to attain some aspects of developed world citizenship by studying abroad, most were not willing to take measures that would reduce their access to Chinese cultural, social, and legal citizenship. They sometimes told me that other Chinese citizens they knew or heard about had illegally overstayed visas or petitioned for political asylum. It was rare, however, for them to tell me about having used these strategies themselves. Such strategies often conflicted with the social, cultural, and legal responsibilities of Chinese citizenship and could take time away from work and study as well as hinder future efforts to return to China; consequently, most of the transnational students in my study told me that the costs of these strategies were too high for them to even consider.

Applying for political asylum in a developed country entailed a difficult, uncertain, time-consuming, and expensive legal process during which the applicant tried to prove to a developed country's government that he or she would face political persecution upon return to China. Participation in the 1989 demonstrations against the Chinese government or in the Falun Gong religious movement banned by the Chinese government seemed to be the most readily recognized by developed countries' governments as legitimate reasons for needing political asylum, because participants in these movements were relatively few and could sometimes have their participation confirmed by other participants who had already been granted political asylum. Some Chinese citizens tried to apply for political asylum because they had criticized the Chinese government or had given birth to more than one child, in violation of the one-child policy, but such applications were rarely successful; developed countries' leaders were reluctant to grant political asylum for actions that could be performed by a large proportion of China's population. None of the transnational students in my study told me that they had applied for political asylum, although some told me about acquaintances who had. Most of the political asylum applicants I heard about were members of Falun Gong. Because all the transnational students in my study wanted to maintain at least some aspects of their Chinese citizenship, they were wary of associating with Falun Gong members or with others who took public stances against the Chinese government. Gaining citizenship in a developed country as a political refugee carried a high price; it could prevent one from returning to China even for visits and could be seen by Chinese citizens as unpatriotic and even immoral. Some transnational students in my study who were critical of the Chinese government were also critical of other Chinese citizens who were applying for asylum. A 24-year-old Chinese ESOL student in Ireland told me three years after he left China, "I do have criticisms of the Chinese government, but I think applying for political asylum is too much. There are people who exaggerate just because they want to stay in Ireland, but they are betraying their own country. No matter how much your mother beats you, she is still your mother and you can't abandon her."

Illegally overstaying a visa had even higher costs. It meant that individuals could not leave the country that granted the visa until they were ready to return to China permanently, after which they might have to pay fines and deal with a record of illegal immigration that would prevent them from getting visas to enter developed countries in the future. Life as an undocumented immigrant also entailed living in constant fear of sudden deportation and consequently not daring to use social services, take advantage of legal rights, work for law-abiding employers, or even make any acquaintance angry, for fear that someone might report the undocumented status to the authorities. Becoming an undocumented immigrant also put individuals in a category that was stigmatized by Chinese citizens in China and abroad and by citizens of the country in which the immigrant was living. Many transnational students in my study refused to share housing with undocumented immigrants because they feared that law enforcement investigations of their housemates could result in thorough examinations of their own legal status. Even those who assumed that their own visas were completely legitimate still worried that such thorough examinations could lead the authorities to make accurate or inaccurate claims about irregularities and violations that could result in their own deportation. Most of the transnational students in my study did not consider undocumented immigration a viable option because it would leave them with even fewer citizenship rights than they had as Chinese citizens before studying abroad and would directly contradict their goal of upgrading to the kind of flexible developed world citizenship that would give them more and better freedoms and capabilities. A 26-year-old singleton Chinese citizen who had attended college in Japan on a student visa was forced to return to China because her student visa had expired and she had failed to find a job with an employer who could sponsor her for a work visa. She told me as we ate ramen at a Japanese style noodle bar in China, "I miss Japan so much. The environment was very clean, and Japanese people's quality is much higher than Chinese people's. Compared to China, Japan was paradise! But I had to return to China when my visa expired. I know other Chinese people who overstayed their visas, but I think they don't respect themselves. I respect myself too much to do that."

Transnational students in my study feared becoming like the undocumented Chinese immigrants (mostly from southern provinces of China, especially Fujian Province) they met abroad who seemed likely to remain indefinitely in low-paying fields in the Chinese-dominated restaurant and sweatshop sectors. Although they sometimes envied the wealth and immigration opportunities attained by their counterparts from southern China, they lacked their established transnational networks and dared not try the illegal, semilegal, or culturally or politically controversial means necessary to attain such wealth and immigration opportunities. They were particularly cautious about living with Fujianese transnationals because of their reputation for living at the margins of legality. A 26-year-old singleton Chinese citizen from Dalian who was attending an ESOL school in Britain told me three years after she left China, "I have a Fujianese classmate who asked to live with us, and I like her personally, but it would be irresponsible for me to bring her in—once you let one Fujianese roommate in, she'll bring all her Fujianese friends, some of whom are illegal or smuggling illegal goods, and if the police come for them, we'll all be arrested and deported."

Conclusion: Minimum-Wage Jobs, Developed World Aspirations, and the Race Against Time

Many transnational students in my study ended up spending more years studying abroad than they had initially planned. Unanticipated obstacles delayed their progress toward their goals, or they redefined their goals, or they became more ambivalent about when and whether they wanted to return to China for permanent residence. They delighted in their acquisition of new capabilities and freedoms, but they also sacrificed a lot in their quest for flexible developed world citizenship. They were reluctant to let go of their legal, cultural, and social Chinese citizenship, but they were also uncertain about which, if any, pathways to social, cultural, and legal citizenship in a developed country they should prioritize. Their floating life conferred some kinds of freedom, but it also entailed insecurity, internal conflicts, and unfulfilled desires.

Some Chinese citizens were dismayed to learn after completing college in developed countries that the developed world credentials they had thought would bring them upward mobility ended up being almost useless. "[One] can't get a good job in China unless [one] already has years of work of experience, but I can't get work experience in China because employers there think I'm overqualified for entry level jobs," a 26-year-old singleton who had left China at age 20 to attend college in Japan told me after he graduated from college in Japan. He had spent several months searching for a job in China and Japan with no result and therefore went back to Japan to attend graduate school. "But I also can't get entry-level jobs in Japan, because they discriminate against Chinese. So I'm still working at the same salesclerk job I had during college, when I thought it would be temporary."

It was difficult for transnational students in my study to get white-collar work in developed countries because they lacked the proficiency in the languages required for such work. They also faced cultural barriers and racial, ethnic, and cultural discrimination when competing with natives of developed countries for white-collar jobs. I knew several Chinese citizens who had earned graduate degrees in developed countries but who were nevertheless working as cooks, waiters, or store clerks in those countries.

Because developed countries made their transitions from high to low fertility earlier than developing countries, they have higher proportions of elderly people than developing countries.[23] One of the ways that developed countries have managed to maintain strong economies despite rising dependency burdens is by attracting young immigrants from the developing world while limiting social welfare costs through immigration policies that allow developed countries to benefit from the labor and intellectual and economic capital of foreign students and workers during the young, productive, healthy periods of their life cycles. Meanwhile, the homelands of these foreign students and workers have to bear the social welfare costs generated by the children, the elderly, the ill, and the disabled who were left behind.[24] Although family reunification and political asylum policies have prevented developed countries' governments from excluding older and less healthy immigrants entirely, most developed countries' policies that regulate student and worker visas aim to prevent sojourners from ever entering categories that would enable them to immigrate and stay past the young, healthy, productive, resourceful, dependent-free stages of their life cycles or to bring their older, less healthy family members to their host countries.

To maintain a valid visa in a developed country, a transnational student without a lot of money must have the physical and psychological resilience to maintain a grueling schedule of study and work. The hardships of the migration process could take a toll on transnational migrants' health.[25] But taking time off for personal or family emergencies could threaten transnational students' student or worker visa status by causing them to be fired from their jobs, to not save enough money to pay for tuition, or to not attend enough classes to qualify for student visa renewals.

Most transnational students in my study started wanting to go abroad when they were adolescents chafing under pressures and constraints from teachers, parents, and relatives. As they became adults abroad, however, they developed a greater appreciation for such pressures and constraints, viewing them as signs of love and concern and as helpful guidance and motivation, even as these pressures and constraints decreased, not just because they were abroad but also because they were now seen as adults capable of making their own decisions. As adolescents in China, they just wanted to be cosmopolitan, capable, and self-reliant; as they reached adulthood abroad, however, they increasingly felt that these attributes were not enough for respectable adulthood. To become respectable adults, they needed to get college degrees, establish careers, marry, and have children, preferably in that order and on the same schedule followed by their peers in China. Many feared that the challenges, uncertainties, and delays they experienced while studying abroad would prevent them from reaching these life-course milestones on time. Every year spent as a low-skilled laborer and language student in a developed country was a year not spent getting the credentials, work experience, and social connections necessary for building a career in China. As a

26-year-old singleton Chinese citizen working at a fast-food restaurant told me five years after he left China to attend an ESOL school in Britain, "As I get older, I have more and more worries. All my friends in China have finished college and are now working in offices. If I go back now, no better than I was at 18, everyone will laugh at me. I keep thinking about the future. I'm not a child anymore; I need to do what men are expected to do. If I keep going on like this, like I am today, just working at [a fast-food restaurant], do you call that a man? If at age 30 I'm still like this, I won't do right by my wife. By the time I'm 35, I'll probably have a child, and I can't be like this then."

The quest for developed world citizenship could potentially open up a brave new world of opportunities unavailable to those who just had Chinese citizenship. Yet full social, cultural, and legal citizenship in the developed world was difficult to attain; therefore many Chinese citizens prolonged their quests in pursuit of it, often far longer than they and their parents had imagined would be necessary. Although they hoped to deploy their hard-won flexible citizenship strategically to enjoy the best of all worlds, it was more common for them to float between worlds. They were glad that life abroad offered new choices, but they also felt lost, fearful of making the wrong choices, and dissatisfied with the choices they did make.

CHAPTER 5

When Migrants from the Same Hometown Meet, Tears Fill Their Eyes

*Freedoms Won and Lost Through
Transnational Migration*

AMARTYA SEN ARGUED that the primary end and principal means of development is freedom, broadly defined to include political freedoms, economic facilities, social opportunities, transparency guarantees, and protective security.[1] Chinese citizens hoped to expand their access to such freedoms by acquiring as many aspects of social, cultural, and legal citizenship in the developed world as they could. But unlike Sen, who focused on freedoms that could be granted or denied by one's own government and society, Chinese citizens in my study focused mainly on gaining freedom from restrictions imposed by the developed world on the developing world. Born and raised to rise to the top of the global neoliberal system, Chinese singletons were frustrated by their parents' and their own low incomes and by the scarcity of educational and professional opportunities that could enable them to take their rightful places as full citizens of the developed world.

Sen defined a country's level of development in terms of the substantive freedoms available to its citizens.[2] Many of the freedoms that Chinese citizens hoped to attain through migration to developed countries were similar to the freedoms Sen described as both the means for and the end of development.[3] Drawing on what Isaiah Berlin called the "positive concept of liberty," which is defined in terms of people's ability "to choose to live as they desire,"[4] Sen argued that the freedoms most important for a person's well-being are the "substantive freedoms he or she enjoys to lead the kind of life he or she has reason to value."[5] For Chinese citizens in my study, such freedoms included the freedom to have the standard of living one wanted, to get the kind of education and work one wanted, to become the kind of person one wanted to become, and to enjoy the lifestyle, food, relationships, and leisure activities one preferred, as well as freedom from poverty, crime, pollution, corruption, health hazards, unpleasant social relationships, and restrictions on transnational mobility.

Substantive freedoms do not guarantee happiness, but they make it more likely that individuals will be able to attain the kind of happiness they desire most. Substantive freedoms are thus more important than happiness itself, Sen argued, because they make it easier for people to adjust their conditions in ways that would give them the kind of happiness they desire if and when they want to pursue that kind of happiness. Recognizing (as psychologists who study happiness do)[6] that the emotional state of happiness is ephemeral, unpredictable, equivocal, relative, and subjective, Sen argued that happiness per se is not as valuable as substantive freedoms that enable individuals to pursue the kind of happiness they desire. An impoverished female member of a stigmatized racial group in a racist, patriarchal, socio-economically stratified society, for instance, may feel happier than a wealthy male member of the dominant race in that same society if she has a job and a spouse that make her happy while he has a job and a spouse that make him unhappy. He may choose not to pursue more happiness because he values staying with his spouse and job more than he values his happiness. But if they ever lose their jobs and spouses, he would have greater freedom than she does to pursue another job or marriage that would lead to happiness.

Although it can be a means to the end of substantive freedoms, freedom from external constraints is not sufficient for the attainment of the substantive freedoms that are most likely to enable someone to find happiness. Even those who have freedom from external constraints cannot use such freedom if they lack capabilities that would enable them to use these freedoms. The ability to pursue happiness, Sen argued, depends not only on freedom from external constraints but also (more importantly) on the capability to achieve valuable functionings, such as being respected and in good health.[7] Capability is the potential to achieve a valued functioning. People exercise agency when they decide which capabilities to convert into functionings. The capability to exercise agency and choose freely is important in the quest for happiness because it maximizes the alternatives available and hence the opportunities to attain happiness. Capabilities are part of developed world social, cultural, and legal citizenship, which offer more and better capabilities than Chinese citizenship alone.

Individuals may differ with regard to which functionings they value most, so their capability to develop the particular set of functionings they prioritize is an integral part of the kind of freedom Sen considers essential to well-being.[8] Capabilities allow individuals to be and do what they want to be and do, even if they choose not to be and do those things at a given moment. Some transnational Chinese students, for example, wanted to get a higher education and white-collar work abroad so that they could become legal citizens of a developed country but then return to China to live the rest of their lives; they thought that they would be happiest if they had both the capability to live in China and the capability to travel to developed countries for work, business, tourism, or education whenever they wanted to. According to Sen's theory, their capability for transnational mobility would enhance their well-being even if they never actually used it after returning to China, because they valued that capability and the functionings it could enable them to have, should they ever want them. As a 22-year-old Chinese student attending college in Australia told me four years after she left China, "Maybe I'll be happier in China, but I don't know what the future will be like. If there are business opportunities abroad, I'll want to be able to pursue them, and if there are problems in China, I'll want to escape them. So I'll feel safer living in China if I just have an Australian passport in my drawer, even if I never use it."

Studying abroad indeed increased Chinese citizens' access to developed world freedoms, such as the freedom to travel, to become more capable, cosmopolitan, and self-reliant, to get a better education and work, to enjoy more civility, safety, health, and upward mobility, and to experience less pollution, corruption, overcrowding, and social pressure. At the same time, however, many were dismayed to learn that the new freedoms they acquired abroad were not as complete, satisfying, or useful as they had hoped and that transnational migration also entailed the loss of many freedoms they had taken for granted in China, such as the freedom to fulfill filial obligations, to spend time with friends and family members, to enjoy Chinese food, culture, city life, and relationships, to finish college, start careers, get married, and have children at the same time as their peers, to avoid the instability and uncertainty associated with the floating life of a migrant, and to live as part of the mainstream middle class rather than the marginal migrant lower class. As many kinds of migrants worldwide have found, even upwardly mobile migration trajectories often entail loss of aspects of their premigration social, cultural, and/or legal citizenship that they did not value until they began losing them.[9]

The sense of loss that transnational Chinese students felt abroad resembled the sentiments expressed in "Migrants from the Same Hometown" (*Lao xiang*), a song that was popular in China in the 1990s and sometimes quoted by transnational students in my study in reference to their own sentiments abroad.[10]

> When migrants from the same hometown meet,
> Tears fill their eyes.
> Migrants from the same hometown ask each other:
> How are you doing?
> Are you feeling well in your heart? Does work keep you busy?
> Actually I'm just like you, dreaming of our hometown
>   every night.
>
> When migrants from the same hometown meet, tears fill
>   their eyes.
> Migrants from the same hometown ask each other:
> Where will you go this time?
> How much bitterness have you experienced?
> How many times were you hurt?
> Actually I'm just like you, always wanting to venture out.
>
> Can you speak this other town's dialect?
> Do you love to sing this other town's songs?
> Are you used to the floating life?
> Do you miss your own hometown?

This song, which describes the homesickness and commiseration rural migrants from the same hometown shared when they met each other in a faraway city, could just as well describe the sentiments of Chinese citizens who were studying in developed countries, who sometimes drew analogies between their experiences and those of the rural migrants who worked in their home cities in China (and provided rental income and home-sale profits that enabled urban youth to study abroad). Some of their experiences, particularly those involving hard work, ambivalence, uncertainty, the quest for upward mobility and more modern lifestyles, and the loss of relationships and lifestyles they valued, were indeed similar to those of rural Chinese citizens who migrated to Chinese cities to study or work.[11] This rural-to-urban migration within China was encouraged by the same global neoliberal system that encouraged Chinese citizens to migrate to developed countries in the quest for even higher levels of developed world citizenship.

Freedom to Become More Capable, Cosmopolitan, and Self-Reliant

Many Chinese citizens wanted to study abroad to develop new capabilities. They told me that going abroad would make them more capable, cosmopolitan, and self-reliant. They thought that the social environments of developed countries were more likely than that of China to encourage these qualities and that they would develop these qualities through the training (*duanlian*) they would experience as they tackled the challenges of traveling, living, studying, and working in difficult new environments without the help of parents, friends, and relatives.

Some parents who worried that they had spoiled their singletons hoped that sending them abroad would make them less spoiled. Parents I knew in China often talked about how the singleton generation, and in many cases their own children, were spoiled as a result of their sheltered, comfortable, convenient lifestyle. Parents felt compelled to provide this lifestyle to give their children advantages in an educational system that had become hypercompetitive as a result of China's integration into the global neoliberal system and a concentration of parental investment and ambitions in each singleton child that made the difficulty and stakes of academic success especially high.[12] Parents hoped, however, that study abroad would make their children more capable and self-reliant. Chen Lei's father told me seven years after he sent his 18-year-old son to attend a Japanese-language school and then a university in Japan, "When we were small, we had to do chores at home and take care of our younger siblings, and then during the Cultural Revolution we were sent away from our families to work in villages among strangers. We ate a lot of bitterness, maybe too much, but it was also a kind of training that made us more capable and self-reliant than our children are. Sometimes when Chen Lei tells me how hard he is working and how lonely he feels abroad, my heart aches, but then I think that it can't possibly be worse than the training I had in my own youth. It was because of that training that I am who I am now, and have all that I have now, so it can't be that bad."

Chinese singletons who had grown up as part of the middle class in China suffered when they went abroad and had to live in poverty while relying on their own incomes from low-paying, often unpleasant jobs. Upon reflection, however, some told me that they considered this a valuable learning experience. "Now that I earn my own money, I don't want to spend my parents' money," 22-year-old college student Zhang Ying told me in Australia, five years after she left her wealthy white-collar parents in China. "I used to not understand what money was worth. Now I realize, if I want to buy a [bottle of] soda, it's half an hour working as a waitress. So I don't buy it."

In response to my 1999 survey question, 40 percent of the 688 junior high school students, 35 percent of the 751 vocational high school students, and 61 percent of the 760 college prep high school students indicated that they usually did not clean, cook, or do laundry at home. Although they complained about having to do these chores while abroad, many transnational Chinese students also told me they valued the self-reliance that they learned from doing them.

They also talked about how going abroad gave them a more cosmopolitan perspective. "In America, people believe they can do whatever they can think of, because their lives and perspectives are broad and open," 24-year-old Chen Shuling told me a year after she left China to attend a university in the United States. "In China everyone is cautious, afraid of this and that, and every time you say you want to do something, your friends and relatives will discourage you by saying it's too hard. But now that I'm abroad, I think that no matter what, I can start over from the beginning and do things, because that's how Americans think. Now I have the courage to do anything I want."

"Leaving our country has given us a different perspective, so we'll be able to see things people in China don't," 27-year-old Jin Weijun told me nine years after he left China to attend college and work in Canada. "Even if we return to China, our thinking will be different from theirs. So when we see some opportunity, we'll be able to take it. We see more than other Chinese because we've been out, we know what's really going on, and we know what's true and what isn't."

"Making 2,000 yuan [US$251] a month sounded good to me in China, but now in Japan I see some people earning 200,000 Japanese yen [US$1,724] a day," said 23-year-old Li Yuenan in 2006, a year after he left China to attend a university in Japan. "I felt very hopeless in China, but abroad I feel like I can do anything I can think of."

In some ways, Chinese students' transnational journeys served as a rite of passage similar to the rites of passage that have been practiced in many societies worldwide. In those societies adolescents became adults by separating from their usual environment, living under conditions of liminality for a set period of time, and then reintegrating into their former environment, but with a newly adult social role.[13] In a world with porous boundaries and the possibility of flexible citizenship, however, rites of passage from one life stage to another do not necessarily end with reintegration into one's former environment. The possibility of permanently changing one's environment as well as oneself is increasingly a possibility in rites of passage, whether they are the journeys that rural Chinese migrants made to Chinese cities, the journeys poor rural children of Sierra Leone made to live as foster children/workers in the families of wealthier urban friends and relatives, the journeys middle-class young adults from developed countries made to developing countries as backpacker tourists, or the journeys that Chinese citizens made to study abroad.[14]

Freedom to Travel

In addition to providing experiences that would make Chinese citizens more cosmopolitan, transnational migration also allowed them to accumulate aspects of developed world cultural, social, economic, and sometimes legal citizenship that would increase their capabilities for future transnational travel. It was difficult for Chinese citizens with no previous transnational migration experience to travel abroad on Chinese passports. Travel from China to any developed country and to most developing countries was much easier for those with permanent residency rights or legal citizenship documents from developed countries. Even a Chinese citizen who lacked permanent residency rights in any developed country but had earned a university degree from a developed country would be more likely to get visas from foreign embassies in the future, because those embassies' officers often surmised that those who had not overstayed their visas during previous trips to developed countries were unlikely to overstay their visas in the future. Transnational travel was also easier for Chinese citizens with developed-world-level incomes and friends, relatives, or colleagues in developed countries who could issue them invitations for temporary stays or sponsor their immigration petitions. Studying abroad could thus serve as the first step toward acquiring the "flexible citizenship"[15] that would enable them to quickly and easily migrate to seize opportunities wherever in the world they appeared and to escape to another country if life in China became unpleasant.

Many Chinese citizens mentioned their desire for transnational mobility as part of their motivation for studying abroad. "I hear there are opportunities in this country or that country, but with a Chinese passport I can't get to them," a 21-year-old singleton Chinese citizen attending college in China lamented to me as he applied for graduate programs at US universities. He hoped to win a fellowship that would also help him obtain a visa. "If I can change my passport to a developed country's passport like the one you have, I'll be able to go anywhere there is an opportunity and return to China if there are opportunities here, but leave again if things get bad here." He failed to get into any of the programs to which he applied, and he has gotten a job as a clerk in a trade company in China, but he still hopes to eventually end up in the United States or another developed country.

Transnational Chinese students also valued international travel for its own sake. They thought that studying abroad would give them new experiences and enable them to "see what the rest of the world is like" and "open their eyes" to insights they could not gain in China. A 16-year-old college prep high school student in China told me a year before she went to Britain to attend an ESOL school, "I don't want to be stuck in China forever, and live and die having seen only one country."

Tourist travel was more affordable for those who were working in developed countries than for those working in China, as even those with minimum-wage part-time jobs in developed countries earned a lot more than most of their counterparts with office jobs in China. Study in a European country was especially likely to open doors to tourist travel in a large number of other European Union countries, because of the countries' close proximity to each other and laws that made it easier for EU residents to visit other EU countries besides the one they were living in. I sometimes saw Chinese citizens who had never been abroad listening with wonder and excitement to the travel stories of friends or relatives who had studied in one European country but had also visited many others.

Losing the Freedom to Return to China

Transnational migration also limited Chinese citizens' freedom to return to China as often and for as long as many would have preferred. Once abroad, many found the costs of return visits to China prohibitively high. Each trip to China cost a great deal of time and money. They had to buy plane tickets, spend time and money on getting reentry visas that would allow them to return to the country in which they were studying, and pay disconnection and reconnection fees for utilities and phone services. They had to use vacation time if they had any or quit their jobs and find new ones after returning, or they had to find someone to substitute for them at their jobs abroad during their time in China if they did not quit their jobs or have vacation time to spare.

They lost the wages they would have earned during that time and lost time that could have been spent improving their foreign-language skills or reading textbooks for their college courses. They had to pay rent to keep their housing abroad while they visited China, or they had to spend time, effort, and money to sublet their housing or move out, store their belongings with friends or at rented storage sites, and get new housing after they returned from abroad. Return trips to China required months of advance planning to minimize expenses and to avoid the loss of jobs, tuition, housing, places in college and graduate programs, and reentry visas. Those applying for permanent residency rights or citizenship in a developed country often had to stay in that country for many years and faced strict limits on how much time they could spend visiting China during those years. Transnational students risked losing everything they had worked for abroad when they had to return to China for personal emergencies (such as injuries or illnesses requiring medical care that was too expensive abroad) or family emergencies (such as the illness or death of a family member).

Some who made such emergency trips to China found that they were unable to get visas to return to the country in which they had been studying. Even a few of those who had thought they had done the proper paperwork to ensure they could go back to the developed country in which they were studying encountered unexpected bureaucratic obstacles. During the SARS epidemic of 2003 and to a lesser extent during the H1N1 epidemic of 2009, fear of the illnesses and of the quarantines China and developed countries might impose on international travelers caused some transnational Chinese students to cancel trips to China that had been planned months or years in advance, losing the time and money they had put into their planning.[16] Those experiences made transnational Chinese students worry about what would happen if longer-term disruptions, such as war or political conflicts, made travel between China and the countries in which they were studying difficult or impossible for even longer periods of time.

Freedom from Pollution and Overcrowding

Even before they left China, Chinese citizens talked about how beautiful and unpolluted developed countries seemed compared to China. This talk was based on what they saw in movies, on TV, and in the photos that acquaintances brought back from those countries. Many were even more impressed once they were living abroad, particularly if they were living in rural or suburban areas of developed countries.

"I want to stay in Ireland and live in one of these beautiful houses," a 25-year-old singleton ESOL student told me as we walked down a suburban Irish street together a year after she left China. "It's so beautiful here, and when I wake up I hear birds singing outside. There are no mosquitoes and very few flies, and it's the same nice temperature in winter and summer. This really is paradise."

"Tell my parents how beautiful this environment is," a 25-year-old singleton Chinese citizen told me four years after she left China to attend a university in the United States. "Since I was a child, my dream was to live in a place like this, next to beautiful natural surroundings. There are no places like this in China; I only imagined this kind of place by reading fairy tales. In China, the countryside has no electricity or water; when I visited a village, there was no air conditioning and it was so hot that I fainted; my parents had to carry me back to a city, and I was so happy to be in a city. But in the US the countryside has everything. No matter how much money you have, you can't find a place like this to live in China."

Even those who lived in developed country cities were impressed with how much cleaner they were than Chinese cities. "In Chinese cities when you blow your nose after a few hours walking around on the streets, the tissue is black from all the soot you breathed in," a 22-year-old singleton Chinese citizen told me three years after he left China to attend college in one of Canada's largest cities. "But that never happens in Canada, even in a big city."

Transnational students in my study also appreciated how even cities in developed countries seemed less crowded and more orderly than Chinese cities. "China has too many people," a 22-year-old singleton Chinese citizen attending a university in one of Australia's largest cities told me four years after he left China. "In China I feel annoyed and can barely breathe, because the buses and stores are so crowded, everyone's arms are touching each other, and there are long lines everywhere you go, whether you're trying to get train tickets, get on buses, or buy groceries. My heart feels more comfortable in Australia, because it has much more space. There are no lines, and not many people anywhere."

Losing the Freedom to Enjoy Chinese Food and City Life

Although they appreciated the open spaces and less polluted air they found in developed countries, transnational Chinese students also missed the convenience, good food, and fun of city life in the densely populated Chinese cities where they had grown up. In China, they had yearned for more access to leisure activities such as international tourism, socializing with foreigners, and meals at McDonald's, Pizza Hut, Starbucks, and Kentucky Fried Chicken. Once abroad and able to access these in abundance, however, they got used to or even tired of such foreign foods, people, and activities and found that they were not as enjoyable as they had imagined while in China. They now missed the easy access to Chinese food and leisure activities—such as karaoke singing, chatting, going to restaurants and bars, and playing soccer, basketball, mah-jongg, or poker with friends and relatives willing to meet up at a moment's notice—that they had taken for granted in China. Although most transnational students in my study grew up in families that were middle class by urban Chinese standards, they often lived in poverty in developed countries, where they roomed in crowded conditions with other Chinese youth in impoverished, high-crime urban neighborhoods or in inconveniently located suburban neighborhoods that added high transportation costs and long commute times to their already overburdened budgets and schedules. Many complained about hunger. They could not afford the same quality and quantity of food they could afford in China. They also had no appetite for many of the foods available in the restaurants and grocery stores of the developed countries in which they were living and missed foods that could be found only in China. They missed the convenience and comforting, delicious taste of the meals their parents used to cook for them every day. Those who lived in rural or suburban areas of developed countries had difficulty getting to grocery stores and restaurants, which were farther away from their homes, more inaccessible by public transportation, and open for fewer hours each day and week than the grocery stores and restaurants in the Chinese cities where they grew up. They also had little time to shop, cook, or go to restaurants because of the many hours they had to spend in school and at work.

"I thought a developed country would be fun and modern, but the buildings here are even older than those in China, and there's nothing to eat and nothing to do," an 18-year-old singleton Chinese citizen told me a few months after she left China to attend college in a small town in Britain.

"I used to think Canada would be like paradise, but after I came here, I realized it was not even as good as Dalian," a 20-year-old singleton Chinese citizen told me two years after she left China to attend college in a small Canadian town. "When it comes to shopping, there are a lot of things that China has that Canada doesn't have, while everything that Canada has, China has as well."

"[This Irish city's] roads and buildings are old and falling apart, but no one bothers to repair them," a 24-year-old singleton Chinese citizen told me six years after he left China to attend an ESOL school and then college in Ireland. "The more I see of Ireland, the more I think it's even less developed than China. When I first came, I thought the Irish government would do things better than the Chinese government, but now I realize that the Chinese government does better at some things, such as roads and construction."

When I visited 20-year-old ESOL student Deng Wei's parents in China before going to visit Deng Wei in Australia two years after she left China, her parents asked me to take some things from China to her because they were hard to find or much more expensive in the Australian city where she lived. These items included contact lenses and a container and cleaning fluid for them, a digital camera and a compact flash card for it, a cell phone, Chinese tea and Chinese teacups, a chopping knife, a wok, clothes, running shoes, gourmet instant noodles, and dried fruit candy. Some of these things were in plastic grocery bags from Carrefour, the French supermarket in China where they had been purchased. Deng Wei was thrilled when I gave these things to her, and she hugged a Carrefour plastic grocery bag with tears in her eyes. "I miss Carrefour so much," she said. "It was cheap and I liked the products. Australian stores are expensive and don't have good stuff and close too early." She then folded the bags carefully and put them on top of the things her parents in China had purchased for her.

Freedom to Be Safe and Healthy

Many Chinese citizens in China and abroad said their health and safety in China were not as good as in developed countries. In China those who could afford to buy food, medicine, toiletries, makeup, toys, and vitamins imported from developed countries often did so even though these products often cost several times more than comparable Chinese products. They told me that they worried about contamination in Chinese products as a result of pollution and unscrupulous Chinese manufacturers, who used dangerously contaminated materials and ingredients to make their products to save on production costs and increase profits. These manufacturers were aided by lax Chinese government regulators who did not want to bother to inspect products as carefully as regulators in developed countries did or who could be bribed to turn a blind eye to contaminated products. They even suspected that imported goods sold in China might be Chinese-made products with fake packaging that claimed they were made abroad. They also suspected that developed countries exported only substandard products to China, saving the best products for their own countries. Chinese citizens in China often asked friends and relatives living in developed countries (including me) to send or bring products from developed countries, particularly during food scares such as the one that began in 2008, when many young children in China were sickened or killed by melamine poisoning in milk products.[17] Chinese and international media reports about this scandal caused great alarm in China and worldwide, and many countries banned the import of Chinese milk products. Transnational students in my study cited food scares, along with the SARS epidemic and various accidents and disasters that they felt were due to or made worse by low safety standards they believed to be common in China, as examples of how China was less conducive to health and safety than developed countries.[18]

"In Japan I feel the food is safe because the standards here are very high, but I'm scared to go back to China," a 23-year-old singleton Chinese citizen attending a university in Japan told me four years after she had left China. "Whenever I go back to China to visit, I'm afraid to eat the food because it might be contaminated."

"Ireland's air and water are especially good for people," a 22-year-old singleton Chinese citizen attending an ESOL school in Ireland told me two years after she left China. "I used to get acne in China, but my skin cleared up as soon as I came to Ireland."

"China will always have epidemics, because China is too dirty and has too many people," a 31-year-old singleton Chinese citizen told me 10 years after he left China to attend a university in Australia, where he eventually received permanent residency rights. "But Australia is clean and spacious, and it's very fitting for human life."

"The American environment makes people healthier," a 23-year-old singleton Chinese citizen told me four years after she left China to attend a university in the United States. "I always get colds and diarrhea when I visit China, but I'm healthy in America."

Transnational students also appreciated the health care that was provided to them in Britain and Ireland. These countries offered universal free health care even to those on student visas who were "ordinarily resident" but not permanent residents or legal citizens. In China, even Chinese citizens had to pay for all their health care in cash and could get only some of their medical expenses reimbursed by their private insurance policies. In Britain and Ireland, though, they could get health care that was not only free but also (some believed) of higher quality than what they could get in China. "In Ireland the doctors truly want to help you and aren't just trying to make money like in China," a 22-year-old singleton Chinese citizen told me two years after she left China to attend college in Ireland. Likewise, three years after she left China to attend an ESOL school in Britain, a 24-year-old singleton Chinese citizen told me that he was impressed with the care he received when he had bronchitis and had to go to a British hospital. "In Britain all the health care is free, and the hospitals are cleaner and the nurses have better attitudes than in China," he told me. "When they give you injections, the needles they use are smaller and don't hurt as much as the needles in Chinese hospitals."

Losing Freedom to Be Safe and Healthy

Other Chinese citizens, however, told me that the health care they received in Britain was not as good as the health care they received in China. A 22-year-old singleton Chinese citizen who had attended an ESOL school while working in a factory in Britain told me that, when he went to a British hospital seeking help for his severe back pain, health care workers just advised him to get more rest. "They didn't even touch me," he told me. "They acted like they didn't want to talk to me. I do not know why they didn't take care of me." After he returned to China a year later, he went to Chinese hospitals and was treated with acupuncture and a combination of Western and Chinese medicines, which he believed were successful in reducing his back pain.

A 21-year-old singleton Chinese citizen attending an ESOL school in Britain told me that she was surprised to find that doctors in a British hospital that tried to treat her seemed less competent than doctors at a hospital in her Chinese hometown. While in Britain, she developed a benign cyst in her buttock, which caused fever, disorientation, and swelling in the lymph nodes in her armpit and neck. "I went to the hospital five different times and saw five different doctors, but they said I was fine," she told me. "They said I just had a cold and should take aspirin and drink fluids and rest. Finally, the sixth time I went, a doctor said I would need surgery, and then they did the surgery, but they didn't remove the cyst completely, so I got sick again. Then I went back to China and had the surgery redone. Now I don't trust British doctors, because a lot of them didn't know what was wrong with me and just told me to sleep, drink plenty of water, and take painkillers. One thought the infection was in my tonsils rather than the lump in my buttocks, even though I didn't feel any pain or itch in my throat. They were bad at surgery, and no one in the whole hospital knew what to do with me the first five times I went there. When I returned to China, my Chinese surgeon was surprised that a British doctor did such a bad job with my surgery. Even the surgical scar from China was smaller than the surgical scar I got in Britain. I used to think health care would be more advanced abroad than in China, but now I think Britain's health care is actually worse than China's."

Other transnational students who lived in high-crime urban areas of developed countries thought that their risk of being victimized by crime was higher than it had been in China. They were annoyed and sometimes frightened by the high crime rates in the areas in which they were studying and told me that they did not feel as safe abroad as they had felt in China.

"In China I wasn't scared to walk around at night, but here I am scared," a 20-year-old singleton Chinese citizen told me a year after she left China to attend a university in a large US city. "Sometimes I'm even scared to walk around during the day. There are a lot of bad people on the streets, and crazy people who yell for no reason."

"I'm shocked by what foreigners [Australian white people] will do," a 22-year-old college student in an Australia city told me five years after she left China. "Once on the train I saw two dirty foreign [Australian white] men talking dirty, and I didn't pay much attention to them. But then I saw a foreign [Australian white] woman screaming 'Help! Call security! Call the police!' and I saw that the woman's boyfriend's face was covered with blood—he had been beaten by the two foreign [Australian white] men. Then the foreign [Australian white] woman stood close to me holding a hypodermic needle and threw up on the floor. I wasn't so scared of the foreign [Australian white] man with the bloody face—that had nothing to do with me—but I was afraid the foreign [Australian white] woman would fall on me and stick me with the needle. I was so scared—this was the first time I saw something like this."

A 27-year-old Chinese citizen who had left China when he was 24 to attend an ESOL school and work at a pub in Ireland told me that he often took indirect routes when walking to and from work and school in order to avoid areas with high concentrations of Irish children who cussed and threw stones at him and his friends and had robbed him and some of his friends of their cell phones and wallets. "I don't like how lax the police are here," he told me. "Irish kids can do anything, and the police won't do anything about them because their law doesn't allow juveniles to be punished for most of the crimes they commit. So they run wild, and all we can do is run away from them."

Political Freedoms and the Intensification of Filial Nationalism

International discourses about China often emphasize the lack of political freedom Chinese people have.[19] Indeed, a common assumption underlying discourses produced by the governments and media outlets of developed countries is that the desire for greater political freedom is a significant motivation for emigration from China. This assumption has been reinforced by biographies and autobiographies of former Chinese citizens who emigrated from China in the 1980s after surviving the violent upheavals of the Cultural Revolution (1966–1976) and of Chinese citizens who applied for refugee status in developed countries, which required them to persuade immigration officials that they were fleeing from political persecution in China.[20]

The complaints that Chinese citizens in my study made about the Chinese government, however, differed significantly from those that international media, developed countries' governments, and human rights organizations commonly assumed they would have. Chinese citizens in my study often talked about their desire to escape corruption as an important reason for wanting to study abroad and in some cases for wanting to spend the rest of their lives abroad. Their desire, however, was less a desire for the political freedoms available in developed countries than a desire to escape from the corruption practiced by teachers, principals, doctors, bureaucrats, and managers in China who controlled access to the resources they needed to have freedom in their everyday lives. They were far less concerned about political persecution than the Chinese citizens who emigrated in the 1980s and then published harrowing autobiographical accounts of political persecution that helped shape international assumptions about Chinese emigrants being motivated by a desire for political freedom.

Desire for the greater political freedoms available in developed countries may well motivate the emigration of political and religious activists who face persecution in China, but such activists were not represented among the Chinese citizens I met in Dalian, a northeastern Chinese city that lacked the large ethnic minority populations common in western provinces of China or the elite liberal arts universities that serve as hotbeds of activism in Beijing and Shanghai. I heard of people in Dalian who were arrested for practicing Falun Gong but did not know any personally; despite heavy Chinese and international media coverage about them, they seemed to constitute a small minority of the population, at least in Dalian. The experiences and desires of Chinese dissidents seem quite different from those of the majority of Chinese citizens in my study, most of whom did not chafe at the tight controls on political activism and religious organizations maintained by the Chinese government or yearn for opportunities to engage in political activism that they might have abroad.

Complaints about the Chinese state's censorship of TV, the news media, and the Internet were widespread in China, but so was the assumption that media discourses from other countries were also biased and/or censored in ways that favored those countries' interests.[21] Some transnational Chinese students with enough time, money, interest, and English-language proficiency to spend much of their leisure time on the Internet got used to easy access to websites such as YouTube, Facebook, Wikipedia, Blogspot, and Google while living abroad. They were dismayed when they found that such websites were sometimes blocked in China and talked about their fondness for such websites as one of their reasons for wanting to stay abroad. Many others, however, told me that they did not care about or were only mildly annoyed by the loss of access to such sites after they returned to live in China, since they did not have enough time, interest, foreign-language proficiency, and money for Internet access to use those websites much even while they were abroad anyway. They were also satisfied with Chinese Internet websites and services, such as Baidu, Youku, Sina, Sohu, QQ, Hudong, Tudou, Weibo, and Renren (formerly Xiaonei), which served many of the same functions that blocked foreign websites served but were entirely in Chinese and therefore easier for them to use. Many Chinese citizens who had never been abroad had not even heard of the foreign websites they could not access in China.

Although a desire to escape China's one-child policy was often cited by Chinese asylum seekers in developed countries, it was rarely mentioned by transnational students in my study as a reason for going or staying abroad. Even the few who mentioned it described it as a minor additional benefit of staying abroad and not as a significant reason for their decisions to go or stay abroad. By 1997, when I started my research in China, most of the urban citizens I met there had come to agree with the rationale behind the one-child policy. Many parents born before the one-child policy told me that, even without that policy, they would not have had enough time, money, and energy to raise more than one child and blamed their own childhood poverty on the large size of their natal families. Even those who told me that they resented the policy's constraints on their own desire for more children said that they believed the policy was necessary for China's development. Some told me that, although they had wanted more children in the early 1980s, the rapid inflation of educational expenses and consumption standards in the 1990s made them glad they had had only one child.

Members of the generation most likely to study abroad were even less averse to the one-child policy because they themselves were singletons who grew up in a society where single-child families were the norm. Fertility limitation policies did not seem to be a significant constraint on their childbearing desires, since most of them will be allowed to have two children because they themselves are singletons and since few of them want more than two children.[22] In response to my 1999 survey question, 32 percent of the 1,215 girls and 16 percent of the 856 boys indicated that they wanted to remain childless all their lives. When I asked 811 of the same respondents when they were between ages 24 and 31 about how many children they would want if China's birth planning policies were abolished, 10 percent of the 415 women and 7 percent of the 396 men indicated that they would want none, 24 percent of the women and 30 percent of the men indicated that they would want one, 62 percent of the women and 59 percent of the men indicated that they would want two, and only 3 percent of the women and 5 percent of the men indicated that they would want three or more.[23]

Chinese citizens in my study rarely complained about their inability to vote in multiparty elections, own guns, or worship, assemble, or express themselves in the media without government interference while in China. Some told me that they might enjoy such freedoms if they became available, but they did not greatly value or miss them. Most had little sympathy for dissidents who engaged in political activism against the Chinese government, and they condoned harsh treatment of people they considered troublemakers, such as leaders of outlawed movements like Falun Gong, Christian churches other than the ones officially sanctioned by the Chinese government,[24] and separatist movements advocating for greater autonomy for Uyghurs or Tibetans (two ethnic groups not represented among the Chinese citizens I knew well).[25] Some cited the chaos prevalent during the Cultural Revolution to illustrate their belief that political activism was dangerous, futile, and a waste of time and effort.

Although many international media and human rights organizations have criticized the Chinese government's frequent use of long prison sentences and the death penalty, transnational students in my study were more likely to complain that the Chinese government was not harsh enough in how it dealt with criminals, particularly well-connected ones. A 28-year-old singleton Chinese citizen who had left China at age 21 to attend an ESOL school and then college in Ireland told me that he disagreed with Irish co-workers at the fast-food restaurant where he worked when they argued that China should abolish the death penalty as Ireland and all other European Union countries had done. "They said the death penalty might cause an innocent person to be killed by mistake, but I said it saves so many more innocent people by serving as a deterrent," he told me. When Chinese citizens in my study complained about their own or their friends' or relatives' mistreatment by police in China, they focused their criticism on the corruption, excessive force, or nonchalance of individual officers rather than on the Chinese state itself.

Even though the greater political and religious freedoms available in developed countries had not been a major draw for them while they were in China, many of the transnational students in my study developed an appreciation for them once abroad. At the same time, however, they became even more defensive of China as they were inundated with critiques of China made by sojourners and immigrants from mainland China, Taiwan, and Hong Kong and by non-Chinese citizens and journalists. They heard such critiques on an almost daily basis from Chinese and non-Chinese teachers, classmates, housemates, co-workers, and friends. They saw on TV and read in newspapers more critical coverage of the Chinese government and saw more sympathetic coverage of Chinese dissidents, members of the outlawed Falun Gong movement and Christian churches without official Chinese approval, activists for Tibetan and Taiwanese independence, and Chinese citizens who protested in Beijing's Tiananmen Square in 1989 than they had ever seen in China. As I walked around the streets of such cities as Boston, Dublin, London, New York, Tokyo, and Sydney with transnational Chinese students during errands and sightseeing and shopping trips, we sometimes ran into protestors denouncing the Chinese government. Many of these protestors seemed to be Chinese immigrants and sojourners from Taiwan, Hong Kong, and mainland China, and they were especially eager to talk with passersby who looked Chinese.

Transnational students in my study often spoke strongly in defense of the Chinese government when confronted with such critics. As I walked on the streets of Dublin with 26-year-old singleton Chen Cheng two years after she left China to attend an ESOL school in Ireland, we were approached by Liu Jun, a 23-year-old woman from China. Liu Jun was standing next to signs stating (in Chinese and English) "The Chinese Communist Party is an evil cult" and "The Chinese Communist Party is a scoundrel." Liu Jun handed us pamphlets in English and Chinese that advocated the overthrow of the Chinese Communist Party rule of China and accused the Chinese government of wrongfully imprisoning and torturing Falun Gong practitioners.

"Do you not love our country?" Chen Cheng scolded Liu Jun. "Foreigners don't distinguish between the Chinese Communist Party and China, so aren't you worried that cursing the Communist Party in front of foreigners will make them behave even more badly towards China?"

"Of course I love our country," Liu Jun retorted. "That's why I oppose the Communist Party. In the Tang dynasty, China was very strong, but even then it eventually weakened and had to be replaced by the Song dynasty. It's like that now—we have to replace the Chinese Communist Party."

"But so many people were killed in the transition from the Tang to the Song," Chen Cheng replied. "Do you want a lot of people to be killed now, to transition from the Chinese Communist Party?"

"A lot of people have already been killed, during the Great Leap Forward, the Cultural Revolution, and June 4," Liu Jun said.[26]

"But those sacrifices have already been made and can't be changed," Chen Cheng responded. "Now people are not being killed. Now, when China has finally gotten strong and prosperous, you want more sacrifices? And if you want to overthrow the Communist Party, what do you want to replace it with? Who do you want to lead China? What would bring the future you want?"

"I want good people to lead China," Liu Jun said. Chen Cheng grabbed my arm and led me away in frustration.

"I want whatever will make China wealthy, powerful, and prosperous and peaceful," Chen Cheng told me later that day. "The Chinese Communist Party has both good and bad parts, but I'd rather have it than what some foolish child like that protester can come up with. If we have another revolution, there will be a lot of deaths, and China's development will stop. I'm glad the protesters' voices exist, saying different things, but I just don't want them to become too loud and interfere with China's development."

Chen Cheng also argued with Irish teachers, classmates, and co-workers when they criticized China. "I never used to speak my mind in China, but now that I'm abroad, my national identity is very strong," Chen Cheng told me. "When my ESOL teacher talked about how 'people are afraid that China will be a threat to other countries, such as Taiwan,' I raised my hand and said 'Excuse me, Taiwan is part of China!' Soon after that, we read an article for class about how China is getting stronger and stronger, that it's the fastest growing economy in the world, and will catch up to the US by 2025. I felt so proud."

Chen Cheng's tendency to defend China was shared by 21-year-old singleton Zhao Miao three years after she left China to study in Britain. "My ESOL teacher used to say Taiwan and Tibet should be independent from China, but now she doesn't dare, because as soon as she says that, I and some other Chinese students will raise our hands and correct her!" she told me.

I had spent time with Chen Cheng, Zhao Miao, and their friends and families in China before Chen Cheng and Zhao Miao studied abroad, and I had never seen them defending China as vehemently in China as they did when confronted by anti-China discourses abroad. This does not mean that they lost all the critical perspectives they had toward China; on the contrary, they became even more critical of many aspects of China (such as the corruption, competition, inequalities, and environmental degradation they wanted to escape by going abroad) that seemed even worse once they started making comparisons to what they experienced abroad. But their frequent encounters with anti-China discourses abroad made them acutely aware of the extent to which their own identity was tied to China and its status on the world stage and of the importance of keeping critiques of China within zones of Chinese cultural intimacy that had to be protected from outsiders who might use them against China.[27]

Transnational students in my study reacted with greater anger when ethnic slurs were directed against them than when they were subjected to more general insults. "When customers say 'fuck,' I pretend not to have heard, because maybe they're just saying it because they're used to it," a 28-year-old singleton food service manager told me nine years after she left China to attend college in New Zealand, where she was now a permanent resident. "But when they say "fucking Chinese," I get angry and yell at them. I can understand if they are just low-quality people who are used to using profanity, but I can't stand when New Zealand people insult Chinese people."

"Usually when I work at [a fast-food restaurant] and customers insult me, I ignore them, pretend I didn't hear," a 24-year-old singleton Chinese citizen told me three years after he left China to attend an ESOL school in Britain. "But once a man called me a "Chinese bitch." I got angry, and said 'What did you say? Do you want to repeat that?' He got scared and claimed that he was just talking to his son. I said 'You called your son a Chinese bitch? What kind of man are you? Do you want your son to grow up learning such bad words? What kind of way is that to educate your child?' I was so angry, I threw his food on the ground. I hate it when people look down on Chinese people. I think every time a Chinese person takes it just to avoid trouble, it just encourages foreigners to think we're easy to bully, and try to scare us and cheat us."

Greater exposure to developed countries' governments and their problems led some Chinese transnationals to extend the same cynicism they had about the Chinese government to developed countries' governments. "When I was in China, I was angry at Chinese leaders for crushing demonstrations on June 4 and thought Western leaders would be better," a 35-year-old small business owner told me 14 years after he left China to study and work in Australia. "But now that I'm abroad and have seen the whole picture, I think any leader, including of the US or Australia, would have responded the same way to demonstrations that threatened to overthrow their government. Now I think the 1989 demonstrations were encouraged by the US media and instigated by Chinese agitators paid by the US, because the US wanted the Chinese government overthrown."

But he also became more critical of some aspects of China. "I understand China's problems better now. It's like how once you go abroad, you notice how everything in China is red. If you're in China all your life, amidst all the red, you don't notice it, because you think it's normal. When you're abroad, you realize it doesn't have to be that way. Going abroad gives you a better, truer perspective."

For instance, he recalled that, before he left China, he had thought that most people in Taiwan wanted Taiwan to reunify with mainland China and that only a few troublemakers backed by anti-China foreigners were advocating for Taiwan's independence. After seeing a lot of Australian news coverage of Taiwan politics and discussing the issues with people from Taiwan who were living in Australia, however, he realized that the desire for independence from China was much more widespread among people in Taiwan than he had assumed. He still hoped that Taiwan would someday voluntarily reunify with mainland China, but he now disapproved of the mainland Chinese government's threats about using military force against Taiwan. "The father shouldn't beat the son if the son doesn't want to have anything to do with the father," he told me. "The father should be patient and hope the son will come back on his own."

Similarly, a 21-year-old singleton Chinese citizen told me that, before she left China to attend an ESOL school in Britain two years earlier, she had thought that "Falun Gong was crazy and scary" because that was how the Chinese media portrayed it, and the few people she had met in China who were zealous enough to risk practicing and proselytizing about it even after it was outlawed did indeed seem crazy. After befriending some sane, successful, and less zealous Chinese students who practiced Falun Gong in Britain, however, she changed her mind. "I don't care whether they're right or wrong," she told me. "I don't think the Chinese government should go after them when all they do is meditate and exercise—they're harmless."

Still, many Chinese citizens remained skeptical of Falun Gong activists' claims even while abroad. "Any Chinese person can believe that police will beat them like they beat any criminal, and it's true that a religious person can be very annoying—if you and I were the police, we'd be annoyed too," a 28-year-old singleton Chinese citizen attending college in Ireland told me. "But making them run naked in freezing temperatures while hosing them with cold water? That's impossible to believe. And if China were really doing these things, foreign governments would condemn China, just like they condemn the African countries from which most of the refugees in Ireland come. But the foreign governments don't say anything, because the allegations can't be proven. They just give money to Falun Gong activists because they don't like China and want to destabilize China."

None of the transnational students in my study had practiced Falun Gong as far as I knew, but some did convert to Christianity while studying abroad. These new Christians appreciated their freedom to worship without the governmental constraints they would face in China. "In China you can only join a Patriotic Church—if you join any other church, you'll be arrested," a 26-year-old singleton Chinese citizen told me three years after he left China to attend an ESOL school in Ireland. When he first arrived in Ireland, he had wanted to stay only long enough to earn a college degree and then return to China to find a high-paying job there. After he converted to Catholicism, however, he became increasingly reluctant to return to China. "The Communist Party shouldn't be managing people's faith," he said.

Yet other Chinese citizens chafed at how Catholicism shaped Irish laws, such as those that made most abortions illegal. Contraception and abortion were inexpensive, convenient, and readily available in China, so Chinese citizens who had unwanted pregnancies while studying in Ireland were surprised and dismayed about the difficulty of getting an abortion there. Unlike Irish citizens, many of whom could quickly and easily travel to other countries to get abortions, Chinese citizens on student visas were deterred by poverty, language barriers, unfamiliarity with European health care systems, the difficulty of getting visas to enter other European countries on short notice, and the fact that sudden return visits to China could jeopardize their finances, jobs, schooling, and visa status in Ireland. "Ireland doesn't allow abortion because it's against their religion, but they shouldn't make that apply to those of us who don't believe in their religion," a singleton Chinese citizen taking language classes told me when she was 22 and had an unwanted pregnancy in Ireland.

None of the transnational students in my study were politically active in China or abroad. Their decisions to go abroad were not motivated by a desire for greater freedom to engage in political activism. Nor did they take advantage of such freedom once abroad. Most had little or no interest in or understanding of local and national elections and political campaigns in the developed countries in which they studied.

Some of them, however, appreciated the effects of multiparty elections on those countries. "In Britain, the people get cheap or free education, free medical care, and good pensions, because there are multiple parties, and each party promises to do more for ordinary people and give them more social welfare, and if they don't fulfill their promises once in office, the voters can vote them out," 24-year-old Tan Yi told her 25-year-old boyfriend Xue Liang three years after they both left China to attend an ESOL school in Britain. "It's not like that in China, where the leaders don't care what ordinary people think, because ordinary people have no say about whether they stay in office. That's why the Chinese Communist Party is so corrupt and keeps letting cadres get rich while cutting back on ordinary people's social welfare."

"Both of us are children of Communist Party members," Xue Liang reminded Tan Yi. "When you criticize the Chinese Communist Party, you are also criticizing your parents. The Communist Party is not a person but a party made up of a lot of different people, including our parents. Some of them are corrupt, but that doesn't mean they all are. I like Britain's system too, but it wouldn't work in China. What if China had a Falun Gong Party, and a separatist party for each ethnicity, and a farmers' party that wanted to end birth planning and bring back arranged marriages? China has too many backward elements. China needs the Communist Party to keep pushing down on them."

Although Tan Yi seemed to favor the British system and Xue Liang seemed to favor the Chinese system in this particular conversation, I also observed many other conversations between them in which their positions were reversed. Their disagreements reflected not only differences between their perspectives of the moment but also the ambivalence that they and many other Chinese citizens in my study felt within themselves. The harsh critiques of China they encountered abroad strengthened and expanded doubts they had about China's political system, but such critiques also intensified their sense of filial nationalism and their desire to protect China.

Freedom from Corruption

Chinese citizens in my study often talked about wanting to go abroad to get away from the corruption they experienced in their everyday lives. But their greatest concerns were not about any corruption in national-level Chinese political processes. Rather, they talked about how going abroad would enable them to get high-quality educational opportunities, jobs, health care, and promotions without having to rely on social connections, gifts, bribes, and favors and how going abroad would free them from the corruption, biases, and unchecked tyranny of the managers, supervisors, and low-level bureaucrats who often made their lives miserable in China. Based on what they heard from friends, relatives, and acquaintances abroad and what they saw in movies, TV shows, news stories, and Internet forums about life in developed countries, they assumed that those countries were culturally and structurally resistant to the corruption they found among resource gatekeepers in China. Their complaints about corruption in China were about doctors and nurses expecting gifts in exchange for decent medical care, bosses and managers expecting gifts and favors in exchange for jobs and promotions, less competent and less experienced co-workers with stronger ties of kinship or friendship to managers getting promoted over them, employers demanding that they work extra hours on weekends, nights, and holidays without extra pay, layoffs and reductions in pay and benefits that they attributed to the mismanagement of co-workers and managers who embezzled and used company resources for personal gain, and university, high school, junior high school, and even elementary school and kindergarten teachers and administrators expecting gifts and favors from parents in exchange for school admissions and even for extra attention during school hours. As a 23-year-old singleton junior college student in China told me two years before she went to Ireland to attend an ESOL school and then a four-year college, "There's so much corruption and unfairness, and you need connections to get anything done, so I don't think there's hope in China for someone like me, from a poor family with no connections. I want to go abroad so I can have a fair chance."

Some Chinese citizens told me that they started thinking about going abroad because of specific instances of corruption. A 17-year-old singleton Chinese citizen in China told me that she had started dreaming about immigrating to the United States at age 15 when she lost a violin contest. She learned from a friend of the judges that the judges felt she had won the contest but nevertheless declared another girl the winner because that girl's parents had bribed them. "I had studied the violin for seven years and felt deeply disappointed with the unfairness of China," she told me. "Before that contest, I had disliked the US and thought it was China's enemy. But after that contest, I wanted to go to the US because I heard it was a much fairer place."

Like Americans who wanted to do "good work," many Chinese singletons in my study believed they would be happier if they could succeed without compromising their ethics.[28] In addition to wanting to go abroad to escape the corruption they associated with China, they feared becoming corrupt themselves if they stayed in China. "I don't want to live in China anymore," Yang Kai, a 22-year-old college student in China, told me. "Chinese people love money too much. As soon as Chinese people become cadres, they try to embezzle and get as many gifts and bribes as possible—even if they thought 90,000 [yuan] was enough, once they have 90,000, they'll want 900,000. No one can turn down money; if I were them, I'd be corrupt too. If I stay in China, the best I can hope for is to become a corrupt cadre like them. But I don't want that—I want to go abroad, where I can make money without being corrupt."

Yang Kai applied for graduate programs in Australia, Canada, and the United States and was admitted to programs in Australia and Canada but without a scholarship. His parents were office workers without enough savings to pay for his tuition abroad, so he was unable to go abroad. Yang Kai attributed his parents' lack of savings to their unwillingness to embezzle and take bribes.

Yang Kai got an office job in China but still hoped to eventually study or work in a developed country. He continued to complain about the corruption he saw around him. "When I want to be a good person while no one else does, I feel like a fool," Yang Kai told me when he was 27. "I want to go abroad so I can feel that being a good person is normal."

Many transnational Chinese students mentioned their desires to escape the widespread corruption in Chinese society as one of their motivations for going abroad. Their newfound freedom from corruption was one of the things they liked most about their lives abroad. "China is so corrupt that if you want to do business there, you have to give bribes to police and to city officials all the time, regardless of whether your business is profitable or not," a 26-year-old singleton Chinese citizen told me four years after he left China to attend an ESOL school in Britain. "Abroad, however, the police and city officials don't expect bribes and won't even accept them if offered, and they treat people fairly. They treat me a bit different because I'm Chinese, but they never forget that I have human rights. So now I understand what human rights are."

Some government leaders, journalists, and activists from developed countries and Chinese dissidents inside and outside China argue that the limitations that the Chinese state places on political freedom are the ultimate cause of the corruption experienced by Chinese people in their everyday lives. Chinese citizens in my study, however, did not assume that limits on political freedom were the main reason for China's corruption. Rather, they attributed such corruption mainly to Chinese culture and viewed the Chinese government's flaws as symptoms of the corruption they believed was endemic to Chinese culture. They were therefore skeptical of the idea that such corruption could be eliminated by the introduction of political freedoms available in many developed countries, such as the freedom to own guns, vote by secret ballot in multicandidate, multiparty elections, organize and protest against the government, publicly criticize the government, disseminate whatever information they wanted in the media, practice whatever religion they wanted, and have as many children as they wanted. Many of them argued that such freedoms would only cause chaos, disunity, and impoverishment in China. A 22-year-old Chinese citizen told me half a year before he left China for a graduate program in Australia, "In Taiwan, even primary school students fight with each other if they belong to different political parties. I don't want that to happen here. If it does, China may be divided. We have so many nationalities in Tibet, Xinjiang, and Taiwan; they might all become separatist without a strong government. We could become like the Soviet Union, which split up after getting multiparty elections, and is now even worse than before."

Chinese citizens in my study talked about how the corruption they personally experienced was exacerbated by the lack of checks and balances in the Chinese government, but the checks and balances they considered most appropriate for China were not necessarily those based on the political freedoms that rein in government excesses in developed countries. Some who grew up under the Maoist government argued that "what China needs is another strong leader like Chairman Mao" who would scare people into avoiding corruption as Mao did. Poorer, older Chinese citizens in my study were especially likely to recall with nostalgia the Maoist egalitarianism prevalent during their youth, even though Maoist policies had also caused them to experience starvation, violence, and chaos. "Nowadays, factory bosses drive cars, use cell phones, and go to fancy restaurants while their workers starve," an unemployed father born in 1951 told his 16-year-old son and me while we ate dinner at their home in China in 2000. "If Chairman Mao were still around, he would execute them all! Nowadays, bosses treat national property like their own private property. When I was young, a boss wouldn't even dare to use the factory's stationery for his private letters, because anyone, even a janitor, could report wrongdoing and have the boss beaten and struggled against. Now that was democracy!"

Younger Chinese citizens were less enthusiastic about the return of Maoism, or any other kind of government that existed in Chinese history, as a solution to corruption, and they were more likely to look for models from developed countries. The aspect of developed countries' governance that they admired most had less to do with political freedoms than with the rule of law (*fazhi*) that seemed more prevalent in developed countries than in China. Instead of hoping for the introduction of more political freedoms into China, they hoped for judicial reforms that would enable the Chinese state to rein in the corruption they saw as endemic in Chinese society. They wanted stricter enforcement of China's existing laws and stronger and more independent, incorruptible, and unbiased judicial and law enforcement institutions that would allow even the poor and powerless to prevail in lawsuits and criminal prosecutions against the rich and powerful. Rather than wanting to go abroad to practice political freedoms unavailable in China, they wanted to go abroad to compete in a fairer system that operated in accordance with the rule of law and to escape the corruption they saw as endemic in China.

Freedom from Friends and Family

Many transnational students in my study told me they wanted to go abroad to gain more freedom (*ziyou*), and those who did go abroad told me that indeed they felt more free (*ziyou*) than they did while they were in China. When they talked about freedom in this way, however, they were almost never talking about political or religious freedoms (which they were more likely to describe in terms of human rights [*renquan*], rule of law [*fazhi*], or democracy [*minzhu*]). Rather, their talk of freedom referred mainly to freedom to pursue a personal lifestyle in which one is free from the competition, gossip, expectations, obligations, and constraints associated with social relationships in China. Their expectation that life abroad would provide such freedom derived partly from movies and television shows they saw about life in developed countries and partly from what they heard about relatives, friends, or acquaintances who had gone abroad and freed themselves from familial and social obligations.

Chinese citizens in my study often chafed at how little of this kind of freedom they had as youth living with their parents. They feared that they would lose even more of this kind of freedom once they established careers, married, and had children of their own. Almost all the Chinese citizens in my study lived with their parents unless they were married, living in college dorms, or working far from where their parents lived. Even if they could afford to rent apartments of their own (which most could not), it would have been considered an insult to their parents for them to choose to live apart from their parents when they did not have to. Some continued to live with their parents even after marriage, because they could not afford neolocal housing or because their parents had health problems and needed them to provide nursing care.

As they reached their mid-20s, Chinese citizens were increasingly pressured by their parents, relatives, and friends to establish careers, marry, and have children of their own (in that order). Many feared that attainment of such life-course milestones would fetter them with even more constraints, pressures, obligations, and expectations. In contrast, peers they knew or heard about who studied abroad seemed free from such constraints, pressures, obligations, and expectations and were able to remain in the seemingly carefree and promising status of single, childless, career-free "student" well into their late 20s. Many Chinese citizens told me that they went abroad partly to escape the sense that they were hurtling toward a conventional life course they considered unsatisfactory. A 20-year-old college student told me a year before she left China to study in the United States, "I could get a job, get married, and have a child, but if I do that soon, my life will be over, and it would have been so boring!"

Once transnational Chinese students were abroad, their parents, relatives, and friends in China had too little contact with them to be able to pressure them as they did in China, and in any case it was generally accepted in China that prolonging the student life stage was a legitimate price transnational students had to pay for the developed world citizenship they were trying to attain. The sheer geographic distance of developed countries from China and the expense of travel between those countries and China seemed to promise an escape from the web of social obligations woven by their friends, family members, co-workers, and relatives. A 20-year-old college student in China who wanted to study in Australia told me as we sat in her family's one-room apartment and looked at a map of the world, "I love the look of Australia, all alone in the sea; it seems like a place where no one would bother you." To Chinese youth who found their current and impending social and familial constraints, pressures, obligations, and expectations suffocating and scary, studying abroad seemed like a good way to escape.

Some transnational Chinese students told me that the most immediate and emotionally salient factor that caused them to study abroad was their desire to escape an undesirable relationship with a specific parent, parent-in-law, boyfriend, girlfriend, or spouse. A desire to escape such a relationship was never the sole motivation for studying abroad, but it was sometimes what tipped the balance in its favor. As a 26-year-old computer programmer explained to me a few months after he left China to work and attend a Japanese-language school in Japan, "My girlfriend and I were always fighting and didn't want to marry each other, but we were together for so long that if I stayed in China, our families would have pushed us to marry. So I left the country to escape that."

Freedom from Chinese Relationships

One of the things the transnational students in my study disliked most about China was the pervasiveness of the instrumental use of social connections (*guanxi*). Trying to keep track of who owed them favors, whom they owed favors, and what various people really wanted from them left them feeling exhausted (*lei*) and irritated (*fan*). Most were motivated to study abroad at least partly by their frustration with problems associated with the close-knit social relations that structured Chinese society. Raised as singletons with developed world aspirations, they associated the neoliberal ideal of the autonomous, self-disciplined individual with sincerity and innocent social relationships and associated the interdependency encouraged by their parents' generation with insincerity and instrumental social relationships.

Their parents also bemoaned the insincerity and instrumentality common in Chinese social relationships but sometimes attributed it to factors associated with increased neoliberalization rather than to factors associated with inadequate neoliberalization that their children assumed was the cause. Chinese citizens who had grown up before the economic reforms that began in the 1980s were happy that material conditions were much better after the economic reforms. Yet they also complained that Chinese people were much more insincere, selfish, uncivil, instrumental, and corrupt than during their own youth.[29] They thought that the political and economic changes that had occurred since their childhood had increased inequalities and instrumentality in Chinese social relationships.

Relationships that are primarily instrumental have little permanence, affection, or moral righteousness. Rather, they are based on the exchange of gifts and favors. Sentimental relationships are chosen, maintained, or abandoned on the basis of how much people enjoy each other's company. Ascribed relationships are based on the moral obligations associated with ascriptive roles. The greater the ascriptive quality of a relationship, the more the instrumental aspect of that relationship is tempered by a sense of permanence and moral righteousness and the more likely it is that sentimental attachments will grow. The most deeply ascriptive relationships are those within the nuclear family—the lifelong ties between siblings, parents and children, husbands and wives. These relationships approach Marshall Sahlins's model of generalized exchange, and their instrumental components are buried under layers of permanence, moral righteousness, and sentimental attachment.[30] To a lesser extent, relationships between other relatives and between co-workers, neighbors, and classmates are also ascriptive, at least more so than relationships between "friends of friends" cultivated for the purpose of gift and favor exchange. The Chinese citizens in my study wanted relationships with a balance of all three components—instrumentality, sentimentality, and ascription. But all too often in an era of rising inequalities, instrumentality was overwhelmingly emphasized at the expense of sentimental attachments and ascribed roles.[31] Social networks seemed increasingly close to Sahlins's model of balanced exchange and offered far less morality, permanence, and sentimental attachment.[32] Social networks were also important before the economic reforms that began in the 1980s, but back then inequalities were smaller. Social networks did not have to be chosen too carefully because most people had gifts and favors of similar value to offer. Relatives, neighbors, and co-workers had similar amounts of wealth, so they could appreciate each other's gifts. Then as now, managers and professionals had more power than ordinary workers and thus could offer their social networks more and better favors.[33] But managers and professionals were not much wealthier than ordinary workers and could appreciate the small gifts of food, clothing, and money given to them by grateful neighbors, co-workers, and relatives.

Increasingly after the 1980s, however, managers, professionals, and owners of large businesses were so much wealthier than workers that they scoffed at the kinds of gifts workers could afford to give. Thus it was hard for workers to maintain long-term relationships of generalized reciprocity with friends and relatives who had become much wealthier. Many who were wealthier thought they had nothing to gain and a lot to lose from maintaining relationships with friends and relatives who were poor; therefore, once they became wealthier, they cultivated new social networks consisting of others of their own socioeconomic status and abandoned their old social networks. This caused bitterness and resentment among those abandoned, who saw it as evidence that Chinese people were insincere. At the same time, those who achieved new, more instrumental relationships were also unhappy about the insincerity of those relationships, because they lacked the sentiment and permanence that characterized ascriptive relationships.

All the Chinese citizens in my study who talked about the exchange of gifts and favors said they disliked it. This raises the question of why the exchanges continued to be so widespread when everyone disliked them. When I asked Chinese citizens in my study why they continued to participate in such exchanges if they disliked them, they said they had no choice because everyone else was doing it. Although they would prefer a system free of corruption and the need to use social connections to get anything done, they felt compelled to participate in the very exchanges that prevented the existence of such a system. As the 47-year-old factory technician father of a teenager in my study told me, "The only kind of people worse than cadres who use official power to benefit their own friends and relatives at the expense of the public are the friends and relatives who have the means to help you but refuse because you don't have enough money or power to repay them." When I asked those who were complaining about someone else's refusal to do a favor whether or not that refusal might be due to a righteous determination to combat the corruption everyone complained about, the response was often something like, "Of course not—they just don't think we're worthy of them—they think we don't have the means to repay the favor," followed by a mention of wealthier, more powerful people who they assumed had been granted the favor they were denied. From a powerful person's perspective, it was hard to avoid doing favors because refusal on moral or legal grounds was often assumed to be an excuse for baser motives (such as the desire to reserve favors for those who could pay more for them). In a system where it was difficult to get anything done without favors, refusal to use one's power to grant favors to friends and relatives could only be seen as treacherous. As a manager in China discussed with his nieces and nephews how he would try to use his influence to give them an edge in their school admissions and job searches, he interspersed his discussion with asides to me denouncing the corruption that made it possible for him to do these favors. "This is why China can never rise up," he said. "Workers are hired and cadres are promoted on the basis of connections rather than ability." At the same time, he said, "I have to help [my nieces and nephews] because everyone else with influence is doing the same thing; if I don't help them, they'll get left behind despite their ability."

Even though educational achievement was important up to a point, connections were the key to securing an especially desirable job within a given field and sometimes the securing of any job at all. This led to both an increasing reliance on instrumental relationships and an increasing sense that society was unfair and corrupt, because those with the right connections were frequently hired over those who were better qualified.

Some parents who grew up under Maoism suggested that these problems actually resulted from post-Mao reforms. They spoke nostalgically about the more egalitarian, less competitive lifestyles of their Maoist youth. They fondly recalled that corruption was rare and severely punished in the strict, austere, egalitarian political culture of Maoism (1949–1976), which rendered cadres so vulnerable and terrified of being denounced that they dared not take bribes or embezzle. Corruption increased in the era of economic reforms, with its more relaxed political atmosphere, rising socioeconomic inequalities, and rampant opportunities to convert political power into wealth and vice versa. This environment also encouraged jealousy and the replacement of sentimental ties and moral obligations (*renqing*) with an increasingly cynical and commodified form of social networking (*guanxi*).[34] Some parents shared their children's tendency to blame the "low quality of Chinese people" for these problems, but other parents blamed the post-Mao economic reforms for the rise of instrumentalism and for selfishness and immorality in general. A Chinese woman born in 1952 told me while I ate dinner at her home in China in 2008, "When I was growing up, there were no thieves and pickpockets; if you dropped a pocketbook, someone would pick it up and run after you, saying you dropped it, or give it to the police station. Everyone listened to Mao Zedong Thought and did what Mao Zedong said, and tried to be good people. If you dropped a piece of clothing, someone would pick it up and find you and give it to you; sometimes they would even wash off the dust before giving it to you. Everyone helped each other—if a family had only one mouthful's worth of food, they would still share a bit of it with neighbors. Our economy was backward, but our thought was advanced. Now our economy is advanced, but our thought is backward."

Chinese singletons born after the 1970s, however, had difficulty understanding such nostalgia. Even though they also disliked corruption, immorality, inequality, and cynical social relationships, they saw these problems as the result of the Chinese population's poverty and low education rather than of China's quest to join the developed world. In 2000, while I was watching the news on TV with an unemployed Chinese citizen, her factory worker husband, and her 15-year-old singleton daughter, the mother, born in 1954, complained that the transition to a market economy was causing corruption and poverty. "If that were so, America and Europe would be the poorest and most corrupt places on earth," her daughter replied. "But they're not, and we are, and it's just because Chinese people's quality is too low." Although Chinese citizens born before the 1970s could recall a time when neoliberalism was taboo and disreputable instead of dominant and pervasive, their children could not. As Ann Anagnost argued, cultural critiques widespread in everyday discourses and in official rhetoric were "reassigning the onus of underdevelopment from Western imperialism to factors endogenous to Chinese society."[35]

No Chinese citizen I knew admitted to enjoying or being good at the art of cultivating and maintaining instrumental social connections (*guanxi*). Even those who were described by others as being especially good at it sometimes complained about how difficult it was. Part of this may have been due to a widespread perception that such a skill, while useful, was not especially admirable. In addition, instrumental social connections were so difficult to navigate that even those who were relatively good at them considered themselves inadequate at times, and it took so much life experience in China to learn their intricacies that most young people were indeed bad at them. Most Chinese singletons were not exposed to the full-blown complexities of instrumental social connections until after they entered the workforce and married and had to trade favors with co-workers, employers, and in-laws. Many found the work of building and maintaining instrumental social connections in a web of intricate workplace and extended family politics intimidating, confusing, and unpleasant. They hoped to escape it by going abroad.

Closely related to the importance of instrumental social connections in China was the pervasiveness of insincerity. As Susan Blum argued, "Chinese tend to emphasize the consequences of the speech, Americans the absolute truthfulness."[36] A teacher in China told me, "Chinese people learn to lie and feel that lying is a good thing—someone who lies well knows how to get things done. For instance, when I thought that meetings to study politics were useless and didn't go to them, the [administrator] got mad at me. So I lied and said the meetings conflicted with a class I was teaching; the [administrator] knew I was lying, but was immediately happy because he could save face. You have to have an excuse, even if it's a lie."

Insincerity was often seen as a necessity in a Chinese society where all aspects of one's life depended on maintaining good social relationships by saving face and ensuring that others save face. But many Chinese citizens told me that they hated how often they had to lie and how often others lied to and around them.

Transnational students in my study left China partly because they believed that doing so would enable them to escape relationships with friends, acquaintances, co-workers, family members, and relatives that they found stressful, restrictive, and exhausting. Once abroad, they indeed gained a great deal of freedom from the close-knit, interdependent Chinese social relationships that were part of the reason for the instrumental social networking, insincerity, and overly onerous social obligations they disliked in China. They greatly appreciated the more carefree social relationships they were able to have once abroad.

"I'm more free abroad," a 23-year-old singleton told me a year after she left China to attend college in the United States. "I can do whatever I like, dress however I like, and no one will say anything to me about it. In China even people who don't know you well will criticize you if you are unusual in any way. Like if you dress unusually, they will tell you what you should be doing."

"In China, I was annoyed by how my Ma always managed me," a 24-year-old singleton told me a year after she left China to attend Japanese-language classes in Japan. "I feel so free now. I've always had wildness in my heart, and going abroad allowed me to let it out."

"When Britons eat together, they split the bill, so no one owes anyone, unlike Chinese people who always treat each other and then feel like they owe each other or have been taken advantage of," a

24-year-old singleton told me two years after he left China to attend an ESOL school in Britain.

"Ireland is more free, and Irish people's relationships are less stressful and more relaxed," a 25-year-old accountant working in Ireland told me six years after she left China to attend college in Ireland. "You don't have to use connections to get things done like you would in China, so when you play with friends you really are just playing and have no ulterior motives."

"In China, neighbors all know everything about each other," a 35-year-old Chinese businessman told me, 14 years after he left China to attend an ESOL school in Australia. "In Australia, I don't even know who my next-door neighbor is. When my fellow Chinese businesspeople ask me, 'How was business today,' I have to think about what to answer: If I say business went well, they might ask me for loans. If I say business went poorly, they might think there are problems with my ability. If Australian businesspeople ask, though, I just answer truthfully; Australians don't think about more than they should. When I take beer to the Australian businessman next door to my business and we drink together, he doesn't think anything of it. Chinese businesspeople would think my business went well today or that I wanted something from them."

Transnational students in my study also appreciated how citizens of developed countries seemed more sincere than their counterparts in China.

"Chinese people lie too much," a 26-year-old singleton Chinese citizen told me, four years after she left China to attend a university in Australia. "They will say things to make themselves look good. Australians are much more honest and don't care what others think of them."

"It's relaxing to be friends with Irish people, because they say whatever is on their minds and I can say whatever is on my mind too, without worrying what they'll think," a 23-year-old singleton told me three years after she left China to attend English-language classes in Ireland.

"I like how honest Americans are," a 25-year-old singleton told me three years after he left China to attend a university in the United States. "They are so much more innocent than Chinese people."

"Britons are honest and trust each other," a middle-aged Chinese businessman told several Chinese citizens who had recently arrived from China and me as we ate dinner at a restaurant in Britain. "Britons

learn from an early age that lying is bad. If you are caught lying, everything will be bad for you. If you lie to one bank, you will never be able
to do business with any bank in Britain." He observed with pride that
his own 10-year-old son, who grew up in Britain, had learned to be
honest as Britons were. "When I needed to pull my son out of school
so we could go on vacation together, I told him to lie to his teacher
and say that he was going to a tutoring class instead of a vacation,"
he said. "But my son refused to lie—he said that lying would be much
worse than skipping school to go on vacation! In China the teacher
would prefer to hear a good excuse even if it were suspected of being
a lie, just to give the teacher face."

Too Much Social Freedom?

Although they enjoyed their newfound freedom from Chinese social
pressures, many Chinese transnational students also lamented that
natives of the countries in which they sojourned seemed so free from
social pressures that they behaved in ways that did not meet Chinese
standards of self-control and responsibility.

"In China I thought Irish people would have much higher quality
than Chinese people, but now I realize that Irish people have even
lower quality than Chinese people," a 26-year-old singleton told me
four years after he left China to attend an ESOL school and work at
a restaurant in Ireland. "Irish people say 'fuck' all the time. In China
there are at least some people with high quality who would not talk
like that, but in Ireland everyone talks like that—even wealthy and
beautiful women!"

"Britons are too casual," a 26-year-old singleton told me four years
after she left China to attend an ESOL school in Britain. "At first I
wanted a British boyfriend because I thought British men were hand-
some and high quality. But when I dated Britons, I was disappointed.
They just wanted to have sex, without caring about consequences. It
was embarrassing when they talked about sex in front of my friends.
They had thick skins, felt no shame, and didn't care what others
thought. They couldn't control themselves like Chinese men can."

"Japanese people are too free about sex," a Chinese citizen told
me in China after returning from Japan, where he had spent three
years working as a waiter and attending a Japanese-language school.
"Their whole society is perverted: The husbands go and find prostitutes, the wives are lonely and look for lovers, and the daughters

become prostitutes; who knows when the dad will end up asking for a prostitute and seeing his own daughter? And this is how they live. It's a pretty place to visit, but I wouldn't want to spend the rest of my life around people who are so perverted."

"Australia hasn't taught me much," a 24-year-old singleton told me six years after he left China to attend an ESOL school and then college in Australia. "I just learned to be lazy and other bad habits here. When I was in high school I tried to control myself and study hard, but when I came to Australia I just wanted to play, because I saw that Australian kids just did whatever they wanted to do at the moment, with no regard to the future, and being around them made me more like them."

"It's hard for me to make friends with foreigners, because I want to study, but all they want to do is go to parties and drink beer," a 22-year-old singleton told me a year after he left China to attend a university in the United States. "They don't have as much discipline as Chinese students have."

"An Irish promise is no promise at all—Irish people forget about a promise very quickly," a 24-year-old singleton told me six years after he left China to attend an ESOL school and then college in Ireland. "Irish people are too casual and don't care about human relationships. In China, at least the people who made the promise would feel they should keep it, even if the laws kept changing. In Ireland, they might say that you'll get one salary or tax or attendance requirement or tuition at the time you sign up, and it will change all of a sudden with no notice, and even the person who made you the promise won't do anything to help you."

Civility Among Strangers

Transnational students in my study had hoped to find greater civility abroad, and in some ways they were not disappointed. They marveled at how people in developed countries waited in orderly lines instead of the pushing and shoving crowds they endured in China, how drivers obeyed traffic laws more than drivers in China did, how salesclerks were much more polite than their counterparts in China, and how strangers said "please" or "thank you" to each other, unlike in China. They marveled at the civility of strangers in these countries.

Liu Shuhua, a 26-year-old singleton Chinese citizen attending an ESOL school in Ireland, told me that a white Irish woman on the street in Dublin, whom Liu Shuhua asked for directions, gave her a ride and even helped her get a job as an elder care aide once she learned that Liu Shuhua was looking for a job. A 25-year-old singleton Chinese citizen attending an ESOL school in Britain told me about an Englishman of "mixed race" who saw him leave his cell phone on a store counter in London and ran down the street after him to give him the phone. A 20-year-old singleton Chinese citizen attending a university in Australia told me about how, when she mistakenly left cash in an ATM slot in Australia on the assumption that the machine was broken, a teenaged white Australian boy who saw her cash in the slot did not steal it but rather ran after her and told her she had forgotten to take her cash. They all talked about how unlikely it would have been for strangers in public places in China to treat them so kindly. They considered such kindness evidence that citizens of the countries in which they studied had more "high quality" (*gao suzhi*) than Chinese citizens.

"Britons are so nice and friendly even to strangers—they treat strangers like friends," a 23-year-old singleton told me a year after she left China to attend an ESOL school in Britain. "Chinese people are very careful around friends because they're afraid of losing face or causing someone else to lose face, but out in public when they don't know anyone, Chinese people become very rude. But Britons are nice to everyone, not because they worry about consequences, but just because they have high quality."

"Americans are so friendly, strangers will smile at you and say hello on the street," a 22-year-old singleton told me three years after she left China to attend a US university. "In China if you do that, people will think you're crazy."

"Canadian streets are safer than Chinese streets, because the drivers follow traffic laws and stop when they see pedestrians," a 22-year-old singleton Chinese citizen told me four years after he left China to attend a Canadian university. "When I go back to China, I can't cross the streets because the cars are too scary—they won't stop for you unless you're right in front of them."

"I don't want to go back to China because Chinese people's quality is too low," a 21-year-old singleton told me a year after she left China to attend an ESOL school and work as a dishwasher in Ireland. "When Chinese cashiers give you change after you buy something, they throw the change at you instead of putting it in your hand; Chinese salespeople ignore you and act like you're bothering them, and sometimes even Chinese store owners are like that. But Irish people are always polite to customers; they treat you like a friend even if it's the first time you ever walked into their store."

"Japanese people have higher quality than Chinese people," a 22-year-old singleton Chinese citizen told me a year after he left China to attend a university in Japan. "Their streets are cleaner because they never throw trash on the ground like Chinese people do. If they eat something and need to throw away the container, they will carry it while walking around, for as long as necessary, until they find a trash can to throw it in."

A 35-year-old businessman told me 14 years after he left China to attend an ESOL school in Australia, "In Australia, I learned to say "Can I have the hamburger?" to the waitress, and then "thank you" when she gave me a hamburger. In China, when I did that, the waitress thought I was strange, I must be crazy or I must have just gotten out of prison or come from elsewhere and so must be easily cheated."

Missing Chinese Relationships

Even though transnational students in my study appreciated the greater honesty and more relaxed social relationships they had with local citizens in developed countries, they were frustrated by the social distance that also resulted. While they marveled at how strangers were treated like friends in these countries, they were also dismayed about how hard it was to develop friendships deeper than the initial friendliness that strangers exhibited toward them in these countries.

"I dislike Britons—they're too cold-blooded," a 25-year-old told me, two years after she left China to attend an ESOL school in Britain. "They're polite, but you can't really be friends with them."

"Britons don't believe in loyalty like Chinese people do," a 24-year-old singleton Chinese citizen told me five years after he left China to attend an ESOL school and then college in Britain. "If my friends were criminals, I would still protect them, because Chinese people are loyal. But a Briton would not be so loyal. Britons would value the rule of law over friendship and turn their friends over to the police."

"My Japanese classmates are polite and smile at me a lot, but they don't really want to talk to me," a 24-year-old singleton told me two years after she left China to attend a university in Japan. "When I try to talk to them, they just say polite things, but nothing deep."

"Chinese people will do more for their friends than Irish people," a 21-year-old singleton Chinese citizen told me two years after he left China to attend an ESOL school in Ireland. "Irish people seem nice when you first meet, but they don't go out of their way to help friends."

"I'm friendly with my classmates, but after a certain point I can't get any closer to them," a 22-year-old singleton Chinese citizen told me a year after she left China to attend a university in the United States. "I have no close friends in the US. No one comes to visit me during the weekend. Maybe it's because everyone lives so far away from each other." She told me she had been invited to a party only once and found it awkward because she could not understand what most people were saying. "I just sat and listened and had nothing to say," she said. "I felt so bad. I couldn't understand them, so I was silent, but I had to pretend to smile and look at whoever was talking. Then they noticed that they were excluding me and asked me a few simple questions about when I came to the US and how I liked it. Then they went back to talking with each other, and I was excluded again."

"Foreign [Canadian] humor and Chinese humor are different," a 24-year-old Chinese singleton attending college in Canada told me four years after he left China. "I feel I know what Chinese people are thinking, but I don't know what [Canadian] foreigners are thinking. When I spend time with Chinese people, I feel relieved and relaxed because I can communicate with them."

A 26-year-old singleton attending vocational training classes in Australia told me five years after he left China, "I can't really make friends with foreigners. When I wear nice clothes and a Chinese person compliments me on them, I feel good, but when a foreigner compliments me, I feel nothing."

"Australians are very nice to you at work, but it's hard to truly become friends with them," a 27-year-old singleton Chinese citizen told me five years after she left China to attend college and then work in an office in Australia. "After work, they just get in their cars and return to their own homes. In China, work friends will have fun together after work and invite each other home. But Australians all live their own lives and they won't invite you to their home even after you know them for a long time. Chinese work friends will talk to each other about their family stuff and things in their heart, but Australian work friends just talk about sports or the weather. If you ask them too much about their personal lives, they'll think you're rude. They have high quality so they're good to you when they're working with you, but if they change jobs they'll forget about you, and you can't rely on them to help you when you really need help."

It was hard to tell the extent to which the differences transnational students in my study observed between social relationships in China and abroad were due to differences between Chinese culture and developed countries' cultures and how much was due to language barriers and differences between their status as natives at home and their status as transnational migrants abroad. It was clear that transnational migrant lifestyles played at least some role in reducing their ability to form deep friendships while studying abroad, because many were at least as dissatisfied with their friendships with fellow Chinese citizens abroad as they were with their friendships with non-Chinese. Some told me with dismay that their relationships with Chinese citizens abroad were based even more on instrumentality and even less on sentiment or morality than their relationships with Chinese citizens in China had been. They also talked about feeling disappointed when their friends and relatives from China did not help them as much as they had hoped.

"One thing I don't like about Australia is that human feelings are lighter here, and friendships not so strong," a 21-year-old singleton told me two years after she left China to attend college prep classes and then college in Australia. The friendships she was talking about were all with other Chinese transnational students. "In China many classmates are good friends, but in Australia classmates don't really know each other. In China people become friends just because they want to become friends, but in Australia people use each other and think about what a friend can do for them."

"It would have been cheaper to go to Australia or New Zealand, but I came to Britain because my cousin was here and I thought he would help me," a 23-year-old singleton Chinese citizen told me four years after she left China to attend a university in Britain. "We were so close when we played together as children, and my Ma was so close to his Ma. But then when I came here, he treated me worse than a stranger and always said he was too busy even to visit me or help me with even the simplest things, like translating job ads or negotiating rent with landlords. My English was so lacking then and his was so much better that it would have been easy for him to help me. It would have made a huge difference for me, but he couldn't be bothered."

Transnational students who failed to help their friends and relatives from China as much as they might have in China felt guilty about this, even though they also felt that their busy, difficult lives made this inevitable. A 20-year-old singleton told me two years after she left China to attend an ESOL school in Ireland, "My good friend from junior high school wanted to follow me here, and her parents agreed to let her because they really liked and trusted me and thought that I would take care of her. When I visited her in China, and her Ma had told her that she should learn to cook, [my friend] joked she didn't have to because I would take care of her. I felt bad, even though it was a joke, because I knew I couldn't take care of her. When she came, she ended up living far away from me, to be close to her ESOL school, so I couldn't take care of her—I had to take two buses and spend 3 euros just to visit her, and I was busy with school and work so I couldn't see her much. She had a hard time after she came to Ireland, so she returned to China after just eight months. I felt so bad, but I couldn't help her."

I often got to hear both the perspectives of newer arrivals from China who felt disappointed at their Chinese friends' and relatives' failure to help them and the perspectives of those friends and relatives who wanted to help but felt their own time and money were too scarce and valuable to allow them to fulfill their friends' and relatives' expectations. Some of these expectations did seem excessive by the standards of the developed countries in which they studied— such as the expectation that a married Chinese transnational student couple should share their bedroom with a newly arrived friend or relative from China who could not find other cheap housing or that a busy, financially strapped Chinese transnational student should take time off from work and drive several hours to pick up or drop off a newly arrived friend or relative from the airport. I had seen financially strapped and busy Chinese citizens (including some of the same ones who refused to do these favors once abroad) do these kinds of favors for friends and relatives while in China, where social pressures (including the nagging of other friends and relatives who insisted that they should help) made them feel obligated to go out of their way to do favors even if they felt taken advantage of or put upon as a result. Indeed, some had told me that a desire to get away from such social pressures was part of their reason for going abroad.

Although they sometimes felt guilty about not fulfilling the expectations they might have fulfilled in China, those who were abroad gradually became used to the lower expectations about how far friends should go to help each other that they found among fellow transnational students and among citizens of the countries in which they studied. They considered these lower expectations reasonable given how little time and money they had. As they spent more time abroad, even some of the Chinese transnational students who had initially complained about the coldness of their more seasoned friends and relatives abroad admitted that their initial expectations had been unrealistic.

Once abroad, many transnational Chinese students mourned the loss of the warmth and care embedded in the Chinese social ties they had taken for granted. They lost touch with Chinese friends who had moved on to the next stage of life. As they adopted more of the cultures of the countries in which they were studying, they had less in common with their Chinese friends and family members. Although they tried to maintain relationships with them through e-mail, phone calls, instant messaging, videoconferencing, and social networking websites, it was hard to maintain communications on a regular basis, given the expense of Internet service and international phone calls. Hectic schedules and time zone differences also made it hard for transnational students to be able to communicate in real time with anyone in China for more than a few hours per week. Transnational students abroad and their loved ones in China usually told each other only about aspects of their lives that were going well. They often hid unpleasant things from each other, such as illnesses, financial difficulties, crime, violence, divorces, abortions, academic failures, job losses, breakups of friendships and romances, and general unhappiness. They feared that the short periods they had to talk would not allow for enough time to explain, much less commiserate over, unpleasant and difficult aspects of their lives. They also thought that discussion of unpleasantness would cause distress and therefore be a poor use of the limited time they had to communicate, that cultural misunderstandings and the necessarily fragmentary nature of any descriptions of unpleasant things would exacerbate such distress, that discussion of problems could invite unwanted advice and conflicts over whether such advice would be taken, and that they might be blamed for causing themselves any problems they experienced.

Chinese singletons studying abroad were especially concerned about the growing distance between them and their parents. Most had little in common with their parents to begin with, given the great differences between the Maoist era in which their parents grew up and the post-Mao era in which they grew up, and studying abroad exacerbated this generation gap. They missed their parents, and some realized more than before how much they loved their parents. They also missed their parents' willingness to do most of the cooking, cleaning, and laundry at home. They even missed their parents' nagging, because they missed having someone care about them. They missed their relatives and the big extended family gatherings they used to find boring or annoying.

Chinese citizens found that making friends abroad was harder than it had been for them in China. Cultural, ethnic, racial, and linguistic barriers made it difficult to become close friends with the non-Chinese majority. It was sometimes even hard for them to become friends with Chinese citizens from other regions of China who spoke different dialects and belonged to other subcultures within China. The friends they did make were aware of the potentially temporary nature of their associations. Some therefore did not feel as obligated to be generous or as fearful of long-term repercussions of bad behavior as they might have been in China. They did not know each other's social networks and therefore felt less social pressure to maintain good relations. In China, anything one did would be remembered and gossiped about by friends, relatives, and co-workers. But abroad there were no such social constraints. The very social expectations that Chinese citizens wanted to get away from while in China had been what sustained the richness, warmth, and moral power of friendships and family relationships that they enjoyed there.

Conclusion: Freedom, Happiness, and Developed World Citizenship

Developed world citizenship offers more freedoms, resources, capabilities, and functionings than Chinese citizenship alone can offer. Chinese citizens in my study went abroad to seek many of the freedoms Sen described. These freedoms could be granted not only by their own government and society, as Sen argued, but also by other governments and societies in a world of flexible citizenship[37] that rendered an individual's relationship with the global neoliberal system at least as important as the individual's relationship with his or her nation-state.

However, the experiences of transnational students in my study also illustrate a persistent problem that social psychologists have repeatedly found in experimental and survey-based studies of how people perceive, experience, and evaluate happiness: People have trouble predicting what will make them happier in the future, and even when they get what they thought would make them happy, they find that such happiness is fleeting because they get used to the circumstances they once thought would make them happier. At the same time, once they get used to something that makes them happy, they cannot bear to part with it, and being deprived of it actually makes them even less happy than they were before they experienced it. Social psychologists found that their US-based research participants made decisions on the basis of mistaken predictions about which actions were likely to maximize future happiness.[38] They found that their research participants overestimated the degree to which major life changes would lead to lasting happiness and underestimated the extent to which they were likely to become used to improved living conditions and take them for granted and that they felt more dissatisfied with their choices if they had many other choices. Their quest for ever elusive goals of happiness can be seen as part of the engine that drives people throughout the global neoliberal system to keep making sacrifices in their quest to join the developed world. This quest is promoted by the global neoliberal system, which motivates many people worldwide, including the transnational Chinese students in my study, to do whatever it takes to become citizens of the developed world.

Many transnational Chinese students believed that migrating to developed countries would enable them to gain access to more prestigious, enjoyable, and useful education, greater purchasing power, better jobs, greater geographic mobility, a healthier and more comfortable physical environment, freedom from social constraints they disliked, and other kinds of "substantive freedoms" that Sen considered the defining features of development.[39] Once abroad, most did gain some of the freedoms they had always wanted. At the same time, however, they lost many of the freedoms they had taken for granted in China. Even though they had imagined that studying abroad would make them happier, many became less happy once they went abroad because they lost the freedoms they had gotten used to in China and found that the freedoms they had gone abroad

to win remained elusive, were not as satisfying as they had anticipated, or were what they had hoped for but no longer seemed so satisfying once they were used to them. Fear of losing the new freedoms
they had abroad, however, made them reluctant to return to China,
even as they lamented the loss of freedoms they had in China.

To be capable of functioning as they want to function, people need
access to resources, such as money, education, knowledge, transportation, legal protections, citizenship rights, and social networks. Sen
argued that these resources are not themselves inherently valuable;
rather, they are valuable only to the extent that they enhance capabilities. The particular resources needed to maximize capabilities vary
depending on the capabilities individuals already have, their values
and priorities, and their sociocultural context and can change as individuals' capabilities, values, and sociocultural contexts change.

This kind of change prevented life abroad from being as happy as
transnational Chinese students in my study had thought it would be
when they were in China. Transnational migration, along with the
transition from adolescence to adulthood, transformed their functionings, values, and sociocultural contexts. The increased access to
developed world resources that would have enabled them to attain
enough functionings to be happy while they were in China were
no longer enough to make them happy after they went abroad. As
they redefined themselves and what it would take to make them
happy, the developed world resources they desired while they lived
in China—such as the foreign foods, less polluted air, and higher
salaries available in developed countries—either became necessary
but insufficient for happiness (because they enjoyed but got used
to these resources and no longer felt especially happy about having
them) or became not even necessary, much less sufficient, for happiness (because they no longer valued them). In addition, many also
found that they lost freedoms they had taken for granted in China,
such as the freedom to fulfill filial obligations and maintain ties
with Chinese friends and family members, enjoy the Chinese food,
entertainment, social activities, and lifestyles they preferred, and
attain qualifications for respectable adulthood (e.g., a college degree,
a career, marriage, and childbearing) at the same ages as their peers
did in China. Looking back on those freedoms, some increasingly
saw China as a paradise lost and the developed country they had
once imagined as paradise as a barren, unsatisfying trap from which

they could not escape because of their desire to recover the costs of transnational migration. The unhappiest transnational Chinese students in my study also failed to gain access to the foreign resources—money, education, knowledge, goods, leisure activities, legal protections, and citizenship rights—they had imagined that transnational migration would provide them, even as they also lost the freedoms they had taken for granted in China.

CHAPTER 6

The Road Home

Decisions About Returning to
China or Staying Abroad

MOST TRANSNATIONAL STUDENTS in my study considered applying for permanent residency rights in a developed country, and some told me it was their paramount goal. Permanent residency rights offered most of the legal and social rights that legal citizenship could provide, including the right to reenter the country in which one was a permanent resident without the expense, uncertainty, and hassle of reapplying for visas, the right to enter other countries almost as easily as legal citizens of developed countries could, and the right to most of the same government-sponsored pensions, health care, and education that legal citizens had. Permanent residency rights could be granted to those who had political asylum, business investments, credentials or work experience that proved they had skills needed by the country, or sponsorship by a family member or an employer (usually in a white-collar profession). Processes of application for permanent residency rights in developed countries were complex, time-consuming, and often expensive. Applications for permanent residency rights usually entailed limitations on how often and how long an applicant could travel outside the country in which he or she wanted to be a permanent resident and in some cases on the applicant's freedom to leave the employer or spouse sponsoring the application. The decision to apply for permanent residency rights was therefore not one that could be made lightly. Many who started out wanting to apply for permanent residency rights in a developed country changed their minds once they realized how many years of their lives they would have to spend trying to structure their education, work, travel, and in some cases family life around permanent residency criteria.

Others persisted in trying to get permanent residency rights. Some told me that they would prefer to live abroad for the rest of their lives and return to China only for brief visits each year. But even they still viewed acquisition of legal citizenship in a developed country ambivalently, because it would entail giving up legal citizenship in China, which many viewed as unpatriotic and likely to lead to a loss of the freedom to visit China freely and easily without applying for visas (particularly important if tensions between China and the country in which they became legal citizens ever intensified). Those who wanted to keep open the possibility of returning to China for permanent residence also worried that becoming naturalized as a legal citizen of another country would subject them to restrictions on the kind of work and business that they could do in China. Permanent residency rights in a developed country were viewed much more favorably, because they were likely to confer most of the rights available to citizens of that country without requiring the holders to give up their legal Chinese citizenship.

Some transnational students in my study wanted to live in China on a permanent basis after studying abroad but with social, cultural, and possibly even legal citizenship in the developed world. They did not believe that life would be much better for them abroad than in China, or they were unwilling to risk having to live apart from their parents (most of whom were unlikely to get permanent residency rights abroad) on a permanent basis. They had wanted to study abroad because they believed that they would have more opportunities to have prestigious, high-paying careers in China once they acquired credentials, skills, cultural and economic capital, and possibly permanent residency rights or legal citizenship from a developed country. Some of their families had enough money to pay for the minimum requirements of a work, business, or student visa to enter a developed country but not enough money to enable them to start successful businesses in China. They hoped that they would be able to save enough money from working abroad to start a business in China. In the long run, though, they believed that they would be happier and have more economic opportunities in China than they would abroad. This view became especially prevalent after the global financial crisis of 2008–2010, when China's relative economic resilience suggested to many in China and abroad that China was likely to become a developed country sooner rather than later.

Before going abroad, most transnational students in my study did not have strong preferences about where they would live on a permanent basis after completing their studies abroad. They were just as willing to live in China as they were to live in any developed country so long as they could have the prestige, incomes, lifestyles, environments, and living standards associated with developed world citizenship. They hoped that going abroad would in the long run enable them to do business with people from developed countries or to secure work that offered developed world incomes, whether in China or in a developed country.

Ambivalence and Vacillation

Many of the participants in my study vacillated over whether they should return to China or stay in a developed country for permanent residence. When Hong Xiaonan first went from China to Ireland in 2004 (when Ireland was experiencing rapid economic growth), she had been uncertain about whether she would want to stay abroad permanently. After spending a year attending an ESOL school while working in the service sector in Ireland, she seemed determined to stay in Ireland. "In Ireland, I feel very free," she told me. "China is too noisy and crowded. In China my heart was too tired. I felt pressure and competition, there were so many other people working hard, and we were still not getting paid enough no matter how hard we worked. Abroad, the harder you work, the more money you earn."

During the global financial crisis of 2008–2010, however, the Irish economy crashed, suffering much more than China's economy did. Although Hong Xiaonan managed to keep working in the service sector part-time to fund her studies as she completed college, she saw many of her friends from China leave because they could no longer find enough work to support themselves, much less pay tuition or accumulate savings. Some were also denied student visa renewals as the Irish government tightened its enforcement of the laws that limited the number of hours foreign students could work and the number of years they could spend in language schools, to prevent them from taking too many jobs away from Irish citizens. By 2010, Hong Xiaonan seemed ready to return to China. "There are a lot more opportunities in China, so my future should be in China," she told me.

I found that even some of the transnational students in my study who started out with strong preferences for returning to China for permanent residence or for settling permanently in a developed country ended up losing their strong preferences while studying abroad. Moreover, even some of those who returned to China after studying abroad and who established a career, married, and had a child there still told me that they hoped to eventually go abroad for permanent residence. Even some of those who established a career, got married, and had a child in a developed country and obtained permanent residency rights or citizenship in that country still told me that they hoped to eventually return to China for permanent residence.

I also observed many Chinese citizens in China downplaying unpleasant aspects of their lives abroad that they had frequently complained about while living abroad. Chinese citizens who had never been abroad thus heard many positive descriptions provided by their friends and relatives who had been abroad, especially if those friends and relatives were not very close to them. I suspect this phenomenon contributed to the discourse about developed countries being like paradise.

"Probably 90 percent of Chinese students abroad think life abroad is not as good as they thought it would be; after just a year in Ireland, I didn't want to stay, but I can't go back because I don't want to waste the money my parents spent on tuition," 23-year-old college student Chen Hong told her friend, 22-year-old Wang Yunhui, and me as we had dinner together in Ireland. Wang Yunhui had come from China to attend an ESOL school in Ireland a year earlier, after hearing Chen Hong talk how much better life in Ireland was than life in China.

"Why didn't you tell me life was so bitter here," Wang Yunhui lamented. "When you were visiting in China last year, you just talked about how much you liked it here. If you had told me life was like this, I wouldn't have come!"

"I didn't want to lose face," Chen Hong replied. "After spending so much money for study abroad, I didn't want to say I didn't like it here. That would sound very bad."

Wang Yunhui returned to China at age 24, after four years of working at low-skill jobs while attending an ESOL school. "Ireland wasn't interesting," she told me a few weeks before she returned to China. "I could make a lot of money just working as a salesclerk, but I was wasting my time. I want to be with my family and friends in China. I want to spend time with them and not just go drinking at a pub with co-workers like I would in Ireland. There are more opportunities for me in China, and life in China is more interesting."

When I had lunch in China with Wang Yunhui and her friend who had never been abroad, however, Wang Yunhui only talked about what she liked about Ireland, "It's beautiful," she told her friend. "The sky is so blue, like you never see in China, and the beaches are much cleaner too. People were friendly, and when you smiled at children, they smiled back."

I later asked Wang Yunhui why she had spoken so positively about Ireland to her friend, even though she usually spoke more negatively about Ireland to me and to her friends in Ireland.

"She's never been abroad and wouldn't have understood why I didn't like it there," Wang Yunhui told me. "And now that I'm in China, I mainly remember the good things about life abroad. I do miss the environment there, and sometimes I also miss the people. I don't remember the bad things about Ireland because they are over, but I notice the bad things about China now because they are in front of my eyes."

I also observed many Chinese citizens speaking fondly about China while they were abroad, despite having complained about China before they left their homeland. They seemed reluctant to talk about unpleasantness of any kind, whether related to study abroad or other aspects of life, to people who were not close to them or who were presumed to not have backgrounds that would enable them to understand and sympathize. This resulted partly from concern about losing face if others who could not understand the circumstances assumed that the unpleasantness resulted from the transnational Chinese citizen's own bad decisions and partly from a tendency to view past experiences with fond nostalgia and present experiences with a more critical eye. Few of the Chinese citizens in my study spoke consistently about preferring life in China or life abroad, and I suspect that those few who did seem to always express consistent views only seemed consistent to me because I had not spent enough time with them in enough different contexts to see when they had less consistent views. Most were ambivalent to some extent, although the amount of ambivalence varied from individual to individual.

Staying Abroad

Some Chinese citizens in my study who were determined to apply for permanent residency rights in a developed country did so because they thought they would be much happier there than in China.

Some told me even before studying abroad that they would prefer to eventually live in a developed country on a permanent basis. They hoped that studying abroad would enable them to acquire the skills, credentials, and cultural capital that would enable them to establish middle-class careers in a developed country, which would enable them to apply for permanent residency rights or legal citizenship in that country, or at least be able to renew work or business visas indefinitely. They were frustrated with many aspects of Chinese life in addition to the dearth of opportunities to earn developed world incomes, and they felt that life in a developed country would be better for themselves and for their future children and perhaps even for their parents (who they dreamed about eventually bringing to a developed country).

A 28-year-old singleton Chinese citizen attending a university and looking for a white-collar job in Ireland told me that she wanted to stay in Ireland permanently after spending four years there because she greatly preferred the natural beauty of her surroundings in Ireland to the surroundings she would have in China. "The moon really is rounder here, because there's less pollution to cover it up," she told me. "If I go back to China, I'll be stuck there forever, and I'll never be able to see such beauty again."

A 28-year-old singleton Chinese citizen who was applying for permanent residency rights in Australia after finishing a technical training program there told me he wanted to stay in Australia because he feared he would not be able to readjust to China after spending seven years abroad. "Most Chinese are afraid of trouble, and won't go to court or the police," he told me. "I'm not like that. I'll fight if I feel I've been wronged. I'm worried about what I would do if I returned to China, now that I'm used to fighting abroad. I always fight; I don't like to let people bully me. In China you can't do that. I don't really want to do business in China because China is so corrupt, and you have to give bribes all the time. I can imagine when the day comes to give bribes, I'll feel angry; why should I give my hard-earned money to them as bribes?"

Many of those who hoped to become permanent residents in a developed country also thought that they would have better opportunities to develop their careers there than they would in China. They told me that their time abroad had made them incompetent at and uncomfortable with "dealing with social connections" (*chuli guanxi*), which was essential for having a successful career in China.[1]

A 26-year-old singleton Chinese citizen who was applying for permanent residency rights in the United States after going there at age 18, completing a college degree, and getting an office job there told me that she would prefer to develop her career in the United States rather than China because she did not want to waste her time dealing with social connections as she would have to do in China. "Sometimes I think that I should just go back to China and get a job there—it would be easier," she told me. "But then I would have to waste time on social connections, so I might as well work hard to spend time on trying to build my career in the US. I'll have to work hard either way. If I return to China, I'll have to work hard all my life at social connections, and I'd hate that."

Transnational students in my study worried that, because they missed out on opportunities to develop the sophisticated social skills their peers developed during the transition from adolescence to adulthood, they would always lag behind their peers in this regard. "Now that I'm used to dealing with simpler relationships [abroad], I can't go back to dealing with the complex relationships in China," a 27-year-old singleton Chinese citizen who received permanent residency rights in New Zealand after he had completed a college degree there told me. "I don't think I can live in China anymore. I don't know how to deal with people anymore. It used to be that if I were sitting in the car in China and others were talking, I would understand what they were talking about without listening very carefully, but now I don't anymore. I have to listen very carefully to figure out what they're talking about. When I go back, I'm still like a child, even though others my age are adults and know all about how to get things done. They're getting better at dealing with social connections every day, while I'm getting worse. Even if I go back and try to catch up, I'll always lag behind them."

Some also thought they would do worse in China than they would abroad because their families lacked powerful connections. A 26-year-old singleton Chinese citizen who was applying for permanent residency rights in Canada after completing a college degree there told me that he had to stay abroad because his family's lack of connections made it unlikely that he would get a job in China that would pay enough to make what his parents invested in his study abroad worthwhile. "My parents spent all their life savings to pay for me to study abroad, and my relatives helped as well," he told me. "If I go back, I may never make enough my whole life to repay that.

I know someone in China who returned to China after study abroad and knows four languages but still couldn't find a job and is now selling vegetables on the street. He could get a job that pays 1,000 yuan per month, but those of us who have studied abroad won't accept work that pays less than what we made abroad. I'd always think, 'I could make this much in a week in Canada as a worker, so why is my salary so low even as a manager in China?' And I may not even get to become a manager in China, because a foreign diploma is better than a Chinese diploma only if you have connections [with powerful people], and I don't. Everyone in my family is just a regular worker. So there's no future for me in China."

Others applied for permanent residency rights or citizenship in a developed country not because they preferred life in that country to life in China but because they had boyfriends, girlfriends, spouses, or children who did. A 29-year-old singleton Chinese citizen who went to Japan to attend college and ended up marrying a Japanese man and then applying for permanent residency rights in Japan based on her status as his wife told me, "When I was working as a waitress and some Japanese customers looked down at me, I used to regret coming to Japan. After I met my husband, though, I felt better about Japan, and I no longer regret coming. Some Chinese people think I married him just because I want to stay in Japan. They call me a traitor for marrying a Japanese man, but they don't understand at all—it was just the opposite. I married him because I really like him, and he makes me happy. I never wanted to stay in Japan until I met him. I want to return to China, but my husband doesn't like living there, so we have to stay in Japan. There are many things I can't get used to in Japan, and I'm giving up a lot by staying here, but it's worth it because of him."

Permanent Residency Rights as Capabilities That Need Not Always Be Used

Wanting permanent residency rights in a developed country did not necessarily mean that a Chinese citizen wanted to live in that country on a permanent basis. Many transnational Chinese students told me that they would prefer to return to China and wanted permanent residency rights only as an escape route (*hou lu*) they could use if they changed their mind and wanted to go abroad again. A 28-year-old singleton Chinese citizen with a degree from an Irish university who was working as an accountant while he applied for permanent residency rights in

Ireland told me, "If Ireland lets me get permanent residency rights here, I'll stay here. Otherwise I'll go to Australia or Canada. I want to get the right to go abroad whenever I want, even if I live in China. But I'll only want to stay abroad 10–20 years; I don't want to stay abroad all my life. I'm Chinese, and I should develop in China eventually; why should I stay in someone else's country forever?"

Most of the Chinese citizens in my study who wanted permanent residency rights or legal citizenship in a developed country did not express strong feelings about wanting to stay in that particular country as opposed to other developed countries. Even after many years of living in a developed country, they sometimes still referred to it as "abroad" (*waiguo*) rather than by the name of the country itself, and they referred to non-Chinese citizens of that country as "foreigners" (*waiguoren*, or, more colloquially, *laowai*), even though it was really they, the Chinese citizens, who were the foreigners in that country. Although that particular country was the only one besides China that they knew well, they assumed that the social and cultural citizenship they had acquired there could be easily transferred to other developed countries and that permanent residency rights or legal citizenship in one developed country would also make it easy for them to get visas, permanent residency rights, or citizenship in other developed countries. A 26-year-old singleton Chinese citizen who had graduated from college in New Zealand and had obtained permanent residency rights there as she worked at an office job told me, "I'm glad I have permanent residency rights now, but I still want to go to graduate school so I can get a better job. It doesn't matter to me where I go next, as long as I have a job that fits me. I could go to Australia, Ireland, Britain, the US, Canada, or China—it doesn't matter. I just want a good job."

Some viewed permanent residency rights as something they should acquire abroad just to make their sojourn seem worthwhile. A 28-year-old singleton Chinese citizen attending a university in Australia told me that he disliked living in Australia but would still probably apply for permanent residency rights there if he met the qualifications. "I feel worse and worse about Australia," he told me. "It's not interesting, and in some ways it's even less developed than China. Staying abroad forever is not interesting. I'm hoping the policy changes by the time I apply for permanent residency rights, so that I'll have an excuse to not apply and not waste time and money. I don't want permanent residency rights, but with some things, even if you don't want them, you have to try to get them. It's a matter of face."

Among the 256 transnational students who answered open-ended questions on my 2008–2010 surveys, 9 percent indicated that they had lived for at least 6 months in each of two or more countries besides China. Some of them hoped from the start to use one country with laxer visa standards and fewer opportunities for gaining permanent residency rights (such as Japan or Ireland) as a stepping-stone to go to another country that had stricter visa standards and more opportunities to gain permanent residency rights (such as the United States, Australia, or Canada). Chinese citizens who did not have enough social and cultural citizenship in the developed world to get a visa to enter the United States, Australia, or Canada sometimes managed to do so after spending several years in another country earning more money, getting a college degree, improving their foreign-language proficiency, marrying a citizen of a developed country, or just demonstrating that they were unlikely to overstay a visa in a developed country. One 18-year-old singleton Chinese citizen, for instance, scored too low on the Chinese college entrance exam to get into a four-year university in China that he and his parents considered prestigious enough to be worth attending, and therefore he wanted to attend college abroad. He preferred the United States, Canada, or Australia because those countries had prestigious colleges and were likely to allow college graduates to get permanent residency rights. However, he was told by his study-abroad broker that, given his limited English proficiency, it would be hard for him to get a visa to enter those countries and that it would be easier for him to get a visa to enter Singapore. His broker knew of a school in Singapore that would be likely to admit him to a two-year program that it ran jointly with an Australian university. If he entered that program, it would be much easier for him to get a visa to enter Australia. Students who got good grades in the Singaporean program could transfer to the Australian university to complete their bachelor's degrees. Most Chinese citizens accepted by that Australian university had been able to get student visas to enter Australia. That would in turn make it easier for him to get into a graduate program at the Australian university, which would in turn make it easier for him to get permanent residency rights in Australia. So he applied for the program in Singapore and got in. He left China at age 19 to attend that program in Singapore for two years, before moving to Australia at age 21 to complete his bachelor's degree. He then began a master's degree program in Australia. After completing his master's degree, he applied for and received permanent residency rights and got an office job in Australia, where he is now applying for legal citizenship.

Others who had not initially intended to move from one developed country to another ended up doing so after discovering that they were unable to accomplish their goals in the first developed country they entered. One Chinese citizen, for instance, left China at age 21, after finishing a three-year adult education college program, to work in a factory in Japan; he hoped to earn enough money to attend a four-year college there. He was so unhappy in Japan, however, that he decided to attend college in Ireland instead. He went to Ireland at age 23 to attend an ESOL school and then a four-year college. He graduated from that college at age 28. After that, he went to Australia to get a master's degree because Australia was more likely to offer permanent residency rights to Chinese citizens than Ireland was. At age 30, he finished his master's degree and applied for and received permanent residency rights in Australia. He returned to China, where he found a job at a transnational corporation. The last time I talked to him, when he was 31, he was in China and still trying to decide whether he wanted to move back to Australia to live for another four years so that he could become a legal citizen of Australia, or stay in China and eventually lose his Australian permanent residency rights by failing to return to Australia. He was torn over his decision. "I don't know if I still want to go through so much trouble," he told me. "I think I'll be happy living the rest of my life in China. I don't want to keep floating from one country to another for too many more years. I want to marry and have a child and stay long enough with my company to get promoted. But then again, Australian citizenship will give me more opportunities, and it's like I walked all the way here, and now I'm here, at the door, and all I have to do is open it, so why not?"

"Changing Passports"

Few of the transnational students in my study ended up applying for legal citizenship in a developed country, and even fewer ended up getting it. Most of them have not yet lived long enough in a developed country to qualify for legal citizenship. Even those who could qualify often did not want it. They could become social and cultural citizens of the developed world even without becoming legal citizens of a developed country. Permanent residency rights usually granted most of the same legal rights that legal citizenship did (besides the right to vote, which most of them did not greatly desire anyway). Those who had obtained permanent residency rights in a developed country therefore found it hard to justify spending the additional time and money it would take to become legal citizens of that country. They were also reluctant to give up their Chinese citizenship. China and most developed countries usually did not allow their citizens to hold dual legal citizenships, so those who gained legal citizenship in a developed country would lose their legal Chinese citizenship. They were concerned about the additional hassle and expense they would experience if, as naturalized legal citizens of developed countries, they had to get visas to reenter China or documents allowing them permanent residency rights in China every time they wanted to spend time in China. They worried about the possibility of being denied visas to reenter China if tensions arose between China and the developed countries in which they had become naturalized legal citizens. Many also thought that the loss of Chinese citizenship would be painful, because it would go against their sense of filial nationalism. "I don't want to change my citizenship; I want to have green card but not be a US citizen," a 24-year-old singleton Chinese citizen attending a university in the United States told me. "If I stop being a Chinese citizen, I'll feel pressure in my heart," he said. "I'm a Chinese person. I don't want to be American person. And I want to go back to China when I'm old, but China doesn't allow its citizens to become Chinese citizens again after giving up Chinese citizenship to take foreign citizenship."

Some who were hoping to replace their legal Chinese citizenship with legal citizenship in a developed country worried that political conflicts could someday make it difficult or impossible for legal citizens of the country in which they were naturalized to get visas or transportation to return to China. A 23-year-old singleton Chinese citizen who was attending a university in the United States and who hoped to eventually marry and bear a child there and send the child back to China for at least a few years told me that she wanted permanent residency rights but not legal citizenship in the United States. "What if the US went to war with China, and US citizens couldn't return to China?" she asked. "My child and parents would be in China, but I would be abroad. That would be too scary."

Even those who were hoping to get or had received legal citizenship in a developed country tried to downplay unpatriotic implications of their decision by calling the process one of "changing passports" (*huan huzhao*) instead of "changing citizenship." Ironically, some of them considered legal citizenship in a developed country preferable to permanent residency rights there because legal citizenship would give them more freedom to live in China or in other countries rather than in the country that granted them legal citizenship. Six years after she left China to attend a university in Australia, a 24-year-old office worker who was applying for permanent residency rights in Australia told me that she intended to stay in Australia only as long as it would take to become an Australian citizen; she would then return to China. "I miss China and don't really like living in Australia," she told me. "I just want to return as an Australian citizen so that I won't have to keep coming back to Australia like I'd have to as an Australian permanent resident. Once I'm an Australian citizen, it will also be easy for me to live in the US or Canada if I want to. But I'll return to China sooner or later."

Although Chinese citizens in my study were most concerned about being trapped in China by their lack of developed world citizenship, those who stayed abroad for a long time were also wary of becoming trapped in a developed country. They feared losing the opportunities, social networks, social competencies, and ability to reach the life-course milestones necessary for a respectable Chinese adulthood that would enable them to live happily in China.

"I'm very unhappy abroad," a 29-year-old singleton Chinese citizen told me 10 years after she left China to attend college and then work at an office job in New Zealand. "I'll need to go back to China soon, because I'll be trapped here if I don't. I want to go back while I'm still young enough to marry and find a good job. If I go back after I'm too old to marry and get a job, everyone will laugh at me."

The risks of staying abroad too long were illustrated by the experiences of Wang Jiansheng, a 35-year-old who had left a college instructor job in China at the age of 21 to study English in Australia, where he became a cook and eventually the owner of a small fast-food business. Wang Jiansheng told me he was unhappy about being divorced, childless, and still not a white-collar professional at age 35. He told me that, despite his hard-won Australian social, cultural, and legal citizenship, he often felt "more miserable than the rural migrants in Chinese cities, because at least they could speak the same language as the people around them." When I asked him if he would make the same decision to go abroad if he could do it over again, he replied, "No, I would have stayed in China. I had a good job and my life would have been quite good. I experienced too much bitterness here.

When Chinese people ask me whether they should go abroad, I tell them not to do it. It's good to visit other countries, but you shouldn't spend half your life in one country and the other half in another. I spent most of my youth eating bitterness. For my first five years in Australia, I kept trying to improve my situation. I wanted to return to my country, but couldn't, because it would make me and my family lose face. I needed to get money before going back. After three months in Australia, I had no money left. I stayed at home, eating instant noodles, staying under the covers trying not to move, because moving would use up more energy and cause me to be hungry again. I went to someone from my hometown and asked to borrow 50 dollars so I could eat, and promised to repay him as soon as I got a job with more hours. After five years, though, when my situation was finally stable enough to let me return to my country, I was no longer used to it. I could no longer cross the street. There were so many cars and motorcycles. The air was dirty, and I couldn't get used to it. I couldn't sleep at night, because there were too many people talking. While abroad, I kept thinking of the snacks from street vendors in China, and how delicious they were, but when I went back to China, I saw that the snacks were covered with exhaust fumes from cars and motorcycles on the street, and dishes were washed in dirty water, so I didn't dare eat them."[2]

Wang Jiansheng was seen by other recent arrivals from China as a model of the flexible citizenship they strove for, but even he was pained by the citizenship trade-offs he had to make. As Don Nonini and Aihwa Ong observed, "Chinese transnationalists seek to elude the localizations imposed on them by nation-state regimes by, above all, moving between national spaces, playing off one nation-state regime against another, seeking tactical advantage—knowing that it is easier to become a citizen here than there, that there are more legal and political rights in country X than in country Y, and so on."[3] This strategy could potentially open up a brave new world of opportunities unavailable to those who just had Chinese citizenship. But the transnational Chinese youth I knew paid a high price for their pursuit of flexible citizenship.

Although Wang Jiansheng had won the developed world citizenship that younger transnational Chinese students aspired to, he thought that the freedoms he gained were not worth the sacrifices he had made for them. By the time transnational migrants like Wang Jiansheng realized this, however, they were too deeply invested in and transformed by their engagement with the developed world to want to return to their old lives in China, even when in retrospect they saw that they had been happier in China than abroad. They made their leap of faith in the global neoliberal system hoping to get the best of all worlds, but they ended up floating between the margins of China and the developed world.

Although transnational students in my study hoped to attain some aspects of developed world citizenship by studying abroad, most were not willing to take measures that could close off the possibility of returning to live as permanent residents of China. They told me that they wanted to return to China for a variety of reasons, including patriotism, a belief that they would be able to get more prestigious jobs in China than they could get abroad, a belief that they would have greater purchasing power in China than abroad, even if their income in China might be lower, a preference for lifestyles in China over lifestyles abroad, and a desire to be close to their friends, relatives, and especially parents. Yet many found the freedoms associated with their social, cultural, and legal Chinese citizenship slipping away as they prolonged their quest for developed world citizenship.

Still, many transnational Chinese students in my study believed that their generation's gambles were more likely than previous generations' gambles to pay off. After all, their generation has the advantages of more concentrated family resources, more ambition, better education, better communication technologies, and stronger linkages between China and the developed world. It remains to be seen whether such advantages will be enough to turn their transnational neoliberal dreams into reality.

The Ones They Left Behind

Legal and financial obstacles along with tight work and school schedules prevented transnational students in my study from making frequent visits to their families in China. It was even more difficult for parents to secure visas to visit their children abroad and for families to come up with enough money to pay for the travel and living expenses of visiting parents from China, most of whom did not have enough language skills or any legal right to work while visiting their children in a developed country. Many parents did not want to leave their rich social and familial networks in China, learn a new language and culture, and develop new social networks at their advanced age. Transnational migration thus entailed long separations between parents and children, most of whom were singletons who assumed that they would eventually have primary responsibility for providing their aging parents with companionship and nursing care. Awareness of this responsibility made transnational Chinese students reluctant to spend the rest of their lives outside China.

Some who wanted to live in a developed country for the rest of their lives hoped to eventually sponsor their parents' immigration to that country as well. But legal citizenship in a developed country was required for sponsoring parents for permanent residency rights in that country. They worried that the process of becoming a legal citizen and then sponsoring a parent for permanent residency rights would take so long that their parents would be dead or too frail to travel by the time it was complete. The parents of the 252 transnational students who indicated their parents' ages on my 1999 surveys were born between 1930 and 1965; by 2010 (when most of their children had not even started applying for permanent residency rights in developed countries), they were between the ages of 45 and 80, with an average age of 55 for mothers and an average age of 56 for fathers.

Shen Shaoling, a Chinese citizen who left China at age 25 to attend an ESOL school while working as an elder care aide in Ireland, told me that she felt sorry for her clients—elderly disabled Irish women who lived alone, yearning for their grown children who seldom came home to visit. Seeing their helplessness made her feel guilty about leaving her own parents and grandparents in China. She told me that she wanted to eventually return to China to take care of her parents in their old age and to retire herself. "When people are old, they long for the things of their childhood," she said. "I don't want to still be speaking someone else's language when I'm old and can't move. I'll want to be with friends and family and chat and play poker and mahjongg with them."

Her parents encouraged her to stay abroad because it seemed to make her happy and wealthy. She hoped to become a permanent resident of Ireland or another developed country and to have a career and family abroad, but she also hoped to return to China eventually to fulfill her filial responsibilities. "Grandma said to my Ma, 'How can you send your child abroad, when you have only one? You'll regret it someday.'" Shen Shaoling told me about her final visit to her grandmother before she left China. "Grandma took out her own brand new underwear and pajamas to give to me to use in Ireland.

She said, 'I don't know if I'll still be alive the next time you return to China.' I felt so sad. I think about what she said whenever I think about staying in Ireland. Grandma has my Ma and my aunts and uncles to take care of her, but my parents only have me. I'd like to stay in Ireland, but I can't throw my parents away. They can never come to Ireland, so I'll have to return to China. Old people are like children, and they'll need us beside them, just like we needed them when we were children."

A 27-year-old singleton Chinese citizen attending a vocational college in Australia had similar sentiments. "My Ma knows the weather where I'm living better than I do; she checks every day, and when it's cold she calls and tells me to put on warmer clothes," he told me. "She always asks me if I'm eating enough, or if I'm too tired. I used to think that after immigrating to Australia, I'd bring my parents over here. But then I realized, if they come here not knowing the language, not having friends, and staying at home all the time, wouldn't that just be like prison? And I wouldn't be able to spend all day with them either, I'd have my own life to live. So now I think it would be best for them to stay in China. But if they stay in China, then I'll want to go back eventually. I'm their only child. When they're old, they won't be able to stand having me so far away, just talking on the phone, or just seeing me once or twice a year."

Returning to China to See an Ill Parent

Most transnational students in my study assumed that they would have many years before they would have to return to China to provide their aging parents with nursing care and companionship. They had left China while their parents were still healthy and socially active. It was extremely rare for singletons to leave China knowing that their parents were ill or disabled and needed their care. In some cases, parents who really wanted their children to study abroad hid or downplayed illnesses and disabilities so that their children would not feel obligated to stay in China, or they did not let their children who were already studying abroad know that they had developed illnesses or disabilities. In one case, a mother did not even let her son who was attending college in Europe know that his father had cancer, for fear that it would cause him to return to China and lose all the time and money he had put into trying to complete a college degree abroad. Even after his father died, his mother feared that grief and regret would make it hard for him to concentrate on his studies, and she therefore kept the death a secret from him until he had finished his college degree, months after his father died. Regardless of whether they had attained the degrees, savings, and permanent residency rights they had hoped to get, most transnational students in my study ended their sojourns abroad as soon as they learned their parents had become seriously ill or disabled.

I observed one of these sudden departures when I shared a room with Xie Aihong and Li Mei, two 22-year-old singleton Chinese citizens in Ireland.[4] They were best friends who had left China together when they were both 21 years old. They had graduated from the same vocational high school and were taking private classes together in preparation for college equivalency exams when they decided to go to Ireland together. They told me they had been motivated both by a desire to see the world and by their belief that studying abroad could lead to opportunities to attain high-paying work, prestigious developed world college degrees, and permanent residency rights in Ireland or somewhere else. Their parents were businesspeople with enough savings to pay for the startup costs of their study abroad but not enough to pay for their tuition and living expenses once there. During the hours when they were not in English classes required for maintaining their visa status, Li Mei worked as a shop clerk and Xie Aihong worked as a hotel housekeeper. They could speak only enough English to hold simple conversations, but they hoped to improve their English skills and save enough money to pay for college tuition in Ireland.

On the wall of the room I shared with them were many pictures of Chinese and Western movie stars, photos of Xie Aihong, Li Mei, and their friends and family members, and a piece of white printer paper with the following words (*sic*):

    HARD WORK!
    HARD STUDY
    EAZY LIFE
    STOP DREAMING!!!

These words were written in English in large, capitalized block letters, colored in with orange and green fluorescent markers, and followed by a specific date in 2004, written in small Chinese characters in red ink. When I asked them what the sign meant, they explained that they had made this sign two months ago, on the day Liu Yuan, another close friend of theirs, had returned to China just eight months after arriving in Ireland. Hoping to earn enough money for college in a short period of time, Liu Yuan had worked constantly at low-level service jobs, where she had been harassed by her bosses and customers. "Liu Yuan couldn't stand Irish people," Xie Aihong told me. "She got sick, and became very fat, and had to go back to China because she couldn't stand life in Ireland. Right after she left, we wrote that sign to remind ourselves that, while we should work hard and study hard, we should also try to have an easy life, live well, be happy, and enjoy life. We should stop dreaming about attending college and just take life one step at a time. If we only think about working and studying hard all the time, we'll feel very unhappy. It will affect us and change us, like it did Liu Yuan."

Xie Aihong and Li Mei tried to avoid such problems by reminding themselves and each other to relax and enjoy the new experiences they were having in Ireland, but they still found the struggle to learn English while living on tight budgets and working many hours at low-paying, physically exhausting jobs stressful. Prolonged separation from loved ones in China was also painful, especially for Xie Aihong, who was close to her mother. "My Ma told me, 'I thought it would be good to send you abroad, but now that you're gone, I realize that a daughter is her mother's blanket,'" Xie Aihong recalled. "Sometimes I think about staying abroad and trying to get permanent residency rights so I can bring my Ma over. But it's so difficult to do that, and life abroad would be such a difficult, different life for her."

One day when I came back to our room, I saw that Xie Aihong was on her way out of the apartment, with tears streaming down her face. After Xie Aihong had left, I asked Li Mei what had happened. Li Mei told me that Xie Aihong had just received a phone call from her uncle, who had revealed that her mother had been diagnosed with cancer. Xie Aihong had rushed out immediately to buy a plane ticket that would allow her to return to China two days later. Over the next two days, Xie Aihong frantically packed, bid her friends farewell, and even worked her final shift as a hotel maid out of a sense of obligation to her supervisors and co-workers. Xie Aihong also arranged to get a reentry visa so that she would be able to return to Ireland if she changed her mind once she was in China.

Several of Xie Aihong's Chinese co-workers, neighbors, and classmates came to our apartment for dinner the night before Xie Aihong left, to say goodbye to her. They tried to act convivial, and some teased Xie Aihong to try to cheer her up. "What did you think of China the last time you went back for a visit?" asked Xie Aihong's friend Li Ting.

"When I went back, I was glad to be at my Mama's side," replied Xie Aihong.

"When I go back for visits, I feel China is lacking a lot; after a month in China, I can't stand it, and I have to come back to Ireland," said Li Ting.

"I just want to be with my family. My Ma used to yell at me and criticize me, but she didn't do that even once the last time I visited her," said Xie Aihong.

Xie Aihong's other friend, Pan Linlin, smiled teasingly and said, "That's because you were just visiting. If you stay with her for good, she'll probably yell at you again."

Xie Aihong smiled with tears in her eyes and said in English, "I like it."

The last time I spoke with her, Xie Aihong was still living in China with her mother, who was recovering from surgery and chemotherapy. Xie Aihong was in the process of taking over her mother's business. Xie Aihong was not planning to return to Ireland, as her reentry visa had expired, and in any case she did not want to leave her mother again.

Goals Redefined

Most of the Chinese citizens in my study ended up failing to reach at least some of the goals they had started out with or acquired during the process of study abroad. Even some of those who had attained all their goals were still dissatisfied, because attainment of these goals did not make them as fully a part of the developed world as they had imagined it would or because their attainment of developed world citizenship had also entailed the loss of aspects of Chinese social, cultural, or legal citizenship that they used to take for granted. Others had to return to China before they accomplished any of their original goals of getting a university degree, saving enough money from work to start a business in China, or getting permanent residency rights in a developed country. For some, the goal of attaining developed world citizenship that they had started out with no longer seemed as important as their goals for establishing a stable career, marrying, having children, and fulfilling their filial responsibilities to their parents, all of which seemed difficult to do while they lived the floating life abroad. When it seemed that the process of trying to attain developed world citizenship was forcing them to stay abroad longer than they wanted to, they chose to cut their losses by returning to China empty-handed instead of continuing to work at low-wage jobs while attending language classes to maintain a student visa in a developed country. Others wanted to keep trying to accomplish their original goals but had their sojourns abroad cut short when their applications for visa renewals were denied and they were unable to secure visas to enter other developed countries in time and unwilling to illegally overstay their expired visas.

Those who returned to China without having met all or any of their original goals were disappointed with themselves and with the countries in which they studied. But some of them tried to console themselves and save face in front of others by redefining their goals for studying abroad and emphasizing that it had not been a waste of time or money because it had given them opportunities for personal growth and learning.

"At least I got to practice English and see foreign countries," a 25-year-old singleton told me after he returned to China from Britain after spending three years there, attending an ESOL school and working at low-skill jobs. Even though he had failed to save enough money to pay for tuition at a British university, he had earned enough to pay his own ESOL school tuition and living expenses and had used the rest of his savings to visit Ireland, France, Germany, and Spain as a tourist. "I got to know European lifestyles, and I got to open my eyes to different ways of thinking. So it was valuable, and even if it doesn't help me get a job in China, I can say I haven't lived my life in vain."

Some told me that studying abroad helped them redefine their standards for happiness. A few months after she returned to China from Ireland, a 25-year-old singleton talked about how studying in Ireland changed her outlook. She had gone there at age 22, after graduating from college in China, with the hope of eventually saving enough money from work to attend a graduate program in Ireland or another developed country. She returned to China after working for three years at a pub in Ireland while attending an ESOL school, because she felt she was unlikely to be able to save enough money to pay for graduate school tuition in Ireland anytime soon. She got an office job in China that paid about 2,000 yuan (US$294) a month, less than what many of her college classmates who had not studied abroad made, but she told me she had no regrets: "Even though I didn't attend a university in Ireland, I learned a lot there. Now I understand that happiness is more important than money. I used to think money was the most important, but in Ireland when I was working at the pub, I met some Irish people who only cared about happiness and not money. They made the lowest wages all their lives, but they didn't want to advance and were happy as long as they could watch TV and drink with friends at the pub. At first I looked down on them, but then the more I understood them, the more I thought the way they lived was pretty good too. But I had to come back to China to do things that made me happy. The three things I love the most in life are first, eating, second, sleeping, and third, singing [karaoke], and I couldn't do them in Ireland. I was sacrificing everything I loved for money, and I felt that it wasn't worth it anymore, so I came back. I'm making a lot less money now, but I'm happy, and that's the most important."

· Others who found that the college degrees they had completed in developed countries brought them no closer to developed world citizenship than they would have been if they had not studied abroad likewise tried to emphasize the noneconomic benefits that studying abroad provided them. "It feels different now that I plan to stay in China permanently," a 26-year-old singleton Chinese citizen told me a year after he returned to China from Australia, where he had spent seven years attending a college prep academy and then completing a college degree. He had found an office job in China that paid only 3,000 yuan (US$440) per month, which was less than what some of his former high school classmates who had not studied abroad were earning, but he said that he still valued his time abroad for what it taught him about resilience. "I feel like I did when I first went abroad—even if I can't get used to things, I will have to, because this is where I plan to live permanently. I ate a lot of bitterness abroad, and it taught me that I can overcome anything. So now when I'm uncomfortable with something in China, I feel I can overcome that too."

Some emphasized that the money they had made while studying abroad was enough to make them feel that they succeeded, even though it was less than what they had originally hoped to earn. A 26-year-old singleton who had left China at age 22 to work at low-skill jobs while attending Japanese-language classes in Japan had to return to China after four years because she could not save enough money to pay for college tuition in Japan. "What is success?" she asked me rhetorically a few months after she returned to China from Japan. "Some people have a lot of money but are still unhappy. I didn't make a lot of money, but I didn't lose any either. I had nothing when I went there—I was from a family of workers. I earned enough there to support myself. I paid my parents back [for what they spent to send me abroad] and haven't been a burden on them. I had experiences that I will never forget, and I can now speak Japanese. So I feel I succeeded."

"I feel happiest when I eat well and eat till full—that's what I want most in life," a 27-year-old singleton Chinese citizen told me. We were eating a delicious meal at a restaurant that she had bought with the money she saved from working for three years as a waitress in Japan while attending Japanese-language classes between ages 21 and 24. She had originally hoped to use her savings from Japan to pay for tuition at a Japanese university but changed her mind because she missed the friends, family, and lifestyle she had in China. She said she was much happier in China than she had been in Japan. "I used to think I would only be happy if I had a college degree and a good job, but now I think that's less important than being around friends and family and having time to enjoy life," she said. "In Japan I was always hungry, because the food was too expensive, and I didn't have time to cook. Sometimes I didn't even have time to eat. I was lonely and didn't have anyone to talk to and cried whenever I thought of home. What kind of life is that?"

Preferring China over Developed Countries

Some transnational students in my study who eventually returned to China told me that they preferred China over developed countries. As they became more disillusioned with life abroad and appreciative of life in China, many of those who attained at least some of their goals abroad, such as receiving a university degree or saving enough money from work to start a business in China, were confident that they could live as social and cultural citizens of the developed world even if they returned to China.

"I always felt China was my home, not New Zealand," a 24-year-old singleton told me a few months after she returned to China with a college degree from New Zealand, where she had been living since age 20. She said she could have gotten a job and eventually permanent residency rights and then citizenship in New Zealand but decided to return to China instead. "I used to think life in foreign countries would be better, but not anymore. I like eating well, dressing well, buying beautiful clothes, and eating good food, and I think China is the best place for that. Even if I had money abroad, I had no place to spend it, and when I bought something, I was just contributing to New Zealand and not China. I can have everything I had in New Zealand here in China—I just have to work a bit harder for it here. New Zealand had good air, and I'll miss that, but if I buy a house in a rural area in China and buy a car to commute to the city for work, the air will be just as good as it was abroad."

Some Chinese citizens had opportunities to prolong their stay abroad but declined so that they could return to China to start establishing their careers and families as soon as possible. "I could have gone to graduate school or gotten a job abroad and continued to float there, but that would not have been interesting," a 27-year-old singleton Chinese citizen told me a year after she returned to China from Britain, where she had stayed for seven years, attending an ESOL school and then completing a college degree while working as a salesclerk. "I want to marry and have a child soon, and it would have been much harder to find a suitable boyfriend abroad. I would have had to come back sooner or later, and if I came back later, I would have missed opportunities in China and wasted my youth abroad. Why stay and be a salesclerk abroad when I can be white collar in China? Even though I make less now in an office job than I did as a salesclerk in Britain, I'll keep getting raises and promotions, and the Chinese yuan is getting stronger, so maybe someday I'll make more than I would have made even if I had gotten an office job abroad. If I had stayed abroad, maybe at age 40 my friends who never left China would be making more money than me, without having eaten as much bitterness. Then I'd feel the unfairness in my heart."

Some Chinese citizens thought that legal citizenship in China could be more valuable than legal citizenship in a developed country if they wanted to build their careers in China. A few days before he returned to China, a 25-year-old singleton Chinese citizen who had left China at age 19 to earn a college degree in Britain and then earned a master's degree in Australia told me and five of his Chinese housemates, classmates, and friends at his farewell dinner, that he did not want to stay in Australia to try to get Australian permanent residency rights and legal citizenship because he would consider that a waste of his time. He hoped to work for a company in China and then eventually go into business on his own. "It will be harder to own a business in China if I get foreign citizenship," he told me. "Right now the Chinese government is good to foreigners because they're needed, but as soon as they're not needed, things will be harder for them. If the [Chinese] government has a special policy to help businesses, it will not let foreign citizens enjoy it."

Some Chinese citizens were increasingly optimistic that China would soon become a developed country and would perhaps develop even faster than some currently developed countries. "Ireland will not develop as fast as China," a 28-year-old singleton Chinese citizen told me in China two years after he returned to China after spending seven years in Ireland, where he had attended an ESOL school and then completed a college degree before working in an office there for two years. He had quit his job in Ireland to return to China, even though he had a valid Irish work visa that he could have continued to extend. He told me that, although his office job in China paid less than a quarter of what he had been paid for similar work in Ireland, he felt much wealthier than he had felt in Ireland because of China's lower cost of living, and he also believed that his income in China would eventually surpass the income he would have earned in Ireland if he had stayed. "In ten years I'll be making more than my friends who stayed in Ireland," he told me. "All of Europe will not develop as fast as China. Before I went abroad, I thought foreigners would have higher quality than Chinese, but now I know that's not true. People with high-quality talent in China are smarter and work harder than anyone in Ireland. But a Chinese person in Ireland would not have been promoted over Irish people, even if he had ability, so I would have been stuck where I was forever. Even if I had gotten citizenship in Ireland, I would not have stayed."

Other Chinese citizens chose to return to China for permanent residence because they considered the lifestyle they would have in China far preferable to what they would have abroad, regardless of other factors. "I would have to give up a lot regardless of where I stayed," a 27-year-old singleton Chinese citizen told me a few weeks before he returned to China after spending seven years in the United States, where he had completed a graduate degree. "But I would have had to give up more if I stayed abroad. I can never get used to habits and lifestyle[abroad]. I'm different from them. China is my home. I'm more used to it. Talking, lifestyle, and habits are all more comfortable in China."

A 27-year-old singleton Chinese citizen who got an office job that paid about 4,000 yuan (US$588) per month in China after living in Japan from age 20 to 26, attending Japanese-language classes and then completing a college degree, told me that it did not matter to her that her salary in China was much lower than what she had expected to get after completing college in Japan, because what really mattered to her was her relationship with her fiancé, who had stayed in China while she studied in Japan and whom she was glad to be reunited with after six years of separation. "What good is it, really, to become a manager and make a lot of money?" she asked me. "How much happiness does that bring you? Won't it bring more happiness if you have a good husband who cares for you, who will be concerned for you if you're ill?"

Conclusion

Part of the power of the global neoliberal system derives from its claim that anyone who acquires the discipline, skills, and affluence of the developed world can become a social and cultural citizen of that world. The legal citizenship embodied by citizenship documents issued by a developed country's government is useful but not necessary or sufficient for becoming part of the developed world. Those who were unable or unwilling to trade their Chinese passports for passports issued by a developed country could still become social and cultural citizens of the developed world by attaining globally recognized credentials and choosing careers that would enable them to earn incomes comparable to those earned by professionals in developed countries. Regardless of whether they lived in China or abroad and whether they had Chinese passports or passports from developed countries, those who had such careers could command respect worldwide, cross national borders with ease, and enjoy a high standard of living.

As pioneers of a brave new world of transnational linkages, transnational Chinese students have helped to reshape China and the developed countries in the image of their own transnational imaginations. Although their motivations, experiences, and trajectories were shaped by the global neoliberal system, they were also the ones who helped to build it, by promoting the standards of the developed world as the proper standards that everyone in the world should strive to attain. As they discovered, created, and embodied new possibilities for flexible developed world citizenship, they also opened up new transnational roads for other Chinese citizens to follow, often literally, as when their friends and family members followed them abroad. Even as they made deeply personal migration decisions, transnational students help to create and disseminate global neoliberal discourses about the superiority of the developed world.

They paid a high price for the new freedoms and capabilities they acquired through study abroad. They tried to get the best of all worlds but often ended up also getting the worst of all worlds. Full developed world citizenship proved elusive, even as the quest for it eroded the Chinese citizenship they had taken for granted. As teenagers and young adults, they had more resources for pursuing upward mobility than at any other point of their lives. In addition to the health, attractiveness, and physical strength characteristic of youth worldwide, they also had special resources associated with the demographic structure that China's one-child policy created for them. That policy enabled their generation to enjoy an unprecedented concentration of family resources and lack of dependents during the critical first two to three decades of their lives. So far, the singleton generation has many working-age parents, aunts, and uncles eager to invest in them, no siblings to compete with for family resources, and, in most cases, no children of their own and no responsibility for taking care of elderly dependents. They are expected to use these resources to launch themselves, their families, and their country into the developed world before dependency costs come due in the form of marriage, childbearing, parental aging, and a social security crisis. Their hope, and the hope of Chinese leaders who created and continue to enforce birth planning policies, is that once they and their country are part of the developed world, they will be able to handle these dependency costs.

In some ways, the gamble that transnational Chinese students made has paid off by giving them increased freedom, mobility, and opportunities. Yet even as they became more mobile, they were still constrained, not only by the developed world's exclusionary policies but also by their own transformed subjectivities and by family responsibilities that were postponed but are now looming. As children and teenagers in China, they imagined that they would be in paradise once they had developed world freedoms. Once abroad, however, they quickly got used to such freedoms but were alarmed at new constraints on their access to Chinese friends, family, lifestyles, and life-course milestones, all of which they had taken for granted while in China. At the same time, though, they became so used to developed world freedoms that they could no longer imagine being happy without them. Because getting a visa to go abroad was so difficult, many feared that they would never be able to go abroad again if they returned to China for permanent residence before they were full citizens of the developed world.

So while their counterparts in China spent their youth earning college degrees, getting married, having children, establishing careers, and fulfilling their filial obligation to provide nursing care and companionship to their aging parents and grandparents, many transnational students in my study postponed these life-course milestones as they devoted their youth to low-skilled work and an expensive but low-prestige education in developed countries. Avoidance of life-course milestones had appealed to them when they were younger, but as they grew older, they increasingly realized that failure to attain such milestones could make them failures in their own eyes and in the eyes of others they cared about, even if they did attain the flexible developed world citizenship they desired. They thought that they could not return to China empty-handed, without a degree from a developed country university, developed world permanent residency rights, or enough savings to justify the sacrifices they had made. As they grew older, though, they saw their opportunities for upward mobility receding and their family responsibilities looming. Even as they gained new opportunities associated with flexible developed world citizenship, many of them lost opportunities to build the careers and families necessary for respectable adult identities in China. They were torn between different, contradictory goals. They wanted to save enough money to start businesses in China, but time and money spent on education abroad could prevent them from accumulating savings. They wanted university degrees from developed countries, but time and money spent on work could prevent them from earning such degrees. They wanted prestigious, high-paying careers in China or abroad, but time spent on study abroad delayed the start of their careers and made them vulnerable to age discrimination. They wanted permanent residency rights in a developed country but had difficulty staying in any one developed country long enough to qualify for those rights. Trying to attain all their goals could ironically cause them to end up with no savings, no university degree, no developed country permanent residency rights, and no good career in China or abroad.

Transnational students in my study were both the products and the producers of the global neoliberalism system. They were both consumers and promoters of discourses that portrayed developed world citizenship as the paradise toward which everyone should be striving. Policies of neoliberalization, including those that promote low fertility, high educational attainment, and transnational migration, are based on faith that the global neoliberal system will reward people and countries for investing in it. Chinese citizens took leaps of faith whenever they sacrificed time, money, and happiness to get themselves or their children into the best schools and jobs possible. Transnational migration was just an especially high-risk extension of these leaps of faith, which were also taken to a lesser extent by their peers who did not go abroad. The birth planning policies that produced the singleton generation were likewise gambles based on the hope that shifting dependency costs from the present to the future would enable Chinese citizens, and China as a whole, to join the developed world by the time the parents were old enough to become dependent on their singleton children.

The experiences of Chinese citizens in my study resonates both with studies that have shown how transnational migration can serve as a powerful strategy for the pursuit of developed world citizenship[5] and those that have highlighted the discrimination, disappointment, and displacement that transnational migrants faced in the process.[6] Although study abroad gave Chinese citizens in my study more freedoms and capabilities than they would have had if they had stayed in China, it also made them disappointed and frustrated when they found that the process of transnational migration also entailed the loss of many freedoms and capabilities they had taken for granted before they left China.

Chinese citizens went abroad hoping to become part of the developed world by acquiring legal citizenship or permanent residency rights in developed countries, earning enough money from work to start lucrative businesses in China, and earning college degrees in developed countries that could help them win prestigious, high-paying jobs in China or in developed countries. Even though the availability of diverse opportunities to become part of the global elite was one of the main advantages of studying abroad, most transnational students in my study told me that they felt torn between these possible paths.

In the process of making decisions about when and whether to return to China, many transnational Chinese students ended up redefining the vision of the developed world paradise that had motivated them to study abroad in the first place. Some came to redefine China as the paradise they had lost while studying abroad. Others learned that the developed countries in which they had studied were indeed more likely than China to allow them to expand their freedoms and capabilities, even if they were not as perfect as the paradise they had imagined. Most, however, found that their study-abroad experience made them more ambivalent about both China and developed countries than they had been before. They became more critical and more fond of China and the developed countries in which they had studied and deeply ambivalent about where they wanted to spend more of their lives. As a 30-year-old singleton Chinese citizen who had returned to China after spending 10 years attending a university and then working at an office job in Japan that she lost because of the global financial crisis of 2008–2010 told me, "Sometimes I think I'll want to go abroad again, to Japan or another country, if I see an opportunity. But sometimes I think that's foolish. There are many things I'm not used to in China anymore, having been abroad for 10 years. But there are also many things I'll never be used to abroad. I'm not used to anywhere anymore."

REFERENCE MATTER

Notes

1. With a population of 2,624,000, Dalian ranked as the fourteenth most populous city in China in 1999, according to China's National Bureau of Statistics (Guojia Tongji Ju, Chengshi Shehui Jingji Diaocha Zongdui 2000: 38).

2. Throughout this book, I present US dollar equivalents of non-US currencies based on the exchange rate prevalent at the time of the transaction or earnings or (when discussing transactions that occurred on more than one date) on the average of the exchange rates (rounded to the nearest whole number) that prevailed during the period over which the transactions occurred (1997–2010, unless otherwise noted).

3. Respondents to questions on my 1999 Dalian survey about their parents' incomes from all sources (including pensions, gifts, subsidies, investments, and business profits) indicated that their 1,855 mothers made an average of 781 yuan (US$94)per month and that their 1,815 fathers made an average of 1,044 yuan (US$126) per month. According to information collected by the Dalian City Archives Office from employers in the Dalian area (which included poorer rural districts as well as urban districts like the ones where I did my research), the average monthly salary in that area was 787 yuan (US$95) in 1999 (Dalian Shi Shi Zhi Bangongshi 2001: 223). According to a representative sample survey conducted in Chinese cities by China's National Bureau of Statistics in 1999, the average annual per capita income was 5,889 yuan (US$711) for all respondents, 12,148 yuan (US$1,467) for the wealthiest 10 percent of respondents, and 2,647 yuan (US$320) for the poorest 10 percent of respondents (Guojia Tongji Ju 2001: 313, 315, 319). According to a 1999 representative sample survey conducted by the Dalian City government, the annual per capita income in urban Dalian was 6,274 yuan (US$758) for all respondents, 11,767 yuan (US$1,421) for the wealthiest 10 percent of respondents, and 3,018 yuan (US$364) for the poorest 10 percent

of respondents. Those respondents included the members of 500 households (the total number of people in these households was not published) (Dalian Shi Shi Zhi Bangongshi 2001: 271). The incomes that respondents to my 1999 survey reported were somewhat higher than the average incomes reported by these government-run surveys because urban citizens had higher incomes than rural citizens (who were included in the national and Dalian-wide surveys), because people in their 40s (e.g., parents of respondents to my 1999 survey) were at the height of their careers and thus had higher incomes than older retired people and younger people just beginning their careers, and because incomes reported to me were likely to include more gifts, subsidies, investments, and business profits, some of which were not legal, than incomes reported to Chinese government survey administrators.

4. Among those who responded to my consumption questions in 1999, 11 percent of the 686 from the junior high school, 13 percent of the 749 from the vocational high school, and 16 percent of the 758 from the college prep high school indicated that their families had computers; and 25 percent of the 686 from the junior high school, 16 percent of the 749 from the vocational high school, and 14 percent of the 760 from the college prep high school indicated that their families had no cell or landline phone.

5. Among the 1,365 who responded to my 2008–2010 survey, 29 percent of the 552 college prep high school alumni, 11 percent of the 485 junior high school alumni, and 18 percent of the 328 vocational high school alumni indicated that they had taken classes outside China at some point; 41 percent of the college prep high school alumni, 21 percent of the junior high school alumni, and 30 percent of the vocational high school alumni indicated that they had left China at some point.

6. Xiang and Wei 2009: 515.

7. Among 2008–2010 respondents who had never been abroad for any reason, 62 percent of the 221 from the college prep high school, 64 percent of the 287 from the junior high school, and 69 percent of the 121 from the vocational high school indicated that they wanted to live abroad someday.

8. Anderson 1991.

9. Ong 1997: 172.

10. Appadurai 1996: 54.

11. Parts of this paragraph are reprinted from Fong (2004a) with permission from the American Anthropological Association.

12. Bai 2008; T.-M. Chen and Barnett 2001.

13. Guo 1998; W. Ye 2001.

14. Altbach and Teichler 2001; McNamee and Faulkner 2001; Scott 2000; Szelényi and Rhoads 2007; Thorstensson 2001.

15. Anderson 1991: 54.

16. See Said's critique of Orientalism (Said 1978).

17. Sassen 2002: 24.

18. I focus on Chinese citizens' perspectives in this book, but my arguments about how the developed world is perceived by those excluded from it may

also resonate with the perspectives of citizens of other developing countries in similar positions of exclusion from the developed world.

19. A comparative study that focused on differences between different developed countries would require a much more specific focus on one particular activity and would need to use methods such as those used by Joseph Tobin and his collaborators in their classic comparisons of beliefs and practices about preschool education held by preschool teachers in Japan, China, and the United States (Tobin et al. 1991, 2009). Such a study is beyond the scope of this book.

20. Although the term *tiantang* (paradise) can have religious connotations in Chinese, as it does in English, it was usually used to refer to a secular vision of happiness by the Chinese citizens in my study, most of whom had no strong religious beliefs.

21. L. Zhang 2010: 2.

22. Anagnost 1997b; Fong 2007a; Kipnis 2006, 2007; Murphy 2006; Woronov 2002, 2007, 2008; H. Yan 2003.

23. Archibugi and Held 1995; Bauböck 1994; Bauder 2008; Bloemraad et al. 2008; Cossman 2007; del Castillo 2002; Ehrkamp and Leitner 2003; Flores and Benmayor 1997; Fong and Murphy 2006; J. Friedman 1994; Levitt and Schiller 2004; Lowe 1996; Mishra 1981; Mitchell 2001; Reed-Danahay and Brettell 2008; Reimers 2010; Sassen 2009; Schiller 2005; Smart and Smart 2001; Soysal 1995.

24. Holston 2008: 5–9, 197–202; Ong 1996, 1999, 2003; Safran 1991.

25. Chu 2004, 2010; Pieke and Mallee 1999; Pieke et al. 2004.

26. Kipnis 2008b.

27. Ong 1999, 2003, 2006.

28. Sen 1992, 1993, 1999.

29. I use the terms *freedoms* and *capabilities* in the sense that Amartya Sen used them, to refer to aspects of one's social environment and oneself that give one the ability to be and do what one wants to be and do (Sen 1992, 1993, 1999).

30. Bulmer and Rees 1996; King and Waldron 1988; Lister 2005; Marshall 1950; Tilly 1998.

31. Bauböck 1994; Dwyer 2003; Falk 1994; Fox 2005; He 2004; Heater 2002; Hutchings and Dannreuther 1999; Michael and Smith 2002.

32. Ong 1997: 138.

33. Castle 2008; Ewing 2008; Holston 2008; Levinson 2010; Maira 2009; Ong 1996, 2003.

34. Fong 2004b.

35. Keyfitz 1990: 729; Sauvy 1952; Tabah 1991: 357; Wolf-Phillips 1987.

36. Wallerstein's discussion of "core regions" and "peripheral regions" can be found in Wallerstein (1974a, 1974b, 1979). I used the terms "First World, "Third World," "core regions," "peripheral regions," and "capitalist world system," in Fong (2004b).

37. I first used "wealthier societies" in Fong (2004a).

38. Hansen 2000: 252.

39. For my use of these terms, see Fong (2004b).

40. Comaroff and Comaroff 1993; Coronil 1996, 1997; di Leonardo 1998; Escobar 1995, 1997, 2007, 2010; Ferguson 1999; Herzfeld 1987; Lowe and Lloyd 1997; Lutz and Collins 1993; Rahnema and Bawtree 1997; Sachs 1992; Scheper-Hughes 1997; Verdery 1991.

41. Ahlburg et al. 1996; Cain 1982; Grant and Behrman 2010; Hess 1988; Jones and Visaria 1997; Maddison 1983; Sardon 2006; Schneider 2005.

42. Harvey 2005: 2.

43. Applbaum 2000; Ong 2006; Rofel 2007.

44. Wallerstein 1974a, 1974b, 1975, 1976, 1979, 1981, 1991.

45. Comaroff and Comaroff 2001; Ferguson and Gupta 2002; Fong 2007a; Greenhalgh 2008; Greenhalgh and Winckler 2005; Harvey 2005; E. Ho 2004; Kipnis 2007; Lutz 2006; Ong 2006; Rofel 2007; H. Yan 2003.

46. Foner 2002; Waldinger and Fitzgerald 2004.

47. Chalfin 2008; Ebron 1999; Frohlick 2007; Lutz and Fernandez 2010; Masquelier 2002; Smart and Smart 2008.

48. Chu 2007; Gamburd 2000, 2008; Hertz 1998; K. Ho 2009; Lemon 1998; Miyazaki 2003; Miyazaki and Riles 2005; Xiang 2006; H. Yan 2008.

49. Bernal 2005; Boellstorf 2008; Constable 2003; Johnson 2007; Rotenberg 2005; Smith 2006.

50. Abu-Lughod 2005; Appadurai 1996, 2002; Armbrust 2000; Ebron 1999; Fong 2007c; Ginsburg et al. 2002; Hannerz 2004; Hasty 2005; Mankekar 1999; Murphy and Fong 2008; Pedelty 1995; Pederson 2003; Rofel 2007; Shryock 2004; Sun 2002; M. M.-H. Yang 1997; Zhan 2006.

51. Ellison 2009; Ferguson and Gupta 2002; Fong 2007a; Greenhalgh and Winckler 2005; Matza 2009; H. Yan 2008.

52. d'Alisera 2004; J. Friedman 1994; Glick-Schiller et al. 1992, 1995; Leonard 2007; Levitt 2001; Linger 2001, 2005; Ong 1999, 2003, 2006; Ong and Nonini 1997; Raj 2003; Small 1997; Tsuda 2003.

53. Of the 2,273 students who completed my survey, 738 were from the junior high school, 753 were from the vocational high school, and 782 were from the college prep high school. For more about this survey and the participant observation I conducted between 1997 and 2002, see my earlier book (Fong 2004b).

54. My survey was completed in Dalian by 94 percent of the 785 students enrolled in eighth or ninth grade at a socioeconomically and academically average junior high school in fall 1999, 91 percent of the 858 students enrolled at a non-keypoint college prep high school in spring or fall 1999, and 88 percent of the 859 students enrolled in the homerooms I surveyed at a vocational high school in fall 1999.

55. The only year I did not visit China between 2002 and 2010 was 2003, when I had to cancel my trip because of restrictions my university placed on travel to China as a result of the SARS epidemic.

56. Quotes from my notes that were written during or right after an interview or participant observation are in quotation marks; comments that are not

direct quotes are paraphrased. Most interviews and participant observations were conducted in Chinese, with occasional English words for emphasis (or when such words were deemed untranslatable); some interviews, however, were conducted in English (with research participants highly proficient in English). I have translated all Chinese quotes into English and have kept most English quotes verbatim except when grammatical corrections are necessary for clarity.

57. I received responses to my 2008–2010 survey from 71 percent of the 782 college prep high school alumni, 66 percent of the 738 junior high school alumni, and 44 percent of the 753 vocational high school alumni. The junior high school and college prep high school had balanced student gender ratios, but the vocational high school students were 70 percent female because their school specialized in female-dominated majors, such as business, public relations, and tourism. The underrepresentation of respondents recruited from the vocational high school among my 2008–2010 survey respondents made the proportion of females slightly lower in my 2008–2010 sample than in my 1999 sample. Respondents were 58 percent female in 1999 (N = 2,273) and 53 percent female in 2008–2010 (N = 1,365). I did not find any larger demographic differences between the 2008–2010 respondents and those who responded in 1999 but not in 2008–2010. Vocational high school alumni were probably underrepresented in my 2008–2010 survey because they had spent less time together and were less enthusiastic about school and thus were less likely to keep in touch with classmates or want to come to the class reunions I organized. Enthusiasm about school was probably also low among the 42 percent of the 387 junior high school respondents who graduated from vocational high schools after my survey and the additional 5 percent of them who did not graduate from any high schools. But respondents recruited from the junior high school were still almost as likely to respond to my survey as those recruited from the college prep high school, probably because their lower enthusiasm for school was balanced by an even greater fondness for their junior high school classmates than that felt by high school alumni for each other. Alumni of all school types told me that they felt closer to their junior high school classmates than they felt toward their vocational or college prep high school classmates, because they had spent more years in the same classroom with their junior high school classmates, were more likely to live close to their junior high school classmates, and felt that junior high school friendships were less marred by competitiveness, insincerity, or instrumentality than high school friendships because they and their friends were more innocent at younger ages.

58. The 782 respondents I first surveyed at the junior high school in 1999 spent grades 7–9 in the same homeroom in which they started seventh grade. Some of them shared a homeroom in both primary school and junior high school and thus spent nine years together. The 753 respondents I first surveyed at the vocational high school in 1999 spent two years together taking classes; then, most spent their third year in internships at various businesses, although 3 percent spent their third year taking additional classes to prepare for the

adult education college exam. Among the 782 respondents I first surveyed at the college prep high school in 1999, those who began tenth grade in 1996 or 1997 chose majors before tenth grade (so all but the few who changed majors midway stayed together all three years of high school); those who began tenth grade in 1998 and 1999, however, started out in one homeroom but in many cases switched to another homeroom as they chose majors at the beginning of eleventh grade.

59. Homerooms from which fewer than four alumni showed up in 2009 were invited to reunions that included other homerooms consisting of students from the same school in 2010.

60. Most respondents who completed the 2008 survey also completed similar surveys in 2009 and 2010, but some respondents were found for the first time in 2009 or 2010 and therefore did not complete earlier surveys, whereas others completed earlier surveys but have not yet had time to complete the 2010 survey. Findings reported in this book are based on data from the most recent survey (2010) when they are available, on data from the 2009 survey if the respondent has not yet completed my 2010 survey, and on data from the 2008 survey if the respondent has not completed my 2009 or 2010 surveys.

61. The only questions that 1999 respondents had to answer to be counted as 2008–2010 respondents were those about their contact information, whether they had ever left China, and, if so, whether they had worked and/or attended classes while abroad. Although 1,365 of them answered these questions, only 1,125 of them completed brief phone or instant messenger surveys, and only 990 of them completed most or all of the full surveys via e-mail or in person. All the basic questions about study abroad, marriage, and childbearing that were asked in 2008 and during brief phone or instant messenger surveys were also asked in the full survey in later years, but some of the more specific questions on the full 2010 survey were not asked in earlier years or during the phone and instant messenger surveys.

62. It is possible that those who wanted to study abroad were overrepresented even in my survey sample because their interest in the United States and English made them more likely to respond to my surveys, in 1999 as well as in 2008–2010, than those who did not. On the other hand, those who studied abroad (and those who moved to other cities in China to pursue better education and work opportunities) may have been underrepresented in my survey sample because they were less likely than those who stayed in China to have come to the class reunions I organized in Dalian, keep in touch with their classmates, or be reachable at the Dalian phone number they gave me in 1999. Those with better jobs in Dalian may have been more likely to come to class reunions and keep in touch with former classmates because they wanted to show off their success to their former classmates; on the other hand, those who were unemployed, underemployed, or lacking career responsibilities outside work hours may have been more likely to come to class reunions and want to keep in touch with classmates because they had more free time and greater need for the help that more successful former classmates

could provide. Parents of respondents from the vocational high school (who were somewhat underrepresented among the 2008–2010 respondents) and the junior high school were of somewhat lower socioeconomic status than parents of respondents from the college prep high school: In 1999, 47 percent of the 672 junior high school respondents, 45 percent of the 723 vocational high school respondents, and 33 percent of the 568 college prep high school respondents had no parents with middle-class jobs (here defined as those whose parents had worked as managers, professionals, or owners of businesses with more than two employees). But those I was not able to reach at the same phone number they gave me in 1999 were also likely to have parents of higher socioeconomic status, because they had moved to pursue better opportunities in other cities, upgraded to a better home in Dalian, sold their home and moved to a less expensive home to make a profit, or disconnected their landline phones because everyone in their family had a cell phone. All urban citizen families had been assigned housing, which they either purchased without a mortgage or continued to live in while paying little for rent and utilities, so it was unlikely for anyone to be forced to move as a result of poverty.

63. Clarke 2010; Ebron 1999; Gewertz and Errington 1991; Graburn 1983; A. Louie 2000, 2004; Lutz and Collins 1993; Sørensen 2003.

64. I avoid identifying which quotes and examples came from respondents to my survey (who might be more recognizable to each other because they were all in grades 8–12 at the same schools in 1999) and which came from the hundreds of other Chinese citizens in my study, in China and abroad. I mention the singleton status of singletons I quote if I know they had no siblings at the time they talked to me, but I refrain from specifying anyone's nonsingleton status because there were so few young nonsingletons in my study that they would be identifiable if I mentioned that they had siblings. I describe jobs they held only in general terms (e.g., office worker instead of accountant, clerk, administrative assistant, engineer, analyst, computer technician, or marketing manager) and only identify the Chinese city that someone came from when it is relevant to the quote or example I present. Otherwise, I describe all the Chinese citizens in my study as having grown up in China (even though the majority of them actually grew up in Dalian, and most of the remainder grew up in other northeastern Chinese cities), because naming their hometowns would make the minority from outside Dalian (especially the few who were not from northeastern Chinese cities) too easily identifiable by those who know they were in my study. I only mention countries in which many Chinese citizens in my study have lived, such as Australia, Britain, Canada, Ireland, Japan, New Zealand, Singapore, and the United States, but not the particular cities or towns they lived in. I avoid discussing the experiences of transnational students who studied in countries in which no other Chinese citizens in my study have studied or who had unusual experiences that no one else in my study had, because they would be too easy for readers who know their community to identify. I have honored the wishes of those who have requested that I not

write about particular things they said and did or that I not write about them at all. Quotes and examples I present are from conversations and activities I observed during participant observation or interviews I conducted in person or by telephone or Internet voice communications between 1997 and 2010, but I only mention the specific year an interview took place or the specific year that an event occurred when an understanding of the historical context of that year is necessary for understanding that quote or example or when currency exchange rates of a particular year are necessary for understanding the value of a particular sum of money described.

65. I use pseudonyms only when they are necessary for avoiding confusion (e.g., when explaining interactions between several different people of the same gender who would be referred to by the same pronoun). More often, quotes and examples are described only in terms of age, gender, student status, singleton status, location, and how long ago someone left China (e.g., "a 24-year-old singleton Chinese citizen who left China two years earlier to attend a university in Australia"), but are not tied to a pseudonym that can link together quotes and actions by the same person that are presented in different parts of this book. This strategy is modeled after a similar strategy used by Sherry Ortner for preserving the anonymity of classmates she interviewed for a study of the socioeconomic trajectories of her high school graduating class (Ortner 2003).

66. Burawoy 2000; Clifford 1997; Constable 2003; d'Alisera 2004; Gupta and Ferguson 1997; Leonard 2007; Marcus 1995; Pieke et al. 2004.

67. Some respondents' parents had more than one child because they gave birth to all their children before the one-child policy began in 1979, because they had multiple births from one pregnancy, because they violated the one-child policy, or because they qualified for exemptions. A couple was allowed to have two children if both husband and wife were singletons or one was an ethnic minority or if their first child was disabled. Students were also likely to have siblings if they were born in rural areas where officials started enforcing the one-child policy later or more laxly than urban Dalian officials did.

68. The population of China in 2000 was 1,265,830,000 (Guojia Tongji Ju 2001: 93).

69. Fong and Murphy 2006; Goldman and Perry 2002; Keane 2001.

70. Murphy 2002, 2004, 2008; Pun 1999, 2005; Solinger 1999; H. Yan 2008; H. Zhang 2007; L. Zhang 2001.

71. Brown 2004; S. Friedman 2010; Newendorp 2008; Pina-Cabral 2002; Smart and Smart 2008; Stafford 1995, 2000.

72. I classify all 2008–2010 survey respondents who answered yes to the question "Have you ever attended any kind of class outside China (including language classes, university classes, technical classes, etc.)?" (*Nin youmeiyou zai waiguo shang guo renhe ke [baokuo yuyan ke, daxue ke, jishu ke, deng deng]?*) as Chinese transnational students.

73. Percentages of those who left China for different reasons add up to 32 percent rather than the 31 percent who went abroad because of missing data

for questions about work outside China and because of the rounding of each percentage to the nearest whole number.

74. Benton and Pieke 1998; S. Chang 2006; Chee 2005; Chu 2004, 2006, 2010; Constable 2003, 2004; Douw et al. 1999; Guest 2003; A. Louie 2004; Newendorp 2008; Nyiri and Saveliev 2002; Ong 1996, 1999, 2006; Ong and Nonini 1997; Pieke and Mallee 1999; Pieke et al. 2004; L. Siu 2005; Tan 2007; Tan et al. 2007; J. L. Watson 1975, 1977a, 1977b.

75. Jiaotong University Institute of Higher Education 2010; Quacquarelli Symonds 2010; The Times Higher Education 2010.

76. Kuhn 2008; W. Ye 2001.

77. Chee 2005; Nonini 1999; Tan 2007; Tan et al. 2007; J. L. Watson 1975, 1977a.

78. Ong and Nonini 1997; Pieke and Mallee 1999; Pieke et al. 2004; L. Siu 2005; Zweig et al. 1995.

79. Benton and Pieke 1998; S. Chang 2006; Chee 2005; Chu 2004, 2006, 2010; Constable 2003, 2004; Douw et al. 1999; Guest 2003; A. Louie 2004; V. Louie 2004; Newendorp 2008; Nyiri and Saveliev 2002; Ong 1996, 1999, 2006; Ong and Nonini 1997; Pieke and Mallee 1999; Pieke et al. 2004; L. Siu 2005; Tan 2007; Tan et al. 2007; J. L. Watson 1975, 1977a, 1977b.

CHAPTER 2

Parts of this chapter have been reprinted from my article, "Filial Nationalism Among Chinese Teenagers with Global Identities" (Fong 2004a), with permission from the American Anthropological Association.

1. Fong 2004a.

2. Greenhalgh 2008; Greenhalgh and Winckler 2005; Rofel 2007; L. Zhang and Ong 2008.

3. Fabian 1983.

4. Wolff 1994.

5. Wallerstein 1974a, 1974b, 1975, 1976, 1979, 1981, 1991.

6. M. M.-H. Yang 1997.

7. For Russia, see Lemon (1998, 2000). For Nicaragua, see Lancaster (1992).

8. Francis and Ryan 1998; S. J. Park and Abelmann 2004.

9. Applbaum 2000: 275.

10. Rofel 1999, 2007.

11. A. Louie 2004.

12. Percentages add up to more than 100% because some respondents were in more than one country for 6 or more months.

13. Dalian's existence as a port city began when Russia started building Dalian's harbor in 1899, after acquiring the area that became Dalian as part of the Liaodong Leasehold in 1898. This area was transferred to Japan in 1905 as a result of the Russo-Japanese War of 1904. The Soviet Union took the area from Japan in 1945 and returned it to China in 1954. Almost all the Japanese and Russian colonizers left by the time China regained official control over Dalian.

14. Among the 22 respondents to the visa and foreign country residence questions on my 2008–2010 survey who had held work visas and had lived in Japan for at least 6 months, 77 percent had also taken classes abroad.

15. Schein 1999, 2000, 2001.   16. Schein 1999: 366–67.

17. Pigg 1996: 163.   18. Fong 2004a.

19. Fong and Murphy 2006; Ong 1997.

20. Parts of the story of Ye Yumei and Hu Jun are reprinted from "Chinese Youth Between the Margins of China and the First World" (Fong 2006), with permission from Routledge.

21. Jiang 2002.

22. Boyer 2003: 258.

23. Goodman 1995; A. Louie 2004: 650; H. Siu 1993: 32.

24. Ong 1999: 25.   25. Y. Zheng 1999: 95.

26. Liu Dehua 1997.   27. H. Siu 1993: 34–35.

28. A. Louie 2000, 2004.

29. Gellner 1991; Shryock 1995, 1997; Tapper 1983.

30. For ideas of Chinese race, see Dikkoter (1992). For ideas of Chinese culturalism, see J. Townsend (1992: 114).

31. Anderson 1991.

32. H. Chang 1987; Harrison 2000; Huang 1972; Lan and Fong 1999; Schwartz 1993; Tang 1996.

33. Duara 1997; W. Ye 2001.

34. Don Nonini argued that the Chinese state is not fully neoliberal or post-socialist but rather an "oligarchic corporate state and Party whose legitimacy is being challenged by disenfranchised classes, but is still in control through its efforts at modernization" (Nonini 2008: 1). Andrew Kipnis has cautioned against perceptions of China as purely neoliberal and post-socialist in light of the continuing power of the Chinese Communist Party and such cultural norms as *guanxi* (social connections) (Kipnis 2007, 2008a, 2008b). These factors, which are keeping China from becoming completely neoliberal, are part of what transnational Chinese students in my study hope to escape by becoming part of the developed world, whether in China or abroad. They have been raised to desire greater participation in the global neoliberal systems for themselves and for China, partly as a result of fertility limitation policies implemented by a Chinese Communist state that is resisting full neoliberalization even as it intensifies its engagement with the global neoliberal system.

35. J. Chang 1991; Gao 1987; Yue and Wakeman 1985.

36. Zito 1997: 185–200.   37. Wolf 1968; Wolf et al. 1975.

38. Sawyer 2002: 162–64.   39. Handler 1988.

40. Among 2,171 respondents to the ethnicity question on my 1999 survey, 98 percent identified as Han.

41. Munasinghe 2002; Verdery 1983, 1995.

42. A. P. Cohen 1996: 805.

43. S. Hall 1997: 21.

44. Dominguez 2000: 365.

45. Fukuyama 1992; Mandelbaum 2002.

46. Huntington 1998.   47. Barber 1995; T. Friedman 2000.
48. Herzfeld 1997: 172.   49. A. P. Cohen 1996: 805.

CHAPTER 3

1. I categorize as middle class all the survey respondents who indicated in 1999 that their parents had at some point worked as managers (including cadres and supervisors), professionals (including all other kinds of civil servants and white-collar workers), or owners of businesses with more than two employees by 1999, as well as all other Chinese citizens in my study whose parents had ever held these kinds of jobs. Among the 1,963 who responded to the question about parents' work histories on my 1999 survey, 42 percent had no middle-class parents, 30 percent had one middle-class parent, and 28 percent had two middle-class parents. The proportions were similar among the 1,139 of them who also responded to my 2008–2010 survey, among whom 40 percent had no middle-class parents, 31 percent had one middle-class parent, and 30 percent had two middle-class parents. I define upper class as those who worked as high officials in the city, province, or national government and/or owned businesses that brought them incomes comparable to those of the middle class in developed countries. Because most Chinese citizens in my study were recruited from nonelite schools or from the social networks of those schools' students, almost none of the Chinese citizens in my study fitted this definition of upper class. Of the 4,349 parents whose educational attainment was reported to me by their children in 1999, only one had a doctorate. Of the 3,670 parents whose incomes were reported to me by their children in 1999, only two earned more than 15,000 yuan (US$1,829) per month in 1999.

2. Jing 2000; Y. Yan 1997.   3. Bourdieu 1977: 78.
4. Fong 2004b.   5. Anagnost 1997a: 124.
6. A grandparent whose grandchild answered no to a 1999 survey question about whether that grandparent could read (*shizi*) was defined as illiterate in my study.

7. Dalian Shi Shi Zhi Bangongshi 2002: 262, 265, 271.

8. Xiang and Wei 2009.

9. Lan and Fong 1999; Mao 1971; Zhou 1980.

10. Fong 2004b; Lin 1999; J. Liu et al. 2000; Peng 2000; Pepper 1990; Seeberg 1993; X. Wang 2003.

11. Dressler 1982, 1990; Dressler and Bindon 2000; Dressler et al. 1987a, 1987b.

12. Smart 1999a, 1999b.

13. Pieke et al. 2004: 86; Xiang and Wei 2009.

14. Pieke et al. 2004: 87.

15. Pieke et al. 2004: 62.

16. Percentages add up to more than 100 because some respondents went abroad several times and used a different visa each time.

17. Pieke et al. 2004.

18. The average annual per capita income in the People's Republic of China in 1999 was 5,889 yuan (US$711) for all respondents, 12,148 yuan (US$1,467) for the wealthiest 10 percent of respondents, and 2,647 yuan (US$320) for the poorest 10 percent of respondents, according to a representative sample survey of 36,000 people conducted in Chinese cities by China's National Bureau of Statistics in 1999 (Guojia Tongji Ju 2001: 313, 315, 319). According to another 1999 representative sample survey conducted by the Dalian city government, the annual per capita income in urban Dalian was 6,274 yuan (US$758) for all respondents, 11,767 yuan (US$1,421) for the wealthiest 10 percent of respondents, and 3,018 yuan (US$364) for the poorest 10 percent of respondents (survey respondents included the members of 500 households; the total number of people in these households was not published) (Dalian Shi Shi Zhi Bangongshi 2001: 271). According to a representative sample survey conducted in Chinese cities by China's National Bureau of Statistics in 2009, the average annual per capita income was 17,175 yuan (US$2,518) for urban citizens and 5,153 yuan (US$756) for rural citizens. According to another representative sample survey conducted by the Dalian city government in 2009, the average annual per capita income in urban Dalian was 17,500.48 yuan (US$2,566), whereas the average annual income of the wealthiest 20 percent of Dalian respondents was 38,825 yuan (US$5,693) and the average annual income of the poorest 20 percent of respondents was 7,716 yuan (US$1,131) (Dalian Shi Shi Zhi Bangongshi 2010). Data collected by the Dalian City Archives Office from Dalian area employers reported that the average annual salary in Dalian was 33,063 yuan (US$4,848) in 2009 (Dalian Shi Shi Zhi Bangongshi 2010: 31). Among the 570 respondents who have never gone abroad and responded to the income question on my 2008–2010 survey, 40 percent earned less than 20,000 yuan (US$2,809) the year before they completed the survey.

19. L. Zhang 2001, 2002, 2006, 2010; L. Zhang and Ong 2008.

20. Chu 2004, 2010.

21. Pieke et al. 2004: 195.

22. For studies of nonstudent transnational migrants from China, see Benton and Pieke (1998), S. Chang (2006), Chee (2005), Chu (2004, 2006, 2010), Constable (2003, 2004), Douw et al. (1999), Guest (2003), A. Louie (2004), Newendorp (2008), Nyiri and Saveliev (2002), Ong (1996, 1999, 2006), Ong and Nonini (1997), Pieke and Mallee (1999), Pieke et al. (2004), L. Siu (2005), Tan (2007), Tan et al. (2007), and J. L. Watson (1975, 1977a, 1977b). For studies of nonstudent transnational migrants from other countries, see Constable (1997), d'Alisera (2004), Gamburd (2000, 2008), George (2005), Leonard (2007), Parrenas (2001, 2005, 2008), Small 1997; and Smart and Smart (2005).

23. Fong 2004b.

24. "Eating spring rice" refers to employment in jobs that provide high incomes to the young, with the guarantee of unemployment once their youth fades (e.g., bar hostesses, sex workers, models, athletes, and hotel security guards) (Hyde 2007; Wang Zheng 2000; Zhang Zhen 2001).

25. For studies of parachute children from wealthier families, see S. Chang (2006) and Ong (2006).

26. Only those who completed the 2010 version of the survey were asked about the year they first went abroad.

27. Benton and Pieke 1998; Chee 2005; Chu 2004, 2006, 2010; Constable 1997, 2003, 2004; Gamburd 2000, 2008; George 2005; Guest 2003; A. Louie 2004; Newendorp 2008; Nyiri and Saveliev 2002; Ong 1996, 1999, 2006; Ong and Nonini 1997; Parrenas 2001, 2005, 2008; Pieke and Mallee 1999; Pieke et al. 2004; L. Siu 2005; Small 1997; Tan 2007; Tan et al. 2007; J. L. Watson 1975, 1977a, 1977b; Xiang 2006.

28. Brownell and Wasserstrom 2002; E. Y. Zhang 2001; T. Zheng 2009.

29. Constable 2003, 2004; S. Friedman 2010; Kelsky 2001; Newendorp 2008.

30. Of those who never left China, 71 percent of the 56 men and 66 percent of the 72 women from the vocational high school, 58 percent of the 147 men and 70 percent of the 140 women from the junior high school, and 55 percent of the 91 men and 68 percent of the 120 women from the college prep high school indicated that they wanted to live abroad someday.

31. Among those who responded to my 2008–2010 survey, 46 percent of the 265 men and 36 percent of the 287 women from the college prep high school, 22 percent of the 240 men and 20 percent of the 245 women from the junior high school, and 29 percent of the 132 men and 30 percent of the 196 women from the vocational high school had been abroad. These figures include 32 percent of the 265 men and 27 percent of the 287 women from the college prep high school, 12 percent of the 240 men and 10 percent of the 245 women from the junior high school, and 21 percent of the 132 men and 16 percent of the 196 women from the vocational high school who had studied abroad.

32. Fong 2002; Shi 2009; H. Zhang 2007.

33. George 2005; Kelsky 2001; Levitt 2001.

34. Such a willingness to gamble with important decisions has also been found in many other communities in China (Hertz 1998) and elsewhere (Malaby 2003; Miyazaki 2003).

35. Abelmann 2003; Abu-Lughod 1993; N. W. Townsend 2002.

36. Benton and Pieke 1998; Chee 2005; Chu 2004, 2010; A. Louie 2004; Pieke and Mallee 1999; Pieke et al. 2004; L. Siu 2005; Tan 2007; Tan et al. 2007.

37. According to responses on the most recent wave of the survey that the 939 respondents to my 2008–2010 survey who had never been abroad completed, 66 percent of the 128 who had two middle-class parents in 1999 indicated that they wanted to live abroad, 68 percent of the 161 who had one middle-class parent in 1999 indicated that they wanted to live abroad, and 63 percent of the 242 who had no middle-class parents in 1999 indicated that they wanted to live abroad.

38. Mabogunje 1970; Massey et al. 1998; Zlotnik 1992.

39. Cornelius et al. 1994; DiPrete and Nonnemaker 1997; Espenshade 1995.

CHAPTER 4

Parts of this chapter have been reprinted from "Chinese Youth Between the Margins of China and the First World" (Fong 2006), with permission from Routledge.

1. Pieke et al. 2004: 195. See also Chu (2004, 2010).
2. Gaetano and Jacka 2004; Solinger 1999; L. Zhang 2001.
3. Shen 1983.
4. Shen 1983: 7.
5. Jin 1996.
6. For the 1999 US poverty level, see Office of the Federal Register (1999: 13,428–30). For the 2009 data, see US Department of Health and Human Services (2010).
7. The 1999 data were collected by China's National Bureau of Statistics from Chinese work units (Guojia Tongji Ju 2001: 135). The 2008 data are from Zhonghua Renmin Gongheguo Guojia Tongjiju (2009).
8. In 2002, for instance, almost 20 percent of Australian college students were not citizens of Australia, and the tuition they paid funded 10 percent of the Australian university system's expenses (Marginson 2002). Australia offered all its own citizens college tuition waivers and even small stipends for their living expenses during college, but it charged noncitizens more than 10,000 Australian dollars in tuition per year.
9. The term *study abroad trash* (*liuxue laji*) was sometimes used in the media and popular discourse to describe youth who returned from study abroad not only empty-handed but also damaged by the psychological problems, bad habits, and sometimes immoral and illegal experiences they had had abroad (Chen Tieyuan 2004).
10. Hayhoe 1996; Lin 1993, 2005; Pepper 1996; Tsang 2000.
11. Parts of Yang Guolin's story and my analysis of it are reprinted from "The Other Side of the Healthy Immigrant Paradox: Chinese Students in Ireland and Britain Who Return to China Due to Personal and Familial Health Crises" (Fong 2008), with permission from Springer.
12. Such children of immigrants did encounter significant obstacles (Yoshikawa 2011), although some scholars have argued that they were more resilient than their native counterparts of the same socioeconomic status as a result of the immigrant optimism and other resources that immigrants had more of than natives (Ogbu 1987; Suárez-Orozco and Suárez-Orozco 1995, 2001).
13. Parts of Liu Yang's story and my analysis of it are reprinted from "The Other Side of the Healthy Immigrant Paradox: Chinese Students in Ireland and Britain Who Return to China Due to Personal and Familial Health Crises" (Fong 2008), with permission from Springer.
14. Constable 2003, 2004.
15. William Jankowiak and his collaborators found that the Chinese women in their study ranked Caucasian male and female models as more attractive than East Asian male and female models, whereas Chinese men did not differentially rank East Asian and Caucasian female models, although they did rank Caucasian men as being more attractive than East Asian models (Jankowiak et al. 2008).
16. DeWoskin 2005.
17. The term *mixed blood* (*hunxue*) usually refers to someone with one white parent and one Chinese parent, although it also occasionally refers more broadly to anyone with parents from more than one ethnicity, nationality, or race. This

term applies solely to people whose parents are of different ethnicities, nationalities, or races; it is not used to describe someone who has two parents of the same ethnicity, nationality, and race but who also has other ancestors of different ethnicities, nationalities, and races. When I asked why people of mixed blood were unusually intelligent and beautiful, some Chinese people I knew said it was logical that children would inherit the best of both of their races/nationalities/ethnicities, whereas other Chinese people I knew could not come up with reasons but cited mixed-blood people they knew or saw in the media as examples of the unusual beauty and intelligence of mixed-blood people.

18. Che 1999.

19. Constable 2003, 2004; Kelsky 2001.

20. Brownell and Wasserstrom 2002; K. Louie 2002; Stafford 2000; Zhong 1994.

21. M. L. Cohen 1976, 1990; Greenhalgh 1985a, 1985b; Sangren 1984; J. L. Watson and Ebrey 1986; R. S. Watson and Ebrey 1991.

22. Davis 1989; Davis and Harrell 1993; Evans 2007; Fong 2002, 2004b.

23. Although China's fertility limitation policies may eventually cause the country to suffer an increase in the proportion of its population who are elderly to proportions similar to those currently found in developed countries, China's population aging is currently not as severe as that found in developed countries, because the state-mandated fertility transition started at least several decades later than the fertility transitions that occurred in most developed countries. As of 2004, only 8 percent of the Chinese population was age 65 or older, compared with 12 percent of the Irish population, 12 percent of the US population, 13 percent of the Australian population, and 16 percent of the British population (Central Intelligence Agency 2005). Yet the proportion of the Chinese population age 14 and younger is similar to the proportions found in developed world countries: As of 2004, 21 percent of the Chinese population was age 14 or younger, compared with 21 percent of the Irish population, 21 percent of the US population, 20 percent of the Australian population, and 18 percent of the British population. These demographic patterns suggest that China's health care and elder care burdens will eventually resemble those currently experienced by developed world countries and may become even worse if the disproportionate emigration of its healthiest, most productive, and most resourceful individuals and families at the peak of their life cycles and familial cycles increases significantly.

24. Constable 1997; Gamburd 2000, 2008; Parrenas 2001, 2005, 2008; Sassen 1991, 1996, 2000; Sassen and Appiah 2000; Xiang 2006.

25. M. J. Ho 2003, 2004; Nachman 1993; J. L. Watson 1975.

CHAPTER 5

1. Sen 1999.

2. Sen 1999.

3. Sen 1999: 75.

4. Berlin 1969: 170.

5. Sen 1999: 87.

6. Ebert et al. 2009; Gilbert 2006; Gilbert and Gill 2000; Gilbert et al. 2004a, 2004b; Lane 2001; Myers 1995, 2000; Morewedge et al. 2009; Wilson and Gilbert 2003; Wilson et al. 2003.

7. Sen 1992: xi.

8. Sen 1992.

9. Constable 1997, 2003, 2004; d'Alisera 2004; Gamburd 2000, 2008; Leonard 2007; Levitt 2001; Linger 2001, 2005; Parrenas 2001, 2005, 2008; Raj 2003; Tsuda 2003; White 1988; Xiang 2006; L. Zhang 2001.

10. Jin 1996.

11. Murphy 2002, 2004, 2008; Pun 1999, 2005; Solinger 1999; H. Yan 2008; H. Zhang 2007; L. Zhang 2001.

12. Anagnost 1997a, 1997b; Fong 2007a, 2007b; Jing 2000; Xiang and Wei 2009; J. Yang 2007.

13. Stafford 2000; Turner 1967; van Gennep 1960.

14. For studies of rural Chinese migrant experiences, see Murphy (2002, 2004, 2008), Pun (1999, 2005), Solinger (1999), H. Yan (2008), H. Zhang 2007, and L. Zhang (2001). For Sierra Leone children's experiences, see Bledsoe (1990). For a study of experiences of backpacker tourists from developed countries, see Graburn (1983) and Sørensen (2003).

15. Ong 1999.

16. Fong 2007c; Kleinman and Watson 2005; Zhan 2006.

17. The deaths triggered investigations by the Chinese government and other governments and researchers around the world. They discovered that many Chinese milk manufacturers were selling milk products that contained dangerously high levels of melamine. It was assumed that some milk processors put this contaminant in milk that had been diluted with water to make the diluted milk appear to have a higher protein content than it actually had (Kuehn 2009; Xin and Stone 2008).

18. Fong 2007c.

19. Broomfield 2003; Hirshberg 1993.

20. See Aird (1990), Aleinikoff (1991), Bhabha (1996), Cheng (1986), Min (1994), Mosher (1993), Thurston (1992), and T.-X. Ye (1998).

21. Fong 2007c; Nyiri et al. 2010; Zhao 2002.

22. Like most other Chinese cities, Dalian has long allowed couples consisting of two singletons to have two children without penalty (Gu et al. 2007). In 2010 the Chinese government announced that, beginning in 2011, couples in which at least one spouse is a singleton will be allowed to have up to two children without penalty in Heilongjiang, Jilin, Zhejiang, Jiangsu, and Liaoning (where most of the Chinese citizens in my study are from) (Garnaut 2010).

23. Although I tried to survey all those who responded to my 1999 survey each of the three years between 2008 and 2010, some responded to the survey only once or twice instead of all three times. For the purpose of this analysis, I counted only the responses they gave on the most recent survey they completed.

24. Chinese citizens can openly participate in Christian organizations affiliated with the Protestant Three-Self Patriotic Movement (*sanzi jiaohui*), the Protestant China Christian Council (*zhongguo jidujiao xiehui*), and the Chinese Patriotic Catholic Association (*zhongguo tianzhujiao aiguo hui*), all of which

are approved and regulated by the Chinese government. Other Christian organizations that lack official approval--such as the "house churches" (*jiating jiaohui*) and the Chinese Catholic Church, which maintains its loyalty to the pope--are illegal, and their leaders are sometimes arrested.

25. Among the 2,171 who responded to the ethnicity question on my 1999 survey, 98 percent were Han, the ethnic group that composed 92 percent of the Chinese population in 2000.

26. "June 4" is shorthand for the Chinese government's repression of demonstrations at Tiananmen Square in Beijing on June 4, 1989.

27. Fong 2007c; Nyiri et al. 2010.

28. For American approaches to "good work," see Gardner (2007) and Gardner et al. (2001).

29. Y. Yan 2010.

30. For a discussion of generalized exchange, see Sahlins (1972). For discussions about generalized exchange in China, see Gold et al. (2002), Kipnis (1997), Smart (1993), Y. Yan (1996), and M. M.-H. Yang (1994).

31. Gold et al. 2002; Kipnis 1997; Smart 1993; Y. Yan 1996, 2010; M. M.-H. Yang 1994.

32. Sahlins 1972.

33. Y. Yan 1996, 2003; M. M.-H. Yang 1994.

34. Gold et al. 2002; Kipnis 1997; Smart 1993; Y. Yan 1996; M. M.-H. Yang 1994.

35. Anagnost 1997b: 119.

36. Blum 2007: 4.

37. Ong 1999.

38. Ebert et al. 2009; Gilbert 2006; Gilbert and Gill 2000; Gilbert et al. 2004a, 2004b; Lane 2001; Morewedge et al. 2009; Myers 1995, 2000; Wilson and Gilbert 2003; Wilson et al. 2003.

39. Sen 1999.

CHAPTER 6

1. Gold et al. 2002; Hoffman 2008; Kipnis 1997; Smart 1993; Y. Yan 1996; M. M.-H. Yang 1994.

2. Wang Jiansheng's comments and my analysis of them are reprinted from "Chinese Youth Between the Margins of China and the First World" (Fong 2006), with permission from Routledge.

3. Nonini and Ong 1997: 23.

4. Parts of Xie Aihong's story and my analysis of it are reprinted from "The Other Side of the Healthy Immigrant Paradox: Chinese Students in Ireland and Britain Who Return to China Due to Personal and Familial Health Crises" (Fong 2008) with permission from Springer.

5. Constable 2003; X. Liu 1997; Ong 1997, 1999; K. Park 1999.

6. Abelmann and Lie 1997; Constable 1997; K. Hall 2002; Malkki 1995; Ong 2003; Ong and Nonini 1997; K. Park 1997; Parrenas 2001, 2005, 2008; Portes and Rumbaut 1996; White 1988.

Works Cited

Abelmann, Nancy. 2003. *The Melodrama of Mobility: Women, Class, and Talk in Contemporary South Korea*. Honolulu: University of Hawaii Press.

Abelmann, Nancy, and John Lie. 1997. *Blue Dreams: Korean Americans and the Los Angeles Riots*. Cambridge, MA: Harvard University Press.

Abu-Lughod, Lila. 1993. *Writing Women's Worlds: Bedouin Stories*. Berkeley: University of California Press.

———. 2005. *Dramas of Nationhood: The Politics of Television in Egypt*. Chicago: University of Chicago Press.

Ahlburg, Dennis A., Allen C. Kelley, and Karen Oppenheim Mason, eds. 1996. *The Impact of Population Growth on Well-Being in Developing Countries*. New York: Springer.

Aird, John S. 1990. *Slaughter of the Innocents: Coercive Birth Control in China*. Washington, DC: AEI Press.

Aleinikoff, T. Alexander. 1991. The Meaning of "Persecution" in United States Asylum Law. *International Journal of Refugee Law* 3(1): 5–29.

Altbach, Philip G., and Ulrich Teichler. 2001. Internationalization and Exchanges in a Globalized University. *Journal of Studies in International Education* 5(1): 5–25.

Anagnost, Ann. 1997a. Children and National Transcendence in China. In *Constructing China: The Interaction of Culture and Economics*, edited by K. G. Lieberthal, S.-F. Lin, and E. P. Young, 195–222. Ann Arbor: Center for Chinese Studies, University of Michigan.

———. 1997b. *National Past-Times: Narrative, Representation, and Power in Modern China*. Durham, NC: Duke University Press.

Anderson, Benedict. 1991. *Imagined Communities: Reflections on the Origin and Spread of Nationalism*, rev. ed. London: Verso.

Appadurai, Arjun. 1996. *Modernity at Large: Cultural Dimensions of Globalization*. Minneapolis: University of Minnesota Press.

———. 2002. *Globalization*. Durham, NC: Duke University Press.

Applbaum, Kalman. 2000. Crossing Borders: Globalization as Myth and Charter in American Transnational Consumer Marketing. *American Ethnologist* 27(2): 257–82.

Archibugi, Daniel, and David Held, eds. 1995. *Cosmopolitan Democracy: An Agenda for a New World Order*. Cambridge, MA: Polity.

Armbrust, Walter. 2000. *Mass Mediations: New Approaches to Popular Culture in the Middle East and Beyond*. Berkeley: University of California Press.

Bai, Limin. 2008. The Influence of Chinese Perceptions of Modernisation on the Value of Education: A Case Study of Chinese Students in New Zealand. *China: An International Journal* 6(2): 208–36.

Barber, Benjamin R. 1995. *Jihad Versus McWorld*. New York: Times Books.

Bauböck, Rainer. 1994. *Transnational Citizenship: Membership and Rights in International Migration*. Aldershot, UK: Edward Elgar.

Bauder, Harald. 2008. Citizenship as Capital: The Distinction of Migrant Labor. *Alternatives* 33: 315–33.

Benton, Gregor, and Frank N. Pieke, eds. 1998. *The Chinese in Europe*. Basingstoke, UK: Macmillan.

Berlin, Isaiah. 1969. *Four Essays on Liberty*. Oxford, UK: Clarendon Press.

Bernal, Victoria. 2005. Eritrea On-Line: Diaspora, Cyberspace, and the Public Sphere. *American Ethnologist* 32(4): 660–75.

Bhabha, Jacqueline. 1996. Embodied Rights: Gender Persecution, State Sovereignty, and Refugees. *Public Culture* 9(1): 3–32.

Bledsoe, Caroline. 1990. "No Success Without Struggle": Social Mobility and Hardship for Foster Children in Sierra Leone. *Man* 25(1): 70–88.

Bloemraad, Irene, Anna Korteweg, and Gökçe Yurdakul. 2008. Citizenship and Immigration: Multiculturalism, Assimilation, and Challenges to the Nation-State. *Annual Review of Sociology* 34: 153–79.

Blum, Susan Debra. 2007. *Lies That Bind: Chinese Truths, Other Truths*. New York: Rowman & Littlefield.

Boellstorf, Tom. 2008. *Coming of Age in Second Life: An Anthropologist Explores the Virtually Human*. Princeton, NJ: Princeton University Press.

Bourdieu, Pierre. 1977. *Outline of a Theory of Practice*, translated by R. Nice. Cambridge, UK: Cambridge University Press.

Boyer, Dominic. 2003. Censorship as a Vocation: The Institutions, Practices, and Cultural Logic of Media Control in the German Democratic Republic. *Comparative Studies in Society and History* 45(3): 511–45.

Broomfield, Emma V. 2003. Perceptions of Danger: The China Threat Theory. *Journal of Contemporary China* 12(35): 265–84.

Brown, Melissa J. 2004. *Is Taiwan Chinese? The Impact of Culture, Power, and Migration on Changing Identities*. Berkeley: University of California Press.

Brownell, Susan, and Jeffrey N. Wasserstrom, eds. 2002. *Chinese Femininities/ Chinese Masculinities*. Berkeley: University of California Press.

Bulmer, Martin, and Anthony M. Rees, eds. 1996. *Citizenship Today: The Contemporary Relevance of T. H. Marshall*. London: Routledge.

Burawoy, Michael. 2000. *Global Ethnography: Forces, Connections, and Imaginations in a Postmodern World*. Berkeley: University of California Press.

Cain, Mead. 1982. Perspectives on Family and Fertility in Developing Countries. *Population Studies* 36(2): 159–75.

Castle, Tomi. 2008. Sexual Citizenship: Articulating Citizenship, Identity, and the Pursuit of the Good Life in Urban Brazil. *PoLAR: Political and Legal Anthropology Review* 31(1): 118–33.

Central Intelligence Agency. 2005. *World Factbook, 2005*. Springfield, VA: Central Intelligence Agency, Office of Public Affairs.

Chalfin, Brenda. 2008. Sovereigns and Citizens in Close Encounter: Airport Anthropology and Customs Regimes in Neoliberal Ghana. *American Ethnologist* 35(4): 519–38.

Chang, Hao. 1987. *Chinese Intellectuals in Crisis: Search for Order and Meaning, 1890–1911*. Berkeley: University of California Press.

Chang, Jung. 1991. *Wild Swans: Three Daughters of China*. New York: Simon & Schuster.

Chang, Shenglin. 2006. *The Global Silicon Valley Home: Lives and Landscapes Within Taiwanese American Trans-Pacific Culture*. Stanford, CA: Stanford University Press.

Che Xing. 1999. *Chang huijia kankan* [Visit home often]. Hebei, China: Hebei Sheng Juyuan [Hebei Province Theater].

Chee, Maria W. L. 2005. *Taiwanese American Transnational Families: Women and Kin Work*. New York: Routledge.

Chen Tieyuan. 2004. *Liuxue yu laji: Laizi zhongguo haiwai liuxuesheng wenti baogao* [Study abroad and trash: The problems of students who return from study abroad]. Beijing: Shijie zhishi chubanshe [World Knowledge Press].

Chen, Tse-Mei, and George A. Barnett. 2001. Research on International Student Flows from a Macro Perspective: A Network Analysis of 1985, 1989 and 1995. *Journal of Studies in International Education* 5(1): 435–53.

Cheng, Nien. 1986. *Life and Death in Shanghai*. London: Grafton.

Chu, Julie [Y.]. 2004. Cosmologies of Credit: Fuzhounese Migration and the Production of Value. Ph.D. dissertation, New York University.

———. 2006. To Be "Emplaced": Fuzhounese Migration and the Politics of Destination. *Identities: Global Studies in Culture and Power* 13(3): 395–425.

———. 2007. Equation Fixations: On the Whole and the Sum of Dollars in Foreign Exchange. In *Money: Ethnographic Encounters*, edited by A. Truitt and S. Senders, 15–25. Oxford, UK: Berg.

———. 2010. *Cosmologies of Credit: Transnational Mobility and the Politics of Destination in China*. Durham, NC: Duke University Press.

Clarke, Kamari. 2010. New Spheres of Transnational Formations: Mobilizations of Humanitarian Diasporas. *Transforming Anthropology* 18(1): 48–65.

Clifford, James. 1997. Spatial Practices: Fieldwork, Travel, and the Disciplining of Anthropology. In *Anthropological Locations: Boundaries and Grounds of a Field Science*, edited by A. Gupta and J. Ferguson, 185–222. Berkeley: University of California Press.

Cohen, Anthony P. 1996. Personal Nationalism: A Scottish View of Some Rites, Rights, and Wrongs. *American Ethnologist* 23(4): 802–15.

Cohen, Myron L. 1976. *House United, House Divided: The Chinese Family in Taiwan.* New York: Columbia University Press.

———. 1990. Lineage Organization in North China. *Journal of Asian Studies* 49(3): 509–34.

Comaroff, Jean, and John L. Comaroff. 1993. *Modernity and Its Malcontents: Ritual and Power in Postcolonial Africa.* Chicago: University of Chicago Press.

———. 2001. *Millennial Capitalism and the Culture of Neoliberalism.* Durham, NC: Duke University Press.

Constable, Nicole. 1997. *Maid to Order in Hong Kong: An Ethnography of Filipina Workers.* Ithaca, NY: Cornell University Press.

———. 2003. *Romance on a Global Stage: Pen Pals, Virtual Ethnography, And "Mail Order" Marriages.* Berkeley: University of California Press.

———. 2004. *Cross-Border Marriages: Gender and Mobility in Transnational Asia.* Philadelphia: University of Pennsylvania Press.

Cornelius, Wayne A., Philip L. Martin, and James F. Hollifield. 1994. *Controlling Immigration: A Global Perspective.* Stanford, CA: Stanford University Press.

Coronil, Fernando. 1996. Beyond Occidentalism: Toward Nonimperial Geohistorical Categories. *Cultural Anthropology* 11(1): 51–87.

———. 1997. *The Magical State: Nature, Money, and Modernity in Venezuela.* Chicago: University of Chicago Press.

Cossman, Brenda. 2007. *Sexual Citizens: The Legal and Cultural Regulation of Sex and Belonging.* Stanford, CA: Stanford University Press.

Dalian Shi Shi Zhi Bangongshi [Dalian City Archives Office]. 2001. *Dalian nianjian, 2000* [Dalian yearbook, 2000]. Dalian, China: Dalian Chubanshe [Dalian Publisher].

———. 2002. *Dalian nianjian, 2001* [Dalian yearbook, 2001]. Dalian, China: Dalian Chubanshe [Dalian Publisher].

———. 2010. *Dalian nianjian, 2009* [Dalian yearbook, 2009]. Dalian, China: Dalian Chubanshe [Dalian Publisher].

d'Alisera, JoAnn. 2004. *An Imagined Geography: Sierra Leonean Muslims in America.* Philadelphia: University of Pennsylvania Press.

Davis, Deborah. 1989. My Mother's House. In *Unofficial China: Popular Culture and Thought in the People's Republic,* edited by E. P. Link, R. Madsen, and P. Pickowicz, 88–100. Boulder, CO: Westview Press.

Davis, Deborah, and Stevan Harrell. 1993. *Chinese Families in the Post-Mao Era.* Berkeley: University of California Press.

del Castillo, Adelaida R. 2002. Illegal Status and Social Citizenship: Thoughts on Mexican Immigrants in a Postnational World. *Aztlán: A Journal of Chicano Studies* 27(2): 9–32.

DeWoskin, Rachel. 2005. *Foreign Babes in Beijing: Behind the Scenes of a New China.* New York: W. W. Norton.

Dikkoter, Frank. 1992. *The Discourse of Race in Modern China*. Stanford, CA: Stanford University Press.

di Leonardo, Micaela. 1998. *Exotics at Home: Anthropology, Others, American Modernity*. Chicago: University of Chicago Press.

DiPrete, Thomas A., and K. Lynn Nonnemaker. 1997. Structural Change, Labor Market Turbulence, and Labor Market Outcomes. *American Sociological Review* 62(3): 386–404.

Dominguez, Virginia R. 2000. For a Politics of Love and Rescue. *Cultural Anthropology* 15(3): 361–93.

Douw, Leo, Cen Huang, and Michael R. Godley, eds. 1999. *Qiaoxiang Ties: Interdisciplinary Approaches to "Cultural Capitalism" in South China*. London: Kegan Paul International.

Dressler, William W. 1982. *Hypertension and Culture Change: Acculturation and Disease in the West Indies*. South Salem, NY: Redgrave.

———. 1990. Lifestyle, Stress, and Blood Pressure in a Southern Black Community. *Psychosomatic Medicine* 52: 182–98.

Dressler, William W., and James R. Bindon. 2000. The Health Consequences of Cultural Consonance: Cultural Dimensions of Lifestyle, Social Support, and Arterial Blood Pressure in an African American Community. *American Anthropologist* 102: 244–60.

Dressler, William W., Jose Ernesto Dos Santos, Philip N. Gallagher Jr., and Fernando E. Viteri. 1987a. Arterial Blood Pressure and Modernization in Brazil. *American Anthropologist* 89: 389–409.

Dressler, William W., Alfonso Mata, Adolfo Chavez, and Fernando E. Viteri. 1987b. Arterial Blood Pressure and Individual Modernization in a Mexican Community. *Social Science and Medicine* 24: 679–87.

Duara, Prasenjit. 1997. Nationalists Among Transnationals: Overseas Chinese and the Idea of China, 1900–1911. In *Ungrounded Empires: The Cultural Politics of Modern Chinese Transnationalism*, edited by A. Ong and D. M. Nonini, 39–60. London: Routledge.

Dwyer, Peter. 2003. *Understanding Social Citizenship: Themes and Perspectives for Policy and Practice*. Bristol, UK: Policy Press.

Ebert, Jane Jenkins, Daniel T. Gilbert, and Tamar Diana Wilson. 2009. Forecasting and Backcasting: Predicting the Impact of Events on the Future. *Journal of Consumer Research* 36: 353–66.

Ebron, Paulla A. 1999. Tourists as Pilgrims: Commercial Fashioning of Transatlantic Politics. *American Ethnologist* 26(4): 910–31.

Ehrkamp, Patricia, and Helga Leitner. 2003. Beyond National Citizenship: Turkish Immigrants and the (Re)Construction of Citizenship in Germany. *Urban Geography* 24(2): 127–46.

Ellison, James. 2009. *Governmentality and the Family: Neoliberal Choices and Emergent Kin Relations in Southern Ethiopia*. American Anthropologist 111(1): 81–92.

Escobar, Arturo. 1995. *Encountering Development: The Making and Unmaking of the Third World*. Princeton, NJ: Princeton University Press.

———. 1997. Anthropology and Development. *International Social Science Journal* 154: 497–516.

———. 2007. Reflections on 50 Years of Development. *Development* 50: 10–12.

———. 2010. Latin America at a Crossroads: Alternative Modernizations, Postliberalism, or Postdevelopment? *Cultural Studies* 24(1): 1–65.

Espenshade, Thomas J. 1995. Unauthorized Immigration to the United States. *Annual Review of Sociology* 21: 195–216.

Evans, Harriet. 2007. *The Subject of Gender: Mothers and Daughters in Urban China*. Lanham, MD: Rowman & Littlefield.

Ewing, Katherine Pratt. 2008. *Stolen Honor: Stigmatizing Muslim Men in Berlin*. Stanford, CA: Stanford University Press.

Fabian, Johannes. 1983. *Time and the Other: How Anthropology Makes Its Object*. New York: Columbia University Press.

Falk, Richard. 1994. The Making of Global Citizenship. In *The Condition of Citizenship*, edited by B. van Steenbergen, 127–40. London: Sage.

Ferguson, James. 1999. *Expectations of Modernity: Myths and Meanings of Urban Life on the Zambian Copperbelt*. Berkeley: University of California Press.

Ferguson, James, and Akhil Gupta. 2002. Spatializing States: Toward an Ethnography of Neoliberal Governmentality. *American Anthropologist* 29(4): 981–1002.

Flores, William Vincent, and Rina Benmayor. 1997. *Latino Cultural Citizenship: Claiming Identity, Space, and Rights*. Boston: Beacon Press.

Foner, Nancy. 2002. *From Ellis Island to JFK: New York's Two Great Waves of Immigration*. New Haven, CT: Yale University Press.

Fong, Vanessa [L.]. 2002. China's One-Child Policy and the Empowerment of Urban Daughters. *American Anthropologist* 104(4): 1098–1109.

———. 2004a. Filial Nationalism Among Chinese Teenagers with Global Identities. *American Ethnologist* 31(4): 629–46.

———. 2004b. *Only Hope: Coming of Age Under China's One-Child Policy*. Stanford, CA: Stanford University Press.

———. 2006. "Chinese Youth Between the Margins of China and the First World." In *Chinese Citizenship: Views from the Margins*, edited by V. L. Fong and R. Murphy, 151–73. London: Routledge.

———. 2007a. Morality, Cosmopolitanism, or Academic Achievement? Discourses on "Quality" and Urban Chinese Only-Children's Claims to Ideal Personhood. *City and Society* 19(1): 86–113.

———. 2007b. Parent-Child Communication Problems and the Perceived Inadequacies of Chinese Only-Children. *Ethos* 35(1): 85–127.

———. 2007c. SARS, a Shipwreck, a NATO Attack, and September 11: Global Information Flows and Chinese Responses to Tragic News Events. *American Ethnologist* 34(3): 521–39.

———. 2008. The Other Side of the Healthy Immigrant Paradox: Chinese Students in Ireland and Britain Who Return to China Due to Personal and Familial Health Crises. *Culture, Medicine, and Psychiatry* 32(4): 627–41.

Fong, Vanessa L., and Rachel Murphy. 2006. *Chinese Citizenship: Views from the Margins*. London: Routledge.

Fox, Jonathan. 2005. Unpacking "Transnational Citizenship." *Annual Review of Political Science* 8: 171–201.

Francis, N., and P. M. Ryan. 1998. English as an International Language of Prestige: Conflicting Cultural Perspectives and Shifting Ethnolinguistic Loyalties. *Anthropology and Education Quarterly* 29(1): 25–43.

Friedman, Jonathan. 1994. *Cultural Identity and Global Process*. Thousand Oaks, CA: Sage.

Friedman, Sara. 2010. Determining "Truth" at the Border: Immigration Interviews, Chinese Marital Migrants, and Taiwan's Sovereignty Dilemmas. *Citizenship Studies* 14(2): 167–83.

Friedman, Thomas. 2000. *The Lexus and the Olive Tree: Understanding Globalization*. New York: Anchor Books.

Frohlick, Susan. 2007. Fluid Exchanges: The Negotiation of Intimacy Between Tourist Women and Local Men in a Transnational Town in Caribbean Costa Rica. *City and Society* 19(1): 139–68.

Fukuyama, Francis. 1992. *The End of History and the Last Man*. New York: Free Press.

Gaetano, Arianne, and Tamara Jacka, eds. 2004. *On the Move: Women and Rural-to-Urban Migration in Contemporary China*. New York: Columbia University Press.

Gamburd, Michele Ruth. 2000. *The Kitchen Spoon's Handle: Transnationalism and Sri Lanka's Migrant Housemaids*. Ithaca, NY: Cornell University Press.

———. 2008. Milk Teeth and Jet Planes: Kin Relations in Families of Sri Lanka's Transnational Domestic Servants. *City and Society* 20(1): 5–31.

Gao, Yuan. 1987. *Born Red: A Chronicle of the Cultural Revolution*. Stanford, CA: Stanford University Press.

Gardner, Howard, ed. 2007. *Responsibility at Work: How Leading Professionals Act (or Don't Act) Responsibly*. San Francisco: Jossey-Bass.

Gardner, Howard E., Mihaly Csikszentmihalhi, and William Damon. 2001. *Good Work: When Excellence and Ethics Meet*. New York: Basic Books.

Garnaut, John. 2010. One-Child Policy's Days Are Numbered. *Sydney Morning Herald*, September 13. http://www.smh.com.au/world/onechild-policys -days-are-numbered-20100912-1571g.html (accessed September 13, 2010).

Gellner, Ernest. 1991. Tribalism and the State in the Middle East. In *Tribes and State Formation in the Middle East*, edited by P. S. Khoury and J. Kostiner, 109–26. Berkeley: University of California Press.

George, Sheba Mariam. 2005. *When Women Come First: Gender and Class in Transnational Migration*. Berkeley: University of California Press.

Gewertz, Deborah, and Frederick Errington. 1991. *Twisted Histories, Altered Contexts: Representing the Chambri in the World System*. Cambridge, UK: Cambridge University Press.

Gilbert, Daniel T. 2006. *Stumbling on Happiness*. New York: Random House.

Gilbert, Daniel T., and Michael J. Gill. 2000. The Momentary Realist. *Psychological Science* 11(5): 394–98.

Gilbert, Daniel T., Matthew D. Lieberman, Carey K. Morewedge, and Timothy D. Wilson. 2004a. The Peculiar Longevity of Things Not So Bad. *Psychological Science* 15(1): 14–19.

Gilbert, Daniel T., Carey K. Morewedge, Jane L. Risen, and Timothy D. Wilson. 2004b. Looking Forward to Looking Backward: The Misprediction of Regret. *Psychological Science* 15(5): 346–50.

Ginsburg, Faye D., Lila Abu-Lughod, and Brian Larkin. 2002. *Media Worlds: Anthropology on New Terrain.* Berkeley: University of California Press.

Glick-Schiller, Nina, Linda Basch, and Cristina Szanton-Blanc. 1992. *Towards a Transnational Perspective on Migration: Race, Class, Ethnicity, and Nationalism Reconsidered.* New York: New York Academy of Sciences.

———. 1995. From Immigrant to Transmigrant: Theorizing Transnational Migration. *Anthropological Quarterly* 68(1): 48–63.

Gold, Thomas B., Doug Guthrie, and David Wank. 2002. *Social Connections in China: Institutions, Culture, and the Changing Nature of Guanxi.* Cambridge, UK: Cambridge University Press.

Goldman, Merle, and Elizabeth J. Perry. 2002. *Changing Meanings of Citizenship in Modern China.* Cambridge, MA: Harvard University Press.

Goodman, Bryna. 1995. The Locality as Microcosm of the Nation? Native Place Networks and Early Urban Nationalism in China. *Modern China* 31(4): 387–420.

Graburn, Nelson H. H. 1983. The Anthropology of Tourism. *Annals of Tourism Research* 10(1): 9–33.

Grant, Monica J., and Jere R. Behrman. 2010. Gender Gaps in Educational Attainment in Less Developed Countries. *Population and Development Review* 36(1): 71–89.

Greenhalgh, Susan. 1985a. Is Inequality Demographically Induced? The Family Cycle and the Distribution of Income in Taiwan. *American Anthropologist* 87(3): 571–94.

———. 1985b. Sexual Stratification: The Other Side of "Growth with Equity." *Population and Development Review* 11: 265–314.

———. 2008. *Just One Child: Science and Policy in Deng's China.* Berkeley: University of California Press.

Greenhalgh, Susan, and Edwin A. Winckler. 2005. *Governing China's Population: From Leninist to Neoliberal Biopolitics.* Stanford, CA: Stanford University Press.

Gu, Baochang, Feng Wang, Zhigang Guo, and Erli Zhang. 2007. China's Local and National Fertility Policies at the End of the Twentieth Century. *Population and Development Review* 33(1): 129–47.

Guest, Kenneth. 2003. Liminal Youth Among Fuzhou Chinese Undocumented Workers. In *Asian American Religions: Borders and Boundaries,* edited by T. Carnes and F. Yang, 55–75. New York: New York University Press.

Guo, Yugui. 1998. The Roles of Returned Foreign-Educated Students in Chinese Higher Education. *Journal of Studies in International Education* 2(2): 35–58.

Guojia Tongji Ju [National Bureau of Statistics]. 2001. *Zhongguo tongji nianjian, 2001* [China statistical yearbook, 2001]. Beijing: Zhongguo Tongji Chubanshe [China Statistics Press].

Guojia Tongji Ju, Chengshi Shehui Jingji Diaocha Zongdui [National Bureau of Statistics, Urban Society and Economy Research Team]. 2000. *Zhongguo chengshi tongji nianjian* [Urban statistical yearbook of China, 1999]. Beijing: Zhongguo Tongji Chubanshe [China Statistics Press].

Gupta, Akhil, and James Ferguson. 1997. *Anthropological Locations: Boundaries and Grounds of a Field Science.* Berkeley: University of California Press.

Hall, Kathleen. 2002. *Lives in Translation: Sikh Youth as British Citizens.* Philadelphia: University of Pennsylvania Press.

Hall, Stuart. 1997. The Local and the Global: Globalization and Ethnicity. In *Culture, Globalization, and the World-System: Contemporary Conditions for the Representation of Identity*, edited by A. D. King, 19–39. Minneapolis: University of Minnesota Press.

Handler, Richard. 1988. *Nationalism and the Politics of Culture in Quebec: New Directions in Anthropological Writing.* Madison: University of Wisconsin Press.

Hannerz, Ulf. 2004. *Foreign News: Exploring the World of Foreign Correspondents.* Chicago: University of Chicago Press.

Hansen, Karen Tranberg. 2000. *Salaula: The World of Secondhand Clothing and Zambia.* Chicago: University of Chicago.

Harrison, Henrietta. 2000. *The Making of the Republican Citizen.* London: Oxford University Press.

Harvey, David. 2005. *A Brief History of Neoliberalism.* Oxford, UK: Oxford University Press.

Hasty, Jennifer. 2005. *The Press and Political Culture in Ghana.* Bloomington: Indiana University Press.

Hayhoe, Ruth. 1996. *China's Universities, 1895–1995: A Century of Cultural Conflict.* New York: Garland Press.

He, Baogang. 2004. World Citizenship and Transnational Activism. In *Transnational Activism in Asia*, edited by N. Piper and A. Uhlin, 78–93. London: Routledge.

Heater, Derek. 2002. *World Citizenship: Cosmopolitan Thinking and Its Opponents.* London: Continuum.

Hertz, Ellen. 1998. *The Trading Crowd: An Ethnography of the Shanghai Stock Market.* Cambridge, UK: Cambridge University Press.

Herzfeld, Michael. 1987. *Anthropology Through the Looking-Glass: Critical Ethnography in the Margins of Europe.* Cambridge, UK: Cambridge University Press.

———. 1997. *Cultural Intimacy: Social Poetics in the Nation-State.* New York: Routledge.

Hess, Peter N. 1988. *Population Growth and Socioeconomic Progress in Less Developed Countries: Determinants of Fertility Transition.* New York: Praeger.

Hirshberg, Matthew S. 1993. Consistency and Change in American Perceptions of China. *Political Behavior* 15(3): 247–63.

Ho, Engseng. 2004. Empire Through Diasporic Eyes: A View from the Other Boat. *Comparative Studies in Society and History* 42(2): 210–46.

Ho, Karen. 2009. *Liquidated: An Ethnography of Wall Street*. Durham, NC: Duke University Press.

Ho, Ming Jung. 2003. Migratory Journeys and Tuberculosis Risk. *Medical Anthropology Quarterly* 17(4): 442–58.

———. 2004. Sociocultural Aspects of Tuberculosis: A Literature Review and a Case Study of Immigrant Tuberculosis. *Social Science and Medicine* 59(4): 753–62.

Hoffman, Lisa. 2008. *Patriotic Professionalism in Urban China: Fostering Talent*. Philadelphia: Temple University Press.

Holston, James. 2008. *Histories and Anthropologies of Citizenship*. Princeton, NJ: Princeton University Press.

Huang, Philip C. 1972. *Liang Qi-Chao and Modern Chinese Liberalism*. Seattle: University of Washington Press.

Huntington, Samuel P. 1998. *The Clash of Civilizations and the Remaking of World Order*. New York: Simon & Schuster.

Hutchings, Kimberly, and Roland Dannreuther, eds. 1999. *Cosmopolitan Citizenship*. New York: St. Martin's.

Hyde, Sandra Teresa. 2007. *Eating Spring Rice: The Cultural Politics of Aids in Southwest China*. Berkeley: University of California Press.

Jankowiak, William, Peter B. Gray, and Kelly Hattman. 2008. Globalizing Evolution: Female Choice, Nationality, and Perception of Sexual Beauty in China. *Cross Cultural Research* 42(3): 248–69.

Jiang Zemin. 2002. Quanmian jianshe xiaokang shehui, kaichuang zhongguo tese shehuizhuyi shiye xin jumian: Zai zhongguo gongchandang di shiliu ci quangguo daibiao dahui shang de baogao [Build a well-off society in an all-round way, work hard to create a new situation in building socialism with Chinese characteristics: Report of the sixteenth Chinese Communist Party Congress]. *Renmin Ribao* [People's daily], November 18, 2002, 1–16.

Jiaotong University Institute of Higher Education. 2010. *Academic Ranking of World Universities, 2010*. Shanghai, China: Jiaotong University Institute of Higher Education http://www.arwu.org/.

Jin Xuefeng. 1996. *Lao xiang jian lao xiang* [When migrants from the same hometown meet]. Shanghai: Shanghai Dongfang Dianshitai [Shanghai Eastern Television Station].

Jing, Jun, ed. 2000. *Feeding China's Little Emperors: Food, Children, and Social Change*. Stanford, CA: Stanford University Press.

Johnson, Ericka. 2007. *Dreaming of a Mail-Order Husband: Russian-American Internet Romance*. Durham, NC: Duke University Press.

Jones, Gavin W., and Pravin M. Visaria. 1997. *Urbanization in Large Developing Countries: China, Indonesia, Brazil, and India*. Oxford, UK: Clarendon Press; and New York: Oxford University Press.

Keane, Michael. 2001. Redefining Citizenship in China. *Economy and Society* 30(1): 1–17.

Kelsky, Karen. 2001. *Women on the Verge: Japanese Women, Western Dreams*. Durham, NC: Duke University Press.

Keyfitz, Nathan. 1990. Alfred Sauvy [in Memoriam]. *Population and Development Review* 16(4): 727–33.

King, Desmond S., and Jeremy Waldron. 1988. Citizenship, Social Citizenship, and the Defence of Welfare Provision. *British Journal of Political Science* 18(4): 415–43.

Kipnis, Andrew [B.]. 1997. *Producing Guanxi: Sentiment, Self, and Subculture in a North China Village.* Durham, NC: Duke University Press.

———. 2006. Suzhi: A Keyword Approach. *China Quarterly* 186: 295–313.

———. 2007. Neoliberalism Reified: Suzhi Discourse and Tropes of Neoliberalism in the PRC. *Journal of the Royal Anthropological Institute* 13: 383–399.

———. 2008a. Audit Cultures: Neoliberal Governmentality, Socialist Legacy, or Technologies of Governing? *American Ethnologist* 35(2): 275–89.

———. 2008b. *China and Postsocialist Anthropology: Theorizing Power and Society After Communism.* Norwalk, CT: Eastbridge.

Kleinman, Arthur, and James L. Watson, eds. 2005. *SARS in China: Prelude to Pandemic?* Stanford, CA: Stanford University Press.

Kuehn, Bridget M. 2009. Melamine Scandals Highlight Hazards of Increasingly Globalized Food Chain. *Journal of the American Medical Association* 301(5): 473–75.

Kuhn, Philip A. 2008. *Chinese Among Others: Emigration in Modern Times.* Lanham, MD: Rowman & Littlefield.

Lan, Hua R., and Vanessa L. Fong, eds. 1999. *Women in Republican China.* Armonk, NY: M. E. Sharpe.

Lancaster, Roger N. 1992. *Life Is Hard: Machismo, Danger, and the Intimacy of Power in Nicaragua.* Berkeley: University of California Press.

Lane, Robert E. 2001. *The Loss of Happiness in Market Democracies.* New Haven, CT: Yale University Press.

Lemon, Alaina. 1998. Your Eyes Are Green Like Dollars: Counterfeit Cash, National Substance, and Currency Apartheid in 1990s Russia. *Cultural Anthropology* 13(1): 22–55.

———. 2000. *Between Two Fires: Gypsy Performance and Romani Memory from Pushkin to Post-Socialism.* Durham, NC: Duke University Press.

Leonard, Karen. 2007. *Locating Home: India's Hyderabadis Abroad.* Stanford, CA: Stanford University Press.

Levinson, Meira. 2010. The Civic Empowerment Gap: Defining the Problem. In *Handbook of Research on the Development of Civic Engagement*, edited by L. R. Sherrod, C. A. Flanagan, and J. Torney-Purta, 331–61. New York: Wiley.

Levitt, Peggy. 2001. *The Transnational Villagers.* Berkeley: University of California Press.

Levitt, Peggy, and Nina Glick Schiller. 2004. Conceptualizing Simultaneity: A Transnational Social Field Perspective on Society. *International Migration Review* 38(3): 1002–39.

Lin, Jing. 1993. *Education in Post-Mao China.* Westport, CT: Praeger.

———. 1999. *Social Transformation and Private Education in China.* Westport, CT: Praeger.

———. 2005. China's Higher Education Reform and the Beida (Beijing University) Debate. *Harvard China Review* 5(2): 132–38.

Linger, Daniel. 2001. *No One Home: Brazilian Selves Remade in Japan.* Stanford, CA: Stanford University Press.

———. 2005. *Anthropology Through a Double Lens: Public and Personal Worlds in Human Theory.* Philadelphia: University of Pennsylvania Press.

Lister, Michael. 2005. "Marshall-ing" Social and Political Citizenship: Towards a Unified Conception of Citizenship. *Government and Opposition: An International Journal of Comparative Politics* 40(4): 471–91.

Liu Dehua. 1997. *Zhongguoren* [Chinese people]. Dalian, China: Liaoning Guangbo Dianshi Yinxiang Chubanshe [Liaoning Radio, Television, and Videotape Publisher].

Liu, Judith, Heidi A. Ross, and Donald P. Kelly. 2000. *The Ethnographic Eye: Interpretive Studies of Education in China.* New York: Falmer Press.

Liu, Xin. 1997. Space, Mobility, and Flexibility: Chinese Villagers and Scholars Negotiate Power at Home and Abroad. In *Ungrounded Empires: The Cultural Politics of Modern Chinese Transnationalism,* edited by A. Ong and D. M. Nonini, 91–114. New York: Routledge.

Louie, Andrea. 2000. Re-Territorializing Transnationalism: Chinese Americans and the Chinese Motherland. *American Ethnologist* 27(3): 645–69.

———. 2004. *Chineseness Across Borders: Renegotiating Chinese Identities in China and the United States.* Durham, NC: Duke University Press.

Louie, Kam. 2002. *Theorising Chinese Masculinity: Society and Gender in China.* Cambridge, UK: Cambridge University Press.

Louie, Vivian. 2004. *Compelled to Excel: Immigration, Education, and Opportunity Among Chinese Americans.* Stanford, CA: Stanford University Press.

Lowe, Lisa. 1996. *Immigrant Acts: On Asian American Cultural Politics.* Durham, NC: Duke University Press.

Lowe, Lisa, and David Lloyd, eds. 1997. *The Politics of Culture in the Shadow of Capital.* Durham, NC: Duke University Press.

Lutz, Catherine. 2006. Empire Is in the Details. *American Ethnologist* 33(4): 593–611.

Lutz, Catherine, and Jane Lou Collins. 1993. *Reading National Geographic.* Chicago: University of Chicago Press.

Lutz, Catherine, and Anne Lutz Fernandez. 2010. *Carjacked: The Culture of the Automobile and Its Effect on Our Lives.* New York: Palgrave Macmillan.

Mabogunje, Akin. 1970. Systems Approach to a Theory of Rural-Urban Migration. *Geographical Analysis* 2: 1–17.

Maddison, Angus. 1983. A Comparison of Levels of GDP Per Capita in Developed and Developing Countries, 1700–1980. *Journal of Economic History* 43: 27–41.

Maira, Sunaina Marr. 2009. *Missing: Youth, Citizenship, and Empire after 9/11.* Durham, NC: Duke University Press.

Malaby, Thomas. 2003. *Gambling Life: Dealing in Contingency in a Greek City.* Chicago: University of Illinois Press.

Malkki, Liisa H. 1995. *Purity and Exile: Violence, Memory, and National Cosmology Among Hutu Refugees in Tanzania.* Chicago: University of Chicago Press.

Mandelbaum, Michael. 2002. *The Ideas That Conquered the World: Peace, Democracy, and Free Markets in the Twenty-First Century.* New York: Public Affairs.

Mankekar, Purnima. 1999. *Screening Culture, Viewing Politics: An Ethnography of Television, Womanhood, and Nation in Postcolonial India.* Durham, NC: Duke University Press.

Mao Zedong. 1971. *Selected Readings from the Works of Mao Tsetung.* Beijing: Foreign Languages Press.

Marcus, George E. 1995. Ethnography in/of the World System: The Emergence of Multi-Sited Ethnography. *Annual Review of Anthropology* 24: 95–117.

Marginson, Simon. 2002. Education in the Global Market: Lessons from Australia. *Academe*, May–June, 22–24.

Marshall, Thomas Humphrey. 1950. *Citizenship and Social Class.* Cambridge, UK: Cambridge University Press.

Masquelier, Adeline. 2002. Road Mythographies: Space, Mobility, and the Historical Imagination in Postcolonial Niger. *American Ethnologist* 29(4): 829–56.

Massey, Douglas S., Joaquin Arango, Graeme Hugo, Ali Kouaouci, Adela Pellegrino, and J. Edward Taylor. 1998. *Worlds in Motion: Understanding International Migration at the End of the Millennium.* Oxford, UK: Oxford University Press.

Matza, Tomas. 2009. Moscow's Echo: Technologies of the Self, Publics, and Politics on the Russian Talk Show. *Cultural Anthropology* 24(3): 489–522.

McNamee, Stephen J., and Gary L. Faulkner. 2001. The International Exchange Experience and the Social Construction of Meaning. *Journal of Studies in International Education* 5(1): 64–78.

Michael, Muetzelfeldt, and Gary Smith. 2002. Civil Society and Global Governance: The Possibilities for Global Citizenship. *Citizenship Studies* 6(1): 55–75.

Min, Anchee. 1994. *Red Azalea.* New York: Pantheon.

Mishra, Ramesh. 1981. *Society and Social Policy.* London: Macmillan.

Mitchell, Katharyne. 2001. Education for Democratic Citizenship: Transnationalism, Multiculturalism, and the Limits of Liberalism. *Harvard Educational Review* 71(1): 51–78.

Miyazaki, Hirokazu. 2003. The Temporalities of the Market. *American Anthropologist* 105(2): 255–65.

Miyazaki, Hirokazu, and Annelise Riles. 2005. Failure as an Endpoint. In *Global Assemblages: Technology, Politics, and Ethics as Anthropological Problems,* edited by A. Ong and S. J. Collier, 320–32. Malden, MA: Blackwell.

Morewedge, Carey K., Lisa L. Shu, Daniel T. Gilbert, and Tamar Diana Wilson. 2009. Bad Riddance or Good Rubbish? Ownership and Not Loss Aversion Causes the Endowment Effect. *Journal of Experimental Social Psychology* 45: 947–51.

Mosher, Steven W. 1993. *A Mother's Ordeal: One Woman's Fight Against China's One-Child Policy.* New York: Harcourt Brace Jovanovich.

Munasinghe, Viranjini. 2002. Nationalism in Hybrid Spaces: The Production of Impurity out of Purity. *American Ethnologist* 29(3): 663–92.

Murphy, Rachel [A.]. 2002. *How Migrant Labor Is Changing Rural China*. Cambridge, UK: Cambridge University Press.

———. 2004. The Impact of Labor Migration on the Well-Being and Agency of Rural Chinese Women: Economic and Cultural Context and the Lifecourse. In *On the Move: Women and Rural-Urban Migration in Contemporary China*, edited by T. Jacka and A. Gaetano, 243–76. New York: Columbia University Press.

———. 2006. Citizenship Education in Rural China: The Dispositional and Technical Training of Cadres and Farmers. In *Chinese Citizenship: Views from the Margins*, edited by V. L. Fong and R. Murphy, 9–26. London: Routledge.

———, ed. 2008. *Labour Migration and Social Development in China*. London: Routledge.

Murphy, Rachel, and Vanessa L. Fong. 2008. *Media, Identity, and Struggle in Twenty-First Century China*. London: Routledge.

Myers, David G. 1995. Who Is Happy? *Psychological Science* 6: 10–19.

———. 2000. The Funds, Friends, and Faith of Happy People. *American Psychologist* 55: 56–67.

Nachman, Steven R. 1993. Wasted Lives: Tuberculosis and Other Health Risks of Being Haitian in a U.S. Detention Camp. *Medical Anthropology Quarterly* 7(3): 227–59.

Newendorp, Nicole. 2008. *Uneasy Reunions: Immigration, Citizenship, and Family Life in Post-1997 Hong Kong*. Stanford, CA: Stanford University Press.

Nonini, Donald [M.]. 1999. The Dialectics Of "Disputatiousness" and "Rice-Eating Money": Class Confrontation and Gendered Imaginaries Among Chinese Men in West Malaysia. *American Ethnologist* 26(1): 47–68.

———. 2008. Is China Becoming Neoliberal? *Critique of Anthropology* 28(2): 145–76.

Nonini, Donald M., and Aihwa Ong. 1997. Introduction: Chinese Transnationalism as an Alternative Modernity. In *Ungrounded Empires: The Cultural Politics of Modern Chinese Transnationalism*, edited by A. Ong and D. M. Nonini, 3–36. London: Routledge.

Nyiri, Pál, and Igor Saveliev. 2002. *Globalizing Chinese Migration: Trends in Europe and Asia*. Aldershot, UK: Ashgate.

Nyiri, Pál, Juan Zhang, and Merriden Verrall. 2010. China's Cosmopolitan Nationalists: "Heroes" and "Traitors" of the 2008 Olympics. *China Journal* 23: 25–55.

Office of the Federal Register. 1999. *The Federal Register* 64(52).

Ogbu, John U. 1987. Variability in Minority School Performance: A Problem in Search of an Explanation. *Anthropology and Education Quarterly* 18(3): 312–34.

Ong, Aihwa. 1996. Cultural Citizenship as Subject-Making: Immigrants Negotiate Racial and Cultural Boundaries in the United States. *Current Anthropology* 37(5): 737–62.

————. 1997. Chinese Modernities: Narratives of Nation and of Capitalism. In *Ungrounded Empires: The Cultural Politics of Modern Chinese Transnationalism*, edited by A. Ong and D. M. Nonini, 171–202. New York: Routledge.

————. 1999. *Flexible Citizenship: The Cultural Logics of Transnationality.* Durham, NC: Duke University Press.

————. 2003. *Buddha Is Hiding: Refugees, Citizenship, the New America.* Berkeley: University of California Press.

————. 2006. *Neoliberalism as Exception: Mutations in Citizenship and Sovereignty.* Durham, NC: Duke University Press.

Ong, Aihwa, and Donald Macon Nonini. 1997. *Ungrounded Empires: The Cultural Politics of Modern Chinese Transnationalism.* New York: Routledge.

Ortner, Sherry B. 2003. *New Jersey Dreaming: Capital, Culture, and the Class of '58.* Durham, NC: Duke University Press.

Park, Kyeyoung. 1997. *The Korean American Dream: Immigrants and Small Business in New York City.* Ithaca, NY: Cornell University Press.

————. 1999. "I'm Floating in the Air": Creation of a Korean Transnational Space Among Korean-Latino-American Re-Migrants. *Positions: East Asia Cultures Critique* 7(3): 667–95.

Park, So Jin, and Nancy Abelmann. 2004. Class and Cosmopolitan Striving: Mothers' Management of English Education in South Korea. *Anthropological Quarterly* 77(4): 645–72.

Parrenas, Rhacel Salazar. 2001. *Servants of Globalization: Women, Migration, and Domestic Work.* Stanford, CA: Stanford University Press.

————. 2005. *Children of Global Migration: Transnational Families and Gendered Woes.* Stanford, CA: Stanford University Press.

————. 2008. *The Force of Domesticity: Filipina Migrants and Globalization.* New York: New York University Press.

Pedelty, Mark. 1995. *War Stories: The Culture of Foreign Correspondents.* New York: Routledge.

Pederson, David. 2003. As Irrational as Bert and Bin Laden: The Production of Categories, Commodities, and Commensurability in the Era of Globalization. *Public Culture* 15(2): 238–59.

Peng, Xizhe. 2000. Education in China. In *The Changing Population of China*, edited by Peng Xizhe and Guo Zhigang, 115–33. Malden, MA: Blackwell.

Pepper, Suzanne. 1990. *China's Education Reform in the 1980s: Policies, Issues, and Historical Perspectives.* Berkeley, CA: Institute of East Asian Studies.

————. 1996. *Radicalism and Education Reform in 20th-Century China: The Search for an Ideal Development Model.* Cambridge, UK: Cambridge University Press.

Pieke, Frank N., and Hein Mallee. 1999. *Internal and International Migration: Chinese Perspectives, Chinese Worlds.* Richmond, UK: Curzon.

Pieke, Frank N., Pál Nyiri, Mette Thunø, and Antonella Ceccagno. 2004. *Transnational Chinese: Fujianese Migrants in Europe.* Stanford, CA: Stanford University Press.

Pigg, Stacey L. 1996. The Credible and the Credulous: The Question of Villagers Beliefs in Nepal. *Cultural Anthropology* 11(2): 160–201.

Pina-Cabral, Joao de. 2002. *Between China and Europe: Person, Culture, and Emotion in Macao*. Oxford, UK: Berg.

Portes, Alejandro, and Ruben G. Rumbaut. 1996. *Immigrant America: A Portrait*, 2nd ed. Berkeley: University of California Press.

Pun, Ngai. 1999. Becoming Dagongmei: The Politics of Identity and Difference in Reform China. *China Journal* 42: 1–19.

———. 2005. *Made in China: Women Factory Workers in a Global Workplace*. Durham, NC: Duke University Press.

Quacquarelli Symonds. 2010. *World's Best Universities: Top 400*. http://www.topuniversities.com/university-rankings/world-university-rankings/home (accessed October 9, 2010).

Rahnema, Majid, and Victoria Bawtree, eds. 1997. *The Post-Development Reader*. London: Zed Books.

Raj, Dhooleka. 2003. *Where Are You From?* Berkeley: University of California Press.

Reed-Danahay, Deborah, and Caroline B. Brettell. 2008. *Citizenship, Political Engagement, and Belonging: Immigrants in Europe and the United States*. Piscataway, NJ: Rutgers University Press.

Reimers, Fernando. 2010. Educating for Global Competency. In *International Perspectives on the Goals of Universal Basic and Secondary Education*, edited by J. E. Cohen and M. B. Malin, 183–202. New York: Routledge.

Rofel, Lisa. 1999. *Other Modernities: Gendered Yearnings in China After Socialism*. Berkeley: University of California Press.

———. 2007. *Desiring China: Experiments in Neoliberalism, Sexuality, and Public Culture*. Durham, NC: Duke University Press.

Rotenberg, Robert. 2005. The Power of Your Influence: Internet Mediated Transnational Urbanism. *City and Society* 17(1): 65–80.

Sachs, Wolfgang, ed. 1992. *The Development Dictionary: A Guide to Knowledge as Power*. London: Zed Books.

Safran, William. 1991. State, Nation, National Identity, and Citizenship: France as a Test Case. *International Political Science Review* 12(3): 219–38.

Sahlins, Marshall. 1972. *Stone Age Economics*. Chicago: Aldine.

Said, Edward. 1978. *Orientalism*. New York: Pantheon Books.

Sangren, P. Steven. 1984. Traditional Chinese Corporations: Beyond Kinship. *Journal of Asian Studies* 43(3): 391–415.

Sardon, Jean-Paul. 2006. Recent Demographic Trends in the Developed Countries. *Population* 61(3): 197–266.

Sassen, Saskia. 1991. *The Global City: New York, London, Tokyo*. Princeton, NJ: Princeton University Press.

———, ed. 1996. *Losing Control? Sovereignty in an Age of Globalization*. New York: Columbia University Press.

———. 2000. *Cities in a World Economy*. Thousand Oaks, CA: Pine Forge Press.

———. 2002. Introduction: Locating Cities on Global Circuits. In *Global Networks, Linked Cities*, edited by S. Sassen, 1–38. New York: Routledge.

———. 2009. Incompleteness and the Possibility of Making: Towards Denationalized Citizenship? In *Political Power and Social Theory*, edited by D. E. Davis and J. Go, 229–58. Bingley, UK: Emerald Group.

Sassen, Saskia, and K. Anthony Appiah. 2000. *Globalization and Its Discontents: Essays on the New Mobility of People and Money.* New York: New Press.

Sauvy, Alfred. 1952. Trois mondes, une planete [Three worlds, one planet]. *l'Observateur,* August 14.

Sawyer, Suzana. 2002. Bobbitizing Texaco: Dis-Membering Corporate Capital and Re-Membering the Nation in Ecuador. *Cultural Anthropology* 17(2): 150–80.

Schein, Louisa. 1999. Performing Modernity. *Cultural Anthropology* 14(3): 361–95.

————. 2000. *Minority Rules: The Miao and the Feminine in China's Cultural Politics, Body, Commodity, Text.* Durham, NC: Duke University Press.

————. 2001. Urbanity, Cosmopolitanism, Consumption. In *China Urban: Ethnographies of Contemporary Culture,* edited by N. N. Chen, C. D. Clark, S. Z. Gottschang, and L. Jeffery, 225–41. Durham, NC: Duke University Press.

Scheper-Hughes, Nancy. 1997. Demography Without Numbers. In *Anthropological Demography: Toward a New Synthesis,* edited by D. I. Kertzer and T. E. Fricke, 201–22. Chicago: University of Chicago Press.

Schiller, Nina Glick. 2005. Transborder Citizenship: An Outcome of Legal Pluralism Within Transnational Social Fields. In *Mobile People, Mobile Law: Expanding Legal Relations in a Contracting World,* edited by F. von Benda-Beckmann, K. von Benda-Beckmann, and A. M. O. Griffiths, 27–50. Aldershot, UK: Ashgate.

Schneider, Patricia Higino. 2005. International Trade, Economic Growth, and Intellectual Property Rights: A Panel Data Study of Developed and Developing Countries. *Journal of Development Economics* 78(2): 529–47.

Schwartz, Benjamin. 1993. Culture, Modernity, and Nationalism: Further Reflections. *Daedalus* 122(summer): 207–26.

Scott, Peter. 2000. Globalization and Higher Education: Challenges for the 21st Century. *Journal of Studies in International Education* 4(1): 3–10.

Seeberg, Vilma. 1993. Access to Higher Education: Targeted Recruitment Reform Under Economic Development Plans in the People's Republic of China. *Higher Education* 25(2): 169–88.

Sen, Amartya [Kumar]. 1992. *Inequality Reexamined.* Cambridge, MA: Harvard University Press.

————. 1993. Capability and Well-Being. In *The Quality of Life,* edited by M. C. Nussbaum and A. K. Sen, 30–53. Oxford, UK: Oxford University Press.

————. 1999. *Development as Freedom.* New York: Random House.

Shen Fu. 1983. *Six Records of a Floating Life,* translated and edited by L. Pratt and Su-Hui Chiang. New York: Penguin Books.

Shi, Lihong. 2009. Little Quilted Vests to Warm Parents' Hearts: Redefining the Gendered Practice of Filial Piety in Rural North-Eastern China. *China Quarterly* 198: 348–63.

Shryock, Andrew. 1995. Popular Genealogical Nationalism: History Writing and Identity Among the Balqa Tribes of Jordan. *Comparative Studies in Society and History* 37(2): 325–57.

————. 1997. *Nationalism and the Genealogical Imagination: Oral History and Textual Authority in Tribal Jordan.* Berkeley: University of California Press.

——, ed. 2004. *Off Stage/on Display: Intimacy and Ethnography in the Age of Public Culture*. Stanford, CA: Stanford University Press.

Siu, Helen F. 1993. Cultural Identity and the Politics of Difference in South China. In *China in Transformation*, edited by W.-M. Tu, 19–44. Cambridge, MA: Harvard University Press.

Siu, Lok. 2005. *Memories of a Future Home: Diasporic Citizenship of Chinese in Panama*. Stanford, CA: Stanford University Press.

Small, Cathy A. 1997. *Voyages: From Tongan Villages to American Suburbs*. Ithaca, NY: Cornell University Press.

Smart, Alan. 1993. Gifts, Bribes, and Guanxi: A Reconsideration of Bourdieu's Social Capital. *Cultural Anthropology* 8(3): 388–408.

——. 1999a. Flexible Accumulation Across the Hong Kong Border: Petty Capitalists as Pioneers of Globalized Accumulation. *Urban Anthropology* 28(3–4): 1–34.

——. 1999b. Participating in the Global: Transnational Social Networks and Urban Anthropology. *City and Society* 11(1): 59–77.

Smart, Alan, and Josephine Smart. 2001. Local Citizenship: Welfare Reform, Urban/Rural Status, and Exclusion in China. *Environment and Planning* 8(33): 1853–69.

——, eds. 2005. *Petty Capitalists and Globalization: Flexibility, Entrepreneurship, and Economic Development*. Albany: State University of New York Press.

——. 2008. Time-Space Puntctuation: Hong Kong's Border Regime and Limits on Mobility. *Pacific Affairs* 81(2): 219–37.

Smith, Daniel Jordan. 2006. Cell Phones, Social Inequality, and Contemporary Culture in Southeastern Nigeria. *Canadian Journal of African Studies* 40(3): 496–523.

Solinger, Dorothy. 1999. *Contesting Citizenship in Urban China: Peasant Migrants, the State, and the Logic of the Market*. Berkeley: University of California Press.

Sørensen, Anders. 2003. Backpacker Ethnography. *Annals of Tourism Research* 30(4): 847–67.

Soysal, Yasemin Nuhoglu. 1995. *Limits of Citizenship: Migrants and Postnational Citizenship in Europe*. Chicago: University of Chicago Press.

Stafford, Charles. 1995. *The Roads of Chinese Childhood: Learning and Identification in Angang*. Cambridge, UK: Cambridge University Press.

——. 2000. *Separation and Reunion in Modern China*. Cambridge, UK: Cambridge University Press.

Suárez-Orozco, Carola, and Marcelo Suárez-Orozco. 1995. *Transformations: Migration, Family Life, and Achievement Motivation Among Latino Adolescents*. Stanford, CA: Stanford University Press.

——. 2001. *Children of Immigration*. Cambridge, MA: Harvard University Press.

Sun, Wanning. 2002. *Leaving China: Media, Migration, and Transnational Imagination*. Lanham, MD: Rowman & Littlefield.

Szelényi, Katalin, and Robert A. Rhoads. 2007. Citizenship in a Global Context: The Perspectives of International Graduate Students in the United States. *Comparative Education Review* 51(1): 25–47.

Tabah, Leon. 1991. Alfred Sauvy: Statistician, Economist, Demographer, and Iconoclast (1898–1990). *Population Studies* 45(2): 353–57.

Tan, Chee-Beng. 2007. *Chinese Transnational Networks.* New York: Routledge.

Tan, Chee-Beng, Colin Storey, and Julia Zimmerman. 2007. *Chinese Overseas: Migration, Research, and Documentation.* Hong Kong: Hong Kong University Press.

Tang, Xiaobing. 1996. *Global Space and the National Discourse of Modernity: The Historical Thinking of Liang Qichao.* Stanford, CA: Stanford University Press.

Tapper, Richard, ed. 1983. *In the Conflict of Tribe and State in Iran and Afghanistan.* London: St. Martin's Press.

Thorstensson, Liv. 2001. This Business of Internationalization: The Academic Experiences of 6 Asian MBA International Students at the University of Minnesota's Carlson School of Management. *Journal of Studies in International Education* 5(4): 317–40.

Thurston, Anne F. 1992. *A Chinese Odyssey: The Life and Times of a Chinese Dissident.* New York: Scribner.

Tilly, Charles. 1998. Where Do Rights Come From? In *Democracy, Revolution and History,* edited by T. Skocpol, 55–72. Ithaca, NY: Cornell University Press.

The Times Higher Education. 2010. *World University Rankings 2010–2011.* http:// www.timeshighereducation.co.uk/world-university-rankings/2010-2011/ top-200.html (accessed September 30, 2010).

Tobin, Joseph, Yeh Hsueh, and Mayumi Karasawa. 2009. *Preschool in Three Cultures Revisited: China, Japan, and the United States.* Chicago: University of Chicago Press.

Tobin, Joseph J., David Y. H. Wu, and Dana H. Davidson. 1991. *Preschool in Three Cultures: Japan, China, and the United States.* New Haven: Yale University Press.

Townsend, James. 1992. Chinese Nationalism. *Australian Journal of Chinese Affairs* 27(January): 97–130.

Townsend, Nicholas W. 2002. *The Package Deal: Marriage, Work, and Fatherhood in Men's Lives.* Philadelphia: Temple University Press.

Tsang, Mun. 2000. Education and National Development in China Since 1949: Oscillating Policies and Enduring Dilemmas. In *China Review 2000,* edited by C.-M. Lau and J. Shen, 579–618. Hong Kong: Chinese University of Hong Kong Press.

Tsuda, Takeyuki. 2003. *Strangers in the Ethnic Homeland: Japanese Brazilian Return Migration in Transnational Perspective.* New York: Columbia University Press.

Turner, Victor. 1967. *Forest of Symbols: Aspects of the Ndembu Ritual.* Ithaca, NY: Cornell University Press.

US Department of Health and Human Services. 2010. *The 2009 HHS Poverty Guidelines.* http://aspe.hhs.gov/poverty/09poverty.shtml (accessed September 30, 2010).

van Gennep, Arnold. 1960 [1909]. *The Rites of Passage*, translated by M. B. Vizedom and G. L. Caffee. Chicago: University of Chicago Press.

Verdery, Katherine. 1983. *Transylvanian Villagers: Three Centuries of Political, Economic, and Ethnic Change*. Berkeley: University of California Press.

———. 1991. *What Was Socialism, and What Comes Next?* Princeton, NJ: Princeton University Press.

———. 1995. *National Ideology and National Character in Interwar Eastern Europe*. New Haven, CT: Yale Center for International and Area Studies.

Waldinger, Roger, and David Fitzgerald. 2004. Transnationalism in Question. *American Journal of Sociology* 109(5): 1177–95.

Wallerstein, Immanuel [Maurice]. 1974a. *The Modern World System: Capitalist Agriculture and the Origins of the European World Economy in the Sixteenth Century*. New York: Academic Press.

———. 1974b. The Rise and Future Demise of the World Capitalist System: Concepts for Comparative Analysis. *Comparative Studies in Society and History* 16(4): 387–415.

———. 1975. *World Inequality: Origins and Perspectives on the World System*. Montreal, Canada: Black Rose Books.

———. 1976. *Class Conflict in the Capitalist World-Economy*. Working Papers, Fernand Braudel Center for the Study of Economies, Historical Systems, and Civilizations. Binghamton: State University of New York.

———. 1979. *The Capitalist World-Economy: Essays*. Cambridge, UK: Cambridge University Press.

———. 1981. *Patterns and Perspectives of the Capitalist World-Economy*. Tokyo: United Nations University.

———. 1991. World System Versus World-Systems: A Critique. *Critique of Anthropology* 11(2): 189–94.

Wang, Xiufang. 2003. *Education in China Since 1976*. Jefferson, NC: McFarland.

Wang Zheng. 2000. Gender, Employment, and Women's Resistance. In *Chinese Society: Change, Conflict, and Resistance*, edited by Elizabeth J. Perry and Mark Selden, 62–82. London: Routledge.

Watson, James L. 1975. *Emigration and the Chinese Lineage: The Mans in Hong Kong and London*. Berkeley: University of California Press.

———. 1977a. *Between Two Cultures: Migrants and Minorities in Britain*. Oxford, UK: Basil Blackwell.

———. 1977b. The Chinese: Hong Kong Villagers in the British Catering Trade. In *Between Two Cultures: Migrants and Minorities in Great Britain*, edited by J. L. Watson, 181–213. Oxford, UK: Blackwell.

Watson, James L., and Patricia Ebrey, eds. 1986. *Kinship Organization in Late Imperial China, 1000–1940*. Berkeley: University of California Press.

Watson, Rubie S., and Patricia Buckley Ebrey, eds. 1991. *Marriage and Inequality in Chinese Society*. Berkeley: University of California Press.

White, Merry. 1988. *The Japanese Overseas: Can They Go Home Again?* New York: Free Press.

Wilson, Timothy D., and Daniel T. Gilbert. 2003. Affective Forecasting. In *Advances in Experimental Social Psychology*, edited by M. P. Zanna, 345–411. New York: Elsevier.

Wilson, Timothy D., Jay Meyers, and Daniel T. Gilbert. 2003. "How Happy Was I, Anyway?" A Retrospective Impact Bias. *Social Cognition* 21: 407–32.

Wolf, Margery. 1968. *The House of Lim: A Study of a Chinese Farm Family*. Englewood Cliffs, NJ: Prentice Hall.

Wolf, Margery, Roxane Witke, and Emily M. Ahern. 1975. *Women in Chinese Society: Studies in Chinese Society*. Stanford, CA: Stanford University Press.

Wolf-Phillips, Leslie. 1987. Why "Third World"? Origin, Definition, and Usage. *Third World Quarterly* 9(4): 1131–39.

Wolff, Larry. 1994. *Inventing Eastern Europe: The Map of Civilization on the Mind of the Enlightenment*. Stanford, CA: Stanford University Press.

Woronov, Terry [E.]. 2002. Transforming the Future: "Quality" Children for the Chinese Nation. Ph.D. dissertation, University of Chicago.

———. 2007. Chinese Children, American Education: Globalizing Child Rearing in Contemporary China. In *Generations and Globalization: Youth, Age, and Family in the New World Economy*, edited by J. Cole and D. Durham, 29–51. Bloomington: Indiana University Press.

———. 2008. Raising Quality, Fostering "Creativity": Ideologies and Practices of Education Reform in Beijing. *Anthropology and Education Quarterly* 39(4): 401–22.

Xiang, Biao. 2006. *Global "Body Shopping": An Indian Labor System in the Information Technology Industry*. Princeton, NJ: Princeton University Press.

Xiang, Biao, and Shen Wei. 2009. International Student Migration and Social Stratification in China. *International Journal of Educational Development* 29(5): 513–22.

Xin, Hao, and Richard Stone. 2008. Tainted Milk Scandal: Chinese Probe Unmasks High-Tech Adulteration with Melamine. *Science* 322(5906): 1310–11.

Yan, Hairong. 2003. Neoliberal Governmentality and Neohumanism: Organizing Suzhi/Value Flow Through Labor Recruitment Networks. *Cultural Anthropology* 18(4): 493–523.

———. 2008. *New Masters, New Servants: Migration, Development, and Women Workers in China*. Durham, NC: Duke University Press.

Yan, Yunxiang. 1996. *The Flow of Gifts: Reciprocity and Social Networks in a Chinese Village*. Stanford, CA: Stanford University Press.

———. 1997. McDonald's in Beijing: The Localization of Americana. In *Golden Arches East: McDonald's in East Asia*, edited by J. L. Watson, 39–76. Stanford, CA: Stanford University Press.

———. 2003. *Private Life Under Socialism: Love, Intimacy, and Family Change in a Chinese Village, 1949–1999*. Stanford, CA: Stanford University Press.

———. 2010. *The Individualization of Chinese Society*. Oxford, UK: Berg.

Yang, Juhua. 2007. The One-Child Policy and School Attendance in China. *Comparative Education Review* 51(4): 471–95.

Yang, Mayfair Mei-Hui. 1994. *Gifts, Favors, and Banquets: The Art of Social Relationships in China*. Ithaca, NY: Cornell University Press.

————. 1997. Mass Media and Transnational Subjectivity in Shanghai. In *Ungrounded Empires: The Cultural Politics of Modern Chinese Transnationalism*, edited by A. Ong and D. M. Nonini, 287–319. New York: Routledge.

Ye, Ting-Xing. 1998. *A Leaf in the Bitter Wind*. Toronto, Canada: Random House.

Ye, Weili. 2001. *Seeking Modernity in China's Name: Chinese Students in the United States, 1900–1927*. Stanford, CA: Stanford University Press.

Yoshikawa, Hirokazu. 2011. *Immigrants Raising Citizens*. New York: Russell Sage.

Yue, Daiyun, and Carolyn Wakeman. 1985. *To the Storm: The Odyssey of a Revolutionary Chinese Woman*. Berkeley: University of California Press.

Zhan, Mei. 2006. Civet Cats, Fried Grasshoppers, and David Beckham's Pajamas: Unruly Bodies After SARS. *American Anthropologist* 107(1): 31–42.

Zhang, Everett Yuehong. 2001. Goudui and the State: Constructing Entrepreneurial Masculinity in Two Cosmopolitan Areas in Southwest China. In *Gendered Modernities*, edited by D. L. Hodgson, 235–66. New York: Palgrave.

Zhang, Hong. 2007. China's New Rural Daughters Coming of Age: Downsizing the Family and Firing up Cash Earning Power in the New Economy. *Signs: Journal of Women in Culture and Society* 32(3): 671–98.

Zhang, Li. 2001. *Strangers in the City: Reconfigurations of Space, Power, and Social Networks Within China's Floating Population*. Stanford, CA: Stanford University Press.

————. 2002. Urban Experiences and Social Belonging Among Chinese Rural Migrants. In *Popular China: Unofficial Culture in a Globalizing Society*, edited by P. Link, R. P. Madsen, and P. G. Pickowicz, 275–300. Lanham, MD: Rowman & Littlefield.

————. 2006. Contesting Spatial Modernity in Late-Socialist China. *Current Anthropology* 47(3): 461–84.

————. 2010. *In Search of Paradise: Middle-Class Living in a Chinese Metropolis*. Ithaca, NY: Cornell University Press.

Zhang, Li, and Aihwa Ong, eds. 2008. *Privatizing China, Socialism from Afar*. Ithaca, NY: Cornell University Press.

Zhang Zhen. 2001. Mediating Time: The "Rice Bowl of Youth" in Fin de Siecle Urban China. In *Globalization*, edited by Arjun Appadurai, 131–54. Durham, NC: Duke University Press.

Zhao, Dingxin. 2002. An Angle on Nationalism in China Today: Attitudes Among Beijing Students After Belgrade 1999. *China Quarterly* 172: 885–905.

Zheng, Tiantian. 2009. *Red Lights: The Lives of Sex Workers in Postsocialist China*. Minneapolis: University of Minnesota Press.

Zheng, Yongnian. 1999. *Discovering Chinese Nationalism in China: Modernization and International Relations*. Cambridge, UK: Cambridge University Press.

Zhong, Xueping. 1994. Male Suffering and Male Desire: The Politics of Reading *Half of Man Is Woman* by Zhang Xianliang. In *Engendering China: Women, Culture, and the State,* edited by C. Gilmartin, G. Hershatter, L. Rofel, and T. White, 175–94. Cambridge, MA: Harvard University Press.

Zhonghua Renmin Gongheguo Guojia Tongjiju [National Bureau of Statistics of China]. 2009. *Zhonghua renmin gongheguo 2009 nian guomin jingji he shehui fazhan tongji gongbao* [PRC 2009 national economic and social development statistical communiqué]. National Bureau of Statistics of China. http://www.stats.gov.cn/tjgb/ndtjgb/qgndtjgb/t20100225_402622945. htm (accessed February 25, 2010).

Zhou Enlai. 1980. *Selected Works of Zhou Enlai.* Beijing: Foreign Languages Press.

Zito, Angela. 1997. *Of Body and Brush: Grand Sacrifice as Text/Performance in Eighteenth Century China.* Chicago: University of Chicago Press.

Zlotnik, Hania. 1992. Empirical Identification of International Migration Systems. In *International Migration Systems: Global Approach,* edited by M. M. Kritz, L. L. Lim, and H. Zlotnik, 19–40. Oxford, UK: Clarendon Press.

Zweig, David, Changgui Chen, and Stanley Rosen. 1995. *China's Brain Drain to the United States: Views of Overseas Chinese Students and Scholars in the 1990s.* China Research Monograph 47. Berkeley, CA: Institute of East Asian Studies.

Index

achievement, 25; academic, 64, 71; educational, 175

aging, 44; parents, 206–207, 217–218

Anderson, Benedict, 5–6, 61

Australia, 16–17, 26–27, 43–44, 79–80, 207, 212; citizenship in, 203–204, 19; permanent residency in, 23, 196, 199–201, 214; stories of transnational Chinese students in, 47–49, 112–113, 119–122, 153–154, 156–157, 163–164, 168–169, 180–184

Bourdieu, Pierre, 68

Britain, 4, 7, 11, 19, 33, 56, 72, 75, 78; stories of transnational Chinese students in, 26–27, 43–44, 48–49, 116–117, 119, 121, 132, 138

brokers, study abroad (*zhongjie*), 4, 47, 76–78, 87, 106, 121, 200

Canada, 11, 16, 19, 82, 102, 124, 131; stories of transnational Chinese students in, 43–44, 47–49, 78–79, 147, 151–153, 197–200, 203, 229

children, 65–66, 67–73, 81–83, 171–173, 175–176, 195–196, 205–207, 217–219; legal rights of, 13

citizenship, 52, 66, 68, 70–71, 73–75, 79, 95–98, 101; ambivalence about, 198–206, 210–212, 214–219; quest for, 113–115, 124–127, 130–132, 135–139, 141, 142,

144–145; social, cultural, and legal, 5–7, 10, 12–17, 19–23, 27–28, 33–36, 39–40, 41–42, 44, 48–50. *See also* flexible citizenship

college, 44–59, 72–82, 84–90, 99–122, 138–141, 147–156, 182–184, 193–203, 211–219

computer, 1, 3; games, 119; programming, 74, 112, 172

cosmopolitanism, 120

dating, 30, 83, 89, 91, 122–123; non-Chinese 127–132, 134

developed country (or countries) 2–8; classification of, 9–12, 14; distinction from developing, 12; as study abroad destination, 11

developing world, 6, 12, 14, 19, 23, 73, 139, 142

discipline: personal, 15, 46, 120, 124, 172, 180, 216; systemic, 40–41

discrimination, 13–14, 16, 46, 139, 219; age, 96, 218; education, 2–8, 24–28, 35–37, 39, 40–42, 47–50, 68–74, 76–78, 80–82, 91–94, 95–97, 102–115, 188–190, 191–192. *See also* college; graduate school; high school; junior high school; primary school

emigration, 38, 52, 58, 75, 82, 93, 157–158; brokers (*zhongjie*), 76. *See also* brokers, study abroad employment: abroad, 109, 114; in China, 92, 109; unemployment, 71. *See also* work

ESOL (English for Speakers of Other Languages), 126–129, 137–138, 153–155, 160–168, 178–183, 193–194, 214–215

Europe(an), 2, 16–17, 41, 96, 102, 112, 124, 176, 207, 215; countries, 11, 19, 36, 43, 49–50, 64, 126, 149, 165; lifestyles, 211. *See also* European Union (EU)

European Union (EU), 9, 50, 149. *See also* Europe(an)

father(s), 69–70, 101–102, 146, 164, 169, 174, 206–208

flexible citizenship, 15, 139 *See also* citizenship; Ong, Aihwa

food, 117–118, 120–121, 143, 152–153, 163, 189, 213–214; Chinese, 144, 151–152, 173, 176, 189; fast-food, 86, 100, 128, 141, 152, 160, 163, 203; scares, 154

freedom(s) 13–16, 111–112, 138–139, 142–144, 148–151, 168–172, 187–190, 191–192, 203–205, 217–220. *See also* Sen, Amartya

friendship(s), 30, 54, 167, 182, 184, 186–187

gender, 13, 24, 71, 83–84, 127, 130, 136, 227

graduate school, 44, 80, 104, 110–113, 115, 139, 199, 211, 214

gifts, 94, 167–168, 173–174

global neoliberal system, 10, 15–17, 19–22, 40–41, 61–62, 64–65, 71–72, 145–146, 187–188

happiness, 74, 96–98, 143, 186–189, 211–212, 216, 219

health, 126–127, 139–140, 143–144, 153–156, 165–171, 192, 207

high school, 1–2, 45–46, 51–52, 81–82, 85–88, 90–94, 95–105, 108–109

Holston, James, 13

Hong Kong, 34–36, 38, 43, 53, 55–56, 60, 98, 160–161

housing: in China, 4, 72, 78–79, 98, 171; abroad, 97, 107, 120–121, 137, 150, 185

hypergamy, 83. *See also* marriage

illness, 13, 92, 116, 150, 186, 207

immigration, 47–48, 50, 74–77, 79–80, 116–117, 125, 137–139, 148, 157

inequality 71, 84, 176

Internet, 3, 8, 31, 42–43, 51, 76, 107, 122, 158, 167, 186; cafes, 47

Ireland, 43, 52, 75–82, 99, 105, 114–116, 125–128, 151–155; stories of transnational Chinese students in, 1–2, 47–49, 88–91, 160–161, 178–181, 193–196, 199–201, 206–212

Japan(ese), 16–19, 26–27, 43–49, 55, 101–102, 134, 182, 198, 216, 220; college degree from, 110; gender ideologies, 127; language, 44–45, 50, 105, 114, 119, 122–123, 134, 146, 172, 177, 212–213, 216; sex industry, 134; stories of transnational Chinese students in, 2, 4, 7–8, 11, 121–124, 133–134, 138–139, 200–201, 212–213

Jiang Zemin, 57

junior high school, 24–25, 45–46, 70, 90, 105, 147, 167, 185

Kipnis, Andrew, 14

Korea, Republic of, 36, 43–44, 50

Laws: abroad, 97, 149, 180, 181; in China, 8, 170; immigration, 117; in Ireland, 125–126, 165, 180, 193; lawsuits, 97, 170; visa, 47

Macao, 34–35, 38, 53, 56, 63

Mao Zedong, 18–19, 62–63, 69, 72, 74, 169, 175–176

Maoism, Maoist-era and/or policies, 18–19, 38, 56, 62, 63–74, 169–170, 175, 187

marriage, 81–83, 92–94, 95–97, 128, 143, 166, 171, 189, 217; abroad, 95, 122–123, 127–136. *See also* hypergamy

medical care, 71, 150, 166–167

mobility, 13, 16, 74, 217; geographic, 14, 19, 27, 143–144, 148, 188. *See also* upward mobility

morality, 173, 175–176, 184

mother(s), 69–70, 87–89, 101–102, 137, 176, 206–207, 209–210

motherland, 54–55, 58, 63, 65–66

nationalism, 5, 52, 56–66, 134, 157, 166, 202

neoliberalism, 176; global, 21, 73, 219

network(s), 38, 123, 138, 205; social, 33, 37, 132–133, 136, 173–175, 177, 186–187

New Zealand, 2, 11, 17, 43, 49, 102, 112; stories of transnational Chinese students in, 122, 163, 184, 197, 199, 203, 213–214

one-child policy, 2, 24, 40, 70, 72–73, 84, 135,159, 217
Ong, Aihwa, 15, 58, 204

patriotic (*aiguo*), 53, 55–56; Church, 165; unpatriotic(ally), 131, 137, 192, 202
patriotism, 54–55, 57, 131, 205. *See also* patriotic (*aiguo*)
permanent residency, 13–20, 48–50, 95–96, 113–115, 191–192, 194–203, 208–210, 218–219.
Pieke, Frank, 14, 75, 80, 95
pollution, 143–144, 150, 153, 196
poverty, 53–54, 71–72, 97–98, 152, 159, 165, 176, 229
primary school, 25, 29, 55, 58, 70, 105, 169

quality (*suzhi*), 27, 41, 52, 55, 70, 72, 99, 109, 115, 138, 152, 155, 163, 173, 175–176, 182, 215; "high-quality" (*gao suzhi*), 12, 55, 111, 167, 179, 181, 184, 215. *See also* inequality

research methods, 23

safety, 85, 144, 153–154,
Sassen, Saskia, 8

Sen, Amartya, 15, 142–144, 187–188
sex(ual), 13, 123, 125–127, 130–132, 134, 179
Singapore, 2, 11, 16–17, 43, 49, 107, 200, 229
strangers, 3, 42, 146; civility among, 180–182

Taiwan(ese), 27, 34–36, 38, 56, 160, 161–162, 164, 169
teacher(s), 24–25, 29–30, 56–58, 89–90, 107–108, 115–116, 161–162
travel, 19–20, 26–27, 148–150, 165, 171, 191–192, 205–206

United States, 43–44, 47–49, 52, 54, 62, 75, 78–79, 121–124; stories of transnational Chinese students in, 149, 151, 154, 167–168, 171, 177–178, 180, 183
upward mobility, 37, 80–81, 98, 101, 126, 139, 144–145, 217–218

visa(s), 49–50, 74–78, 96–97, 126–127, 137, 140, 208–210, 218; student, 2, 44, 48, 75, 86, 90–92, 104, 106, 114–117, 123, 138, 140, 149, 165, 192–193, 211; tourist, 19, 75; work, 52, 138, 140, 215

Wallerstein, Immanuel, 17, 21–22
work, 35–38, 44–47, 67–79, 86–93, 106–110, 117–120, 135–141, 146–147, 166–168, 191–198